BRICK CITY

LEGO® FOR GROWN UPS

WARREN ELSMORE

MITCHELL BEAZLEY

Brick City
by Warren Elsmore

First published in Great Britain in 2013 by Mitchell Beazley,
an imprint of Octopus Publishing Group Limited,
Endeavour House, 189 Shaftesbury Avenue, London WC2H 8JY
www.octopusbooks.co.uk

An Hachette UK Company
www.hachette.co.uk

A CIP record for this book is available from the British Library.
ISBN: 978 1 84533 812 1
QTT.BCNY

This book was conceived, designed, and produced by
Quintet Publishing Limited
6 Blundell Street
London N7 9BH
United Kingdom

Photographer: Michael Wolchover (unless otherwise stated)
Lead Designer: Gareth Butterworth
Assistant Designer: Ceyda Cemal
with design contributions from: Rehab Designs
Additional text: Bruno Vincent
Art Director: Michael Charles
Editor: Ross Fulton
Editorial Assistant: Hazel Eriksson
Commissioning Editor: Sonya Patel Ellis
Editorial Director: Donna Gregory
Publisher: Mark Searle

10 9 8 7 6 5 4 3 2 1

Set in Gill Sans

Printed in China by Toppan Leefung

CONTENTS

INTRODUCTION

BRICK CITIES

WELCOME TO BRICK CITY

I've been a LEGO® fan since before I can remember. Even my parents can't recall when this started – I just always seemed to love it. I wasn't content with the simple models, though. As soon as I had mastered those, I wanted to create a whole city. Every January I would pore over the LEGO catalogue planning a whole year in advance and deciding which ones to ask for as birthday and Christmas presents, and which to save up for myself.

Before too long, my bedroom was filled with a huge city layout. It was planned to the last detail so that it really fitted together as a town. It had not only the traditional LEGO® models of the fire and police stations, but also an airport, a garage, shops and a railway station – even if the track only ran around the city and back to the station again. It even had old ruined city walls, re-purposed from the LEGO castle range to add character.

Sadly, I moved away from LEGO as I grew up, and only came back to it in my twenties, discovering my passion was stronger than ever. This time I built the city I had always wanted to build as a child. My station had multiple platforms and more than one train – even though they technically didn't go anywhere. Next, I painstakingly built a copy of our house, scaled so that the LEGO minifigures could be placed inside. Then I built the train that occasionally took me to London and, after that, a working model of the 2.4-kilometre (1½-mile)-long Forth Bridge for my new train to travel over – a beast of 3 metres (9 feet and 10 inches) long. By then I wanted to show these models off at events, so I decided to start on something more ambitious. Eighteen months and 120,000 bricks later, I unveiled my model of London's St. Pancras railway station at the LEGO fair in Denmark. This showpiece has since toured both the UK and Europe, been featured on BBC television, and paved the way to a new career as an independent LEGO artist.

Brick City is the result of my lifelong love affair with LEGO. It is both a celebration of amazing global architecture and my love of the possibilities of LEGO bricks. In this book, you will find some huge projects: my St. Pancras model complete with Eurostar trains waiting to depart; and the London Olympic Park, which was on display at the Paralympic GB 2012 headquarters. *Brick City* also features some of my favourite models from other LEGO builders from around the globe, such as Westminster Abbey, commissioned to celebrate the wedding of Prince William and Kate Middleton. But more than that, each chapter will highlight iconic images from different cities, whether it's the San Francisco cable car, cherry blossom in Tokyo, or the yellow New York taxi. The book also includes full instructions for many of these models, so no matter what age you are on the outside, you can let the LEGO-loving kid within take over, get out those LEGO bricks and start building. Welcome to *Brick City*!

Warren Elsmore

THE STORY OF LEGO®

The story begins in 1916, when Ole Kirk Christiansen started a woodworking business in Billund, Denmark. He made wooden toys at first, and by the 1930s had dubbed the company 'Lego' after an abbreviation of the Danish phrase that means 'play well.' The company moved into plastics in 1947, and in 1949 it began producing plastic interlocking bricks under the name 'Automatic Binding Bricks.'

The early designs were not quite the bricks we know today, but in 1954, Ole Kirk's son, Godtfred, realised that with the addition of doors and windows, LEGO® bricks (as they were re-named in 1953) had almost limitless creative potential. The first town plan system was released soon after, but LEGO bricks were still not the company's core business. The stud-and-tube interlocking system was developed and patented in 1958, and bricks from this era are still compatible with the ones on sale today – the most important innovation was that when they were snapped together, they remained in place. 1958 was also the year Ole Kirk died, and the business passed to Godtfred.

In 1960, a warehouse fire destroyed much of Lego's remaining stock of wooden toys, and production of them was discontinued. The company, by then composed of more than 400 employees, was poised to enter the U.S., Canada, and Italy. Within a few years, it spread to a host of other countries, including Finland, the Netherlands, Hong Kong, Australia, Morocco and Japan. The LEGO invasion had begun.

By 1966, the toys were sold in forty-two countries, and the first LEGO train had been introduced, running on a four-and-a-half volt motor. This was also the year that the first LEGOLAND® Park was opened, in Billund, receiving 3,000 visitors on its first day.

LEGO sets have continued to be released on many different themes, from spacecraft to pirate ships, and many technical elements have been incorporated, such as motors, magnets and sensors. LEGO® DUPLO® – larger bricks for younger children – was released in 1977, and the following year, miniature figures ('minifigs') were introduced, allowing humanoid shapes to inhabit LEGO landscapes for the first time.

LEGO has inspired many people to accomplish extraordinary feats over the years and encouraged so much energetic innovation that few records set for LEGO creations last very long. One that has lasted (so far) is the largest LEGO structure, which is a statue of Sitting Bull at LEGOLAND, Denmark, which stands almost 7.5 metres (25 feet) tall and was made from one and a half million bricks. At the time of writing, the tallest LEGO tower is a staggering 32.5 metres (106 feet and 8 inches) tall. And I'm proud to say that the largest mosaic in the world was 472 square metres (1,549 square feet and 3 square inches), achieved at my LEGO show in May 2012, meaning that I'm the happy owner of a Guinness World Record certificate. The following month, however, the record was smashed and now stands at 820 square metres (2,690 square feet, 98 square inches). Such is the fervour of LEGO builders, these records are often broken just as fast as they are set.

WHY LEGO®?

THE STRUCTURAL QUALITIES OF LEGO® BRICKS

It's amazing how often you come across the exact same problems in a LEGO® model that you would with real materials. There are common architectural structures, such as arches, trusses and cantilevers, that have to be dealt with both in real buildings and in LEGO models. Let's use the St. Pancras International railway station in London (featured on p.104–5) as an example.

The real St. Pancras station is made up of two elements: a large hotel and a huge overarching train 'shed'. The hotel is a standard building, and replicating it is quite a straightforward task: the bricks are placed 'studs up' to create the walls and laid out in what is known as a 'stretcher bond' (the overlapping pattern we see in the walls of ordinary houses). By overlapping, the bricks strengthen each other and form a stronger whole.

The stretcher bond is only one brick thick, and doubling up the bricks would be too heavy, so, just as in a real building, it's commonly tied into a supporting wall or structural beam. To add structural integrity to the LEGO model, a LEGO Technic beam is added behind the wall to tie these courses together in exactly the same way as internal walls or steel beams might in a modern brick building.

The train shed of St. Pancras station presents another challenge. When it opened in 1868, the William Barlow-designed station featured the largest unsupported arch in the world, at 75 metres (245 feet). It's still very impressive today. The great weight of the steel arch would typically cause the outside walls to push apart unless they were held down by a great weight. The engineers used the floor of the station to act as huge tie beams, pulling in the sides of the arch and keeping the roof high.

Building an arch in LEGO at this scale (over 1.5 metres, or 5 feet, wide) brings the same problems as the St. Pancras engineers experienced. As accurate and well fitting as LEGO bricks are (and they are very,

very accurate), there is a slight 'give' in the connections, which solves the problem. When two LEGO plates are joined by a third plate underneath, there is a small gap between them. This allows the toys to be easily constructed and pulled apart, but also gives the modeller the chance to flex the elements very slightly. The 1.5-metre (5-foot)-wide arch is therefore constructed by a single line of plates, overlapping by only a single stud. There's just enough flex in that line to bend it into an arch, and enough strength to keep it in shape. But the walls must be strong enough not to push apart. This is solved by making the arch slot into the floor so that the floor takes the tension – exactly the same way as it does in the real building.

THE 10 MOST USEFUL BRICKS

These are the exciting bricks that open up whole new possibilities in LEGO® building. In my experience, the most useful bricks are those that change the direction of the studs or give fine detailing to models. It seems like no matter how many of these bricks I have, they're never enough.

1X4 PLATE HINGE

These are the little brothers of the hinge bricks that I remember as a child – small but strong hinges that let you choose the exact angle for your creation.

1X2 PLATE WITH ONE STUD, OR 'JUMPER'

When one stud is just too much! Jumpers are excellent for creating a half-stud offset for fine details. Check out the 2x2 Jumper, too.

1X1 'HEADLIGHT' BRICK

(Officially called an 'Earling' after the brick's inventor)
The original 'Studs Not On Top' (SNOT) brick, used for headlights on millions of cars. Its geometry is very clever – the depth of the recess is exactly the height of two plates.

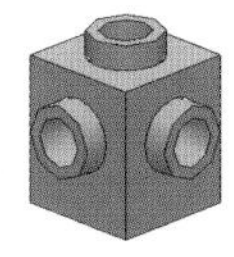

1X1 BRICK WITH STUDS ON FOUR SIDES

Nicknamed the 'dalek' in the UK, these are fantastic for creating small columns, as they let you point plates out in four directions. Overlap them and you have eight directions.

1X1 BRICK WITH A STUD ON ONE SIDE

(Nicknamed a 'ross,' as it is half a 'davros' – which, as you will know if you watch *Doctor Who*, might be described as a half-dalek!) These bricks give you a simple way of attaching a plate to the side of a brick – for detailing or to use a special brick in an unexpected manner.

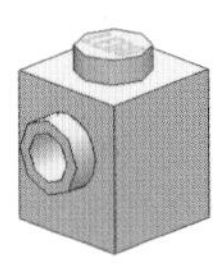

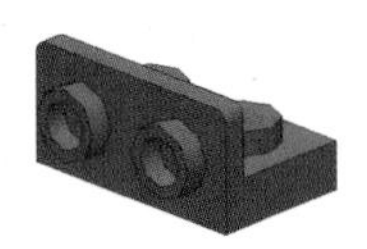

1X2 BRACKET

A new piece introduced in 2012, but so useful! These pieces help where other brackets can't, and add real strength to your model.

1X1 ROUND PLATE WITH HOLE

Only available in the LEGO® games sets, these parts are suitable for anchoring rods into the floor.

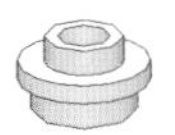

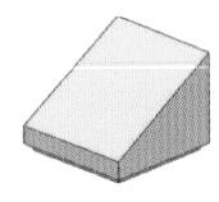

1X1X$^{2}/_{3}$ SLOPE (OR 'CHEESE' SLOPE)

A great piece that gives models a really smooth, modern look. These are useful for modelling buildings, vehicles, and even animals.

TECHNIC PIN JOINER

Structural steelwork plays a huge part in modern architecture, and these pieces joined together are just the right shape to model that in LEGO form.

And finally...

2X4 BRICK

The oldest brick around, and still my personal favourite. Strong, compact, and great for providing structure underneath something delicate.

WHERE TO BUY YOUR BRICKS

HOW TO FIND THE BRICKS YOU'LL NEED

Real-world architecture is much more serious than the LEGO® sets you find in stores, so many of the models in this book use repeating patterns of bricks – or, huge numbers of the same piece. This is where your special LEGO-buying skills come in.

My first piece of advice is to pool together all the bricks you currently have. LEGO is such a popular toy, it's almost certain that somewhere in your attic, basement or parents' house, there are boxes of LEGO parts lying around. Dig through, see if you have the bricks you need or bricks that will do (if you can't find a certain brick – for example a 2x4 brick – try a substitute, such as two 2x2 bricks), and get building. Chances are that you will find most of the bricks you need and, if you can forgive a little colour variation, you're all set.

But of course, there are models that just have to be built in the right colour and/or the right bricks. Buckingham Palace looks great in white, and tan would probably work just as well, but the impact would be lost if twelve colours were used to make the frontage. So where would a true craftsman source bricks?

If you live in the U.S., U.K. or certain other countries you may have a local LEGO brand store or LEGOLAND® theme park. These stores have special 'Pick a Brick' areas: a wall of containers all holding different parts. Need some lime green 2x4 bricks? Here you can buy them by the bucket load. If that sounds similar to picking sweets at the cinema, that's because it is. Pick a Brick walls are a great resource – because they typically sell bricks by volume or weight, they usually work out to be a highly cost-effective way to buy the bricks you need.

If you're not near a LEGO store or LEGOLAND park, don't despair; you can still access Pick a Brick online, which is available though LEGO's website at *lego.com* and delivers to a wide range of countries. The online shop charges per part, so you should determine precisely what you need before placing an order.

The vast majority of the models with instructions in this book are designed so that you can build them from parts available either online or in a LEGO store. However, sometimes a specific part is needed to make a model work, and although they were all made by LEGO, not every part has remained in production throughout the company's history. The answer is to be found on *bricklink.com*, the brainchild of an enterprising young LEGO enthusiast, Dan Jekel (who is sadly no longer with us). Here, thousands of traders worldwide list the parts they want to sell so that LEGO fans can source whichever parts they need (you will need a Paypal account to buy from most sellers, and this is encouraged as it has built-in protection). You should also always take note of the seller's location, as while a part might be cheap, additional shipping prices and import duty can make the purchase much less appealing. You may also want to keep an eye on your wallet – once you get used to the luxury of unlimited LEGO parts being available at the press of a button, it can get expensive very quickly.

See p.255 for details of an additional online resource to help you source the bricks required for the buildable projects featured in *Brick City*.

SCALE

Scale is a perennial issue for LEGO® artists trying to represent real buildings or designs. It can be equally difficult within the pages of a book to clearly communicate the scale of each of these projects: when photographed, some of the best LEGO models can easily be mistaken for their real-life counterparts at first or even second glance. The scale diagram below shows how some of the projects featured in the book stack up against each other, and will perhaps help give a sense of porportion.

Where we have featured towers or other particularly large models we've used the illustration below to give a better sense of its scale. These show how many minifigs you would need to stack on top of each other to reach the equivalent height, or line up shoulder-to-shoulder to make up an equal width, of that model. In a couple of cases like the Sydney Harbour Bridge they are lying down in a line, head to toe (which isn't all that unlikely in real life – there's an annual picnic on the bridge!)

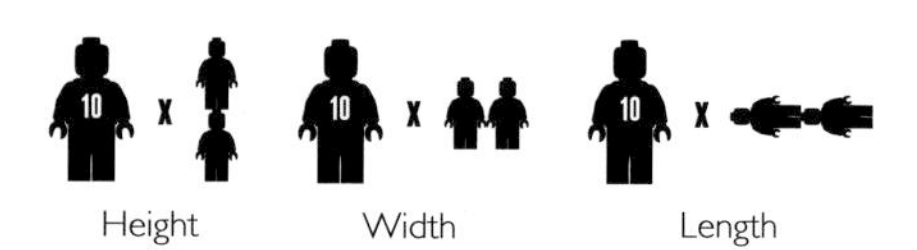

Parisian Café Coffee Machine (p.152)

Chac Mool (p.76)

Sagrada Família (p.128)

Abraham Lincoln Memorial (p.68)

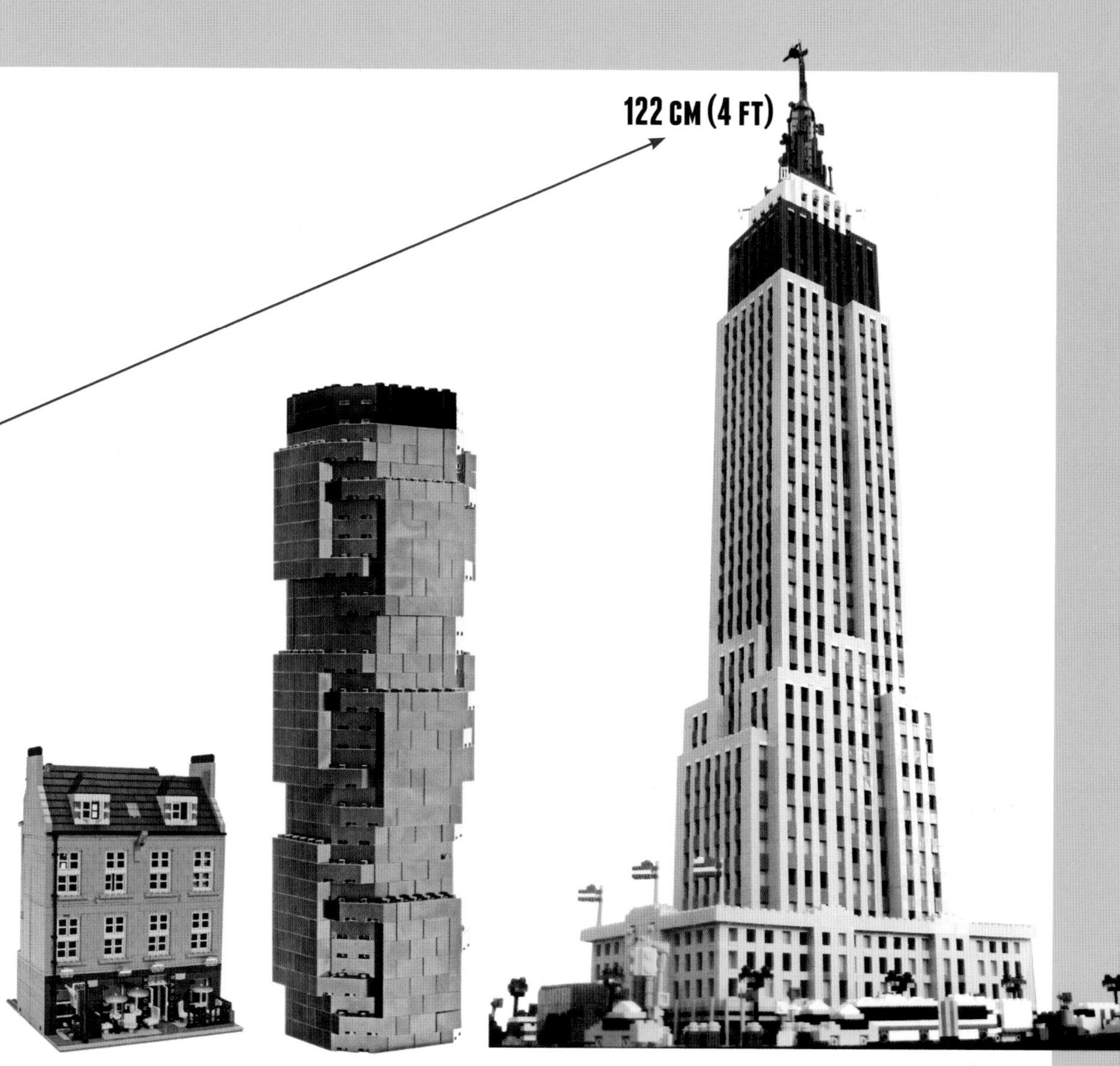

Edinburgh Tenement
(p.90)

Lippo Centre
(p.234)

The Empire State Building
(p.44)

A GUIDE TO THE MINIFIG SCALE AND OTHER APPROACHES TO SCALE IN LEGO® MODELLING

Since its launch, the LEGO® minifigure, or 'minifig', has become the globally recognisable symbol of the LEGO company. Minifigs add character, make models look more lifelike and, most importantly, let children (and adults) act out their own stories. Many of the models in this book are built to make the minifigs look human-sized, and this is called 'minifig scale', which is generally agreed to be somewhere between 1:40 and 1:50. LEGO minifigures are much wider and shorter than the average person, so it's a difficult comparison to make accurately. But sometimes to make a model work, the scale has to be very cleverly played with, and here our demonstration building, St. Pancras International station, comes back again.

The minifig scale model is massive, over 2 metres (6½ feet) wide and 4 metres (13 feet) long, with six working platforms and hundreds of minifig passengers going about their normal lives. But compare this with the real station and you'll notice a big difference. The real St. Pancras station is long and narrow, the brick building perhaps ten times longer than it is wide. Yet although the model looks accurate, it is hardly five times longer than it is wide.

Many of the larger models in this book use a technique called 'selective compression', and without even knowing it, you will have seen it before in real life. The next time you're in any major theme park, take a close look at the buildings. The ground floor is as you would expect – you can walk through the doors and look through the windows. But look at the third or fourth floor, and you start to notice the upper floors aren't as tall as the ground floor – they've been compressed to make the building look larger than it really is. The same technique is used by LEGO builders to make large models look correct rather than be strictly accurate in terms of scale. This means that minifig scale can often vary from 1:40 or 1:50 to 1:100. As long as the minifigs don't look out of place, the eye is deceived.

What about the smaller models that do not include minifigs? With buildings such as the Las Vegas hotels or Chichen Itza in Mexico which are very large in real life, it wouldn't be feasible to build models to minifig scale, so a smaller one has to be sought. This is often referred to as a 'microscale'. As with the minifig scale, rather than enforce a strict numerical scale, a microscale uses common LEGO elements to represent real objects. Although a microscale varies more widely than a minifig scale, it is generally based on the use of a 1x1 brick, or plate, as a person. More recently, the small figures that are used in the LEGO games sets have also been used to bridge the gap between the microscale and the minifig scale, creating greater variation in the possibilities of scale in LEGO models.

There are a variety of models in this book that are at too small a scale to even contemplate representing people. How to decide on a scale for the Arc de Triomphe, for instance? The hard-learned trick (which takes a lot of trial and error) is to have a sense for how large a model will have to be in order to look like its real-world counterpart – in the same way as you have to stand far back enough from a digital image before the pixels gel into a recognisable image. If you get the key defining elements right, then the rest is likely to follow.

CAD MODELLING

Computer-Aided Design (CAD) software lets you play with virtual LEGO® bricks to explore and plan the model you want to build, before you build it. With an unlimited number of bricks and any colour at your disposal, a world of planning awaits. If you're going to build ambitious projects, like many of those in this book, using CAD will tell you in advance how many of each brick you will need. There are two main types of LEGO CAD systems, and both are free!

LEGO Digital Designer (LDD) (*ldd.lego.com*) can be downloaded from LEGO and is available for Mac or PC. Once installed, it will download a full list of all the (currently) available LEGO bricks. LDD helps you build creations that will work in the real world, so bricks will be automatically connected for you as you place them. Once finished, LDD can automatically create online instructions to build the actual model – just switch into 'Building Guide Mode' and follow the steps.

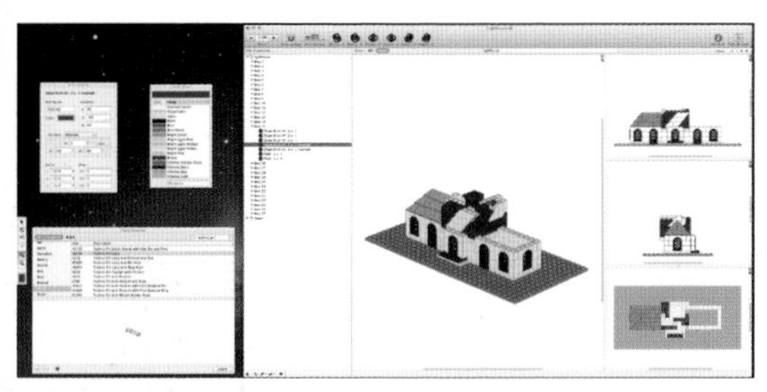

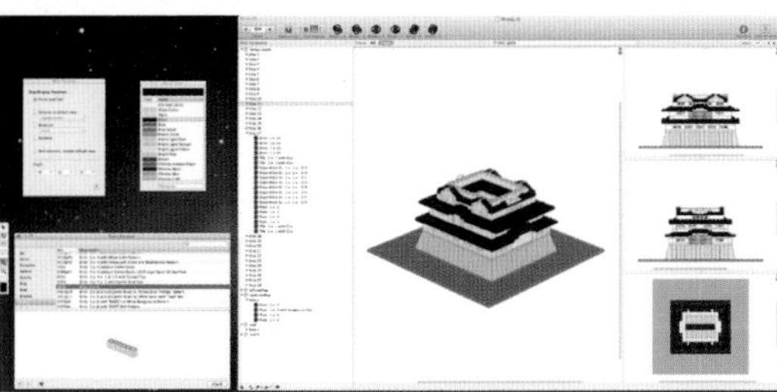

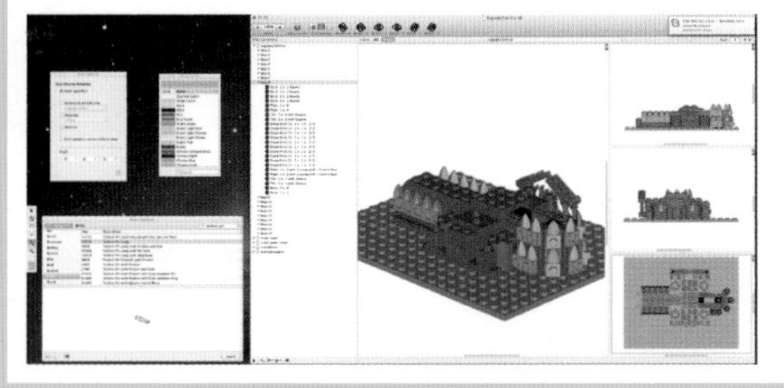

The LDraw system (*ldraw.org*; pictured below) predates LDD, and, rather than being written by LEGO, it has been created and maintained by the LEGO community. It does have a few significant advantages over the official software. First, almost any part ever made is available in LDraw – a much larger list than LDD provides. Second, LDraw is far more flexible and will let you create models that wouldn't really work in the real world. For instance, when designing a model I sometimes use 1x1 bricks for everything, just until I get the look right. Of course, this would fall apart if I tried to build it, so once I get the look that I want, I put in the proper bricks that would allow the model to stand. Doing it this way can be somewhat labour-intensive, but it's a useful planning technique.

The LDraw system contains a number of different tools that you can use to create both models and instructions. For this book, I used the Bricksmith editor on the Mac to create all the models and the LPub tool to create their instructions. I am extremely grateful to all those involved in creating this software and to everyone at *LDraw.org*.

Left, from top: the Green Point Lighthouse, Himeji Castle, and the Sagrada Família under consruction in LDraw.

BUILDING FREESTYLE

BUILD LEGO® FREESTYLE, WITHOUT A SET OF INSTRUCTIONS

Free building is a little like free climbing – there's no safety net. The majority of the models in this book are not free builds because they have to be as precise as possible and require a lot of work, so instructions should be used. But the truth is, freestyle is how most people build with, and get fun out of, LEGO®.

Anything can be free-built. A child might build a spaceship out of whichever parts are available and believe it is one. But as we get older, we may start to get fixed ideas about what a spaceship looks like, and might decide in advance whether it has rockets, blasters and a sleek, domed cockpit. The trick to enjoying free building is to try and forget that strict, specific approach and the need for exact accuracy, and to reinvent your creations with that childlike imagination.

Here's a good tip to encourage yourself to free build. At your next grown-up dinner party, go to your local toy store and find some small sets, getting one for every guest. Something from LEGO's Creator range is good – they tend to have lots of pieces and a low price point. Now, your challenge is to free-build from that set only. Perhaps choose a spaceship (or robot, car or house) as a theme, and sit back. You'll be amazed what you and your guests can come up with – even if their childhood technically ended decades ago.

LEGO® BUILDING TIPS

One thing you might notice as you flip through this book is that the LEGO® models featured don't look like the LEGO models you might see on the shelves of your local toy store. Well, there's a reason for that! The first question I'm asked about a model is usually, 'Is that really all LEGO?' The answer is yes. Every model you see here is made from 100 per cent LEGO elements. But the way in which these bricks are assembled might vary significantly from what you're used to.

Many of the icons within these pages are built 'studs up' – that is, each brick is stacked on top of the one beneath it. Many other models, however, are not built this way. To understand why not, we need to go back to school.

There are two basic types of LEGO elements from which nearly all other elements are derived: bricks and plates. One LEGO brick is equal in height to three LEGO plates. Plates give models more rigidity (for instance, they make great floors), but they also allow you to have three times the colour variation or detail in the same space as a simple brick. Smaller elements mean more accurate designs, so many of the models in this book use plates instead of bricks. For instance, a coloured stripe can be introduced by using three plates of contrasting colours rather than a single brick (see the illustration below).

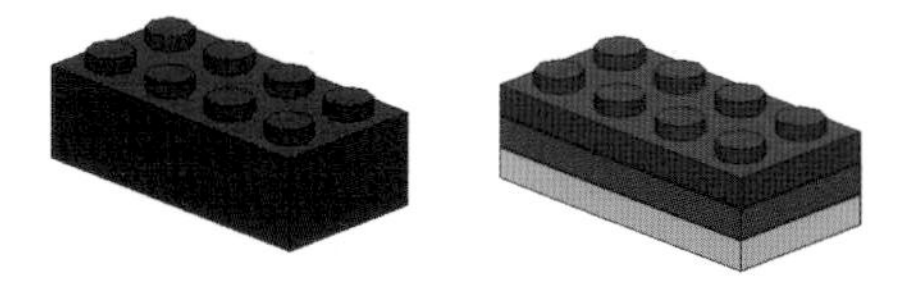

Yet making models out of plates will only take us so far. Skyscrapers and flat-sided vehicles adapt well, but what about curved surfaces, thin extrusions and structural steelwork? How do we model those in LEGO? Thankfully there are many other bricks that can help us out – thousands of types of elements, dating back over fifty years. Roofs can be made out of sloped bricks, for example, and steel columns can be represented by LEGO Technic elements – you will see many more inventive uses of different parts in our instruction illustrations. Choosing the right elements can help create a model using a surprisingly small number of parts.

There is another important technique that LEGO fans use to put bricks together, which is nicknamed (perhaps unfortunately) 'SNOT'. This is not a rather unsanitary method of sticking bricks together; rather, it stands for 'Studs Not On Top' – this is a method of turning bricks or plates sideways to allow countless possibilities.

SNOT relies on another simple principle of LEGO geometry. Whereas a LEGO brick is three times the height of a LEGO plate, it is also two and a half times as wide as that plate is high. Or, the width of two bricks is equal to the height of five plates (illustration below). Using plates and SNOT, the accuracy of your modelling can be increased threefold, in all directions.

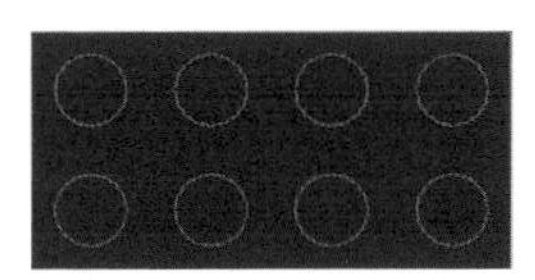

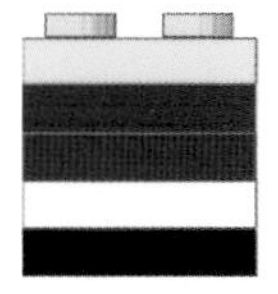

This offers even more interesting possibilities. Perhaps a model needs a circular shape which is not available from LEGO as an existing element? While it would be possible to use plates to model this curve – and they would work well for part of the circle – this method is not so useful where the curve becomes steeper. But turn half of the plates sideways and suddenly our model is far more accurate (see below).

To hold these sideways elements in place, we need some special pieces that can hold elements on one side, two sides or even all four sides of a brick, and luckily a number of these exist (see 'The 10 Most Useful Bricks' section on p.9). In the end, a combination of bricks and plates, and the use of all the available slopes, hinges and curves, and of course SNOT, enables us to make the models in this book possible.

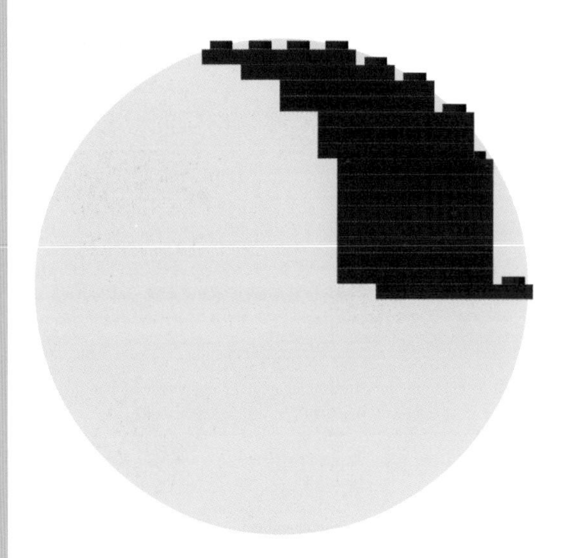

Modelling a curve without SNOT

Modelling a curve using SNOT

LEGO® COLOURS

Re-creating a building with LEGO® always throws up one challenge in particular: with so many LEGO colours to choose from, which should you use? When I first started using LEGO as a child, there were very few colours, and those that were available were mainly bright colours like Red, Yellow and Blue. But as LEGO developed, greys were introduced, followed by Tan (a beige colour) and now there is a whole spectrum of colours to choose from.

So how to choose a colour? Well, the obvious choice will be to choose the LEGO colour that matches your building as closely as possible – but beware! Not all parts exist in all colours, and in fact some very common parts have never been made in some of the obvious colours. How often a part has been manufactured and made available in a particular colour can dramatically affect its value as well: rare part/colour combinations can be very expensive on Bricklink.

I find that the easiest way to choose a colour is to first decide which of the more than 140 LEGO colours would best match your model. Is the stonework Tan, White or Grey? Can you represent a gold tower block with dark orange bricks? Narrow down your choices to one of the LEGO colours available, then take a look at your model. Which are the important parts that really define the model? Make sure that the colour you choose has those pieces available!

To help you choose, below and over the page is a guide to some, but not all, of the colours available, using their Bricklink names rather than the official LEGO ones.

Yellow

Green

Turquoise

Light Bluish-Grey

Light Yellow

Bright Green

Sand Green

Sand Blue

Black

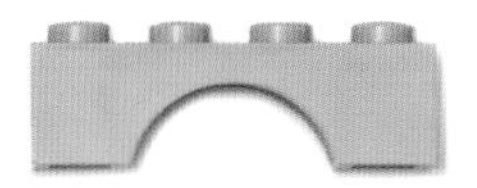

Lime Green

Dark Bluish-Grey

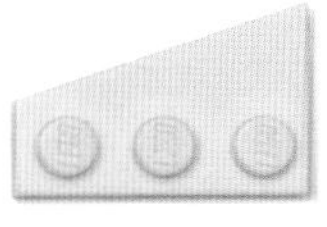

White

Dark Turquoise

Dark Green

Trans-Black

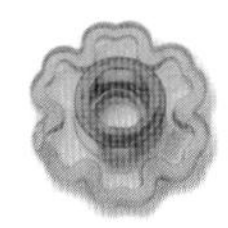
Trans-Pink

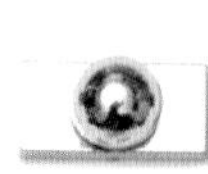
Chrome Silver

Dark Red

Trans-Clear

Trans-Red

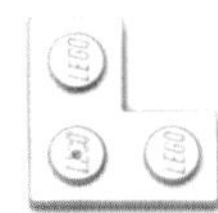
Pearl Silver

Red

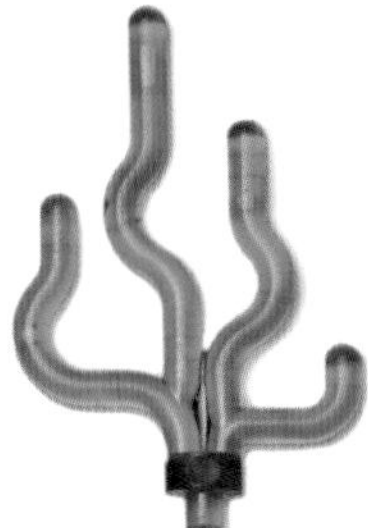
Trans-Green

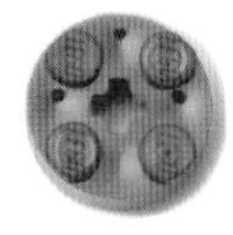
Trans-Neon Orange

Marbled Silver

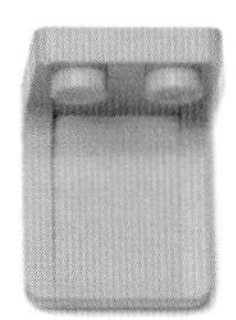
Pink

Trans-Light Blue

Trans-Orange

Pearl Light Grey

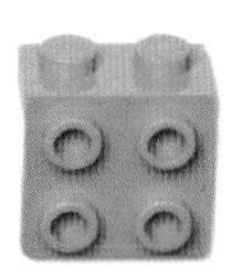
Medium Dark Pink

Trans-Dark Blue

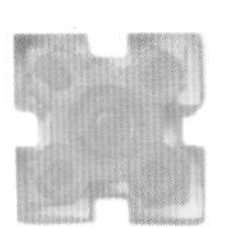
Trans-Yellow

Pearl Black

Light Purple

Trans-Blue

Trans-Neon Green

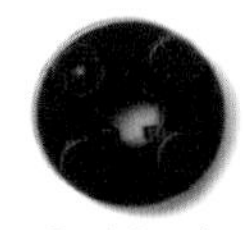
Dark Purple

Bright Pink

Trans-Purple

Pearl Gold

Purple

Dark Pink

Aqua

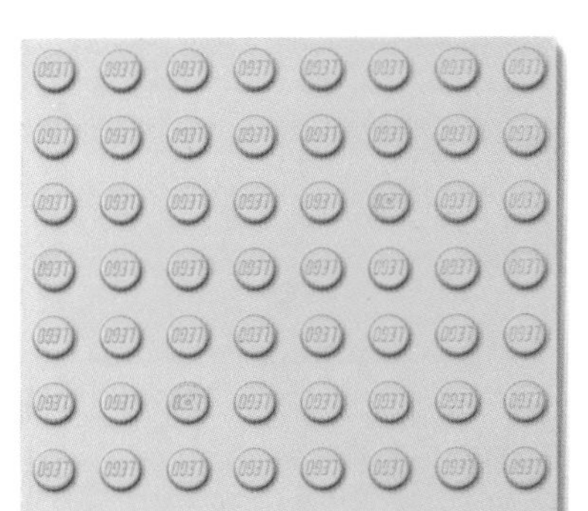

Bright Light Blue

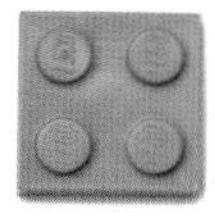

Dark Azure

Medium Blue

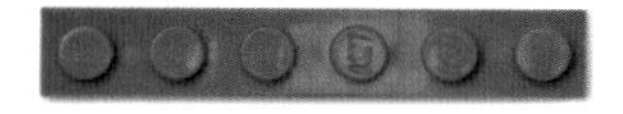

Maersk Blue

Violet

Bright Light Yellow

Bright Yellow

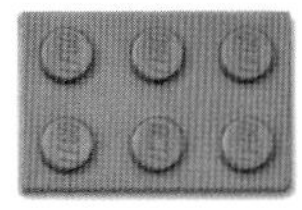

Light Orange

Dark Flesh

Orange

Dark Blue

Blue

Dark Brown

Reddish Brown

Earth Orange

Dark Orange

Dark Tan

Olive Green

Tan

PRACTICE PROJECT

Before we begin our world trip, it might be worth brushing up on some of those LEGO® building skills. The models in this book use a few advanced techniques that you might not remember from your childhood. So to begin, how about a simple bungalow? The house you see opposite is a small LEGO house, just like any other. But I've used a few techniques to give it more detail and a more customised look. Let's see how it's built.

The first thing you'll notice is that this model isn't to 'minifig scale'. I've made it smaller so it's easier to build, but that brings its own problems. Building smaller than minifig scale meant that I needed to build my own door. Rather than just choose bricks of different colours, I wanted to add a door frame and some texture. Using bricks around the door would be too large – so I've opted to use plates instead. Building the door sideways with plates is a SNOT technique ('Studs Not On Top,' see p.17–18). This allowed me to add fine detail to the model. Remembering that five plates is equal to two studs allowed me to ensure that the door fitted in. To create the door frame, I used the 1x2 Plate with door rail (part 32028). This sticks out enough to create a frame. And the door itself is made not from standard bricks, but the 1x2 brick with grill (2877), which gives a lovely wooden effect.

The windows present similar problems to the builder. LEGO minifig scale windows would have looked too large and ungainly, so I opted to create windows from bricks. In this instance, I used four of the headlight bricks (4070) but facing backwards – to create window panes. Notice that on the front windows I've also added a window ledge. This could have been created using the same 1x2 plates with rail as I used on the door, but for variety in this case I used the 'jumper' plate instead (3794). I placed two of these under the window, so that I could put the rear hole of another two jumpers on the studs I'd created. Going half a stud back means I'm now half a stud forwards for the ledge. The second pair of jumpers put the window back in the right place – not that they have to be!

As you complete the walls of the bungalow, you'll notice that the plates I've put above the door aren't actually connected to anything! This is a common technique that LEGO fans use but which the LEGO company avoids (it's too difficult to explain sometimes – and awkward to put into instructions). These plates are held in place by the next layer of plates above. So when the building is complete, the pieces are held in place, but I don't need to worry about the lack of studs in my door.

The final part of any building is the roof. Again, I did not use the standard LEGO technique you might think of (roof bricks). In this case, I've used some LEGO technic elements to angle the sides of the roof downwards. This is quite a common technique for a number of reasons. It uses fewer bricks than LEGO roof bricks so it is cheaper. More importantly, though, this technique allows the builder to angle the roof just how he or she wants it to be. This is even more important when it comes to complex roof shapes.

So, now that you've built your bungalow, you're ready for the whole Brick City! Where to start?

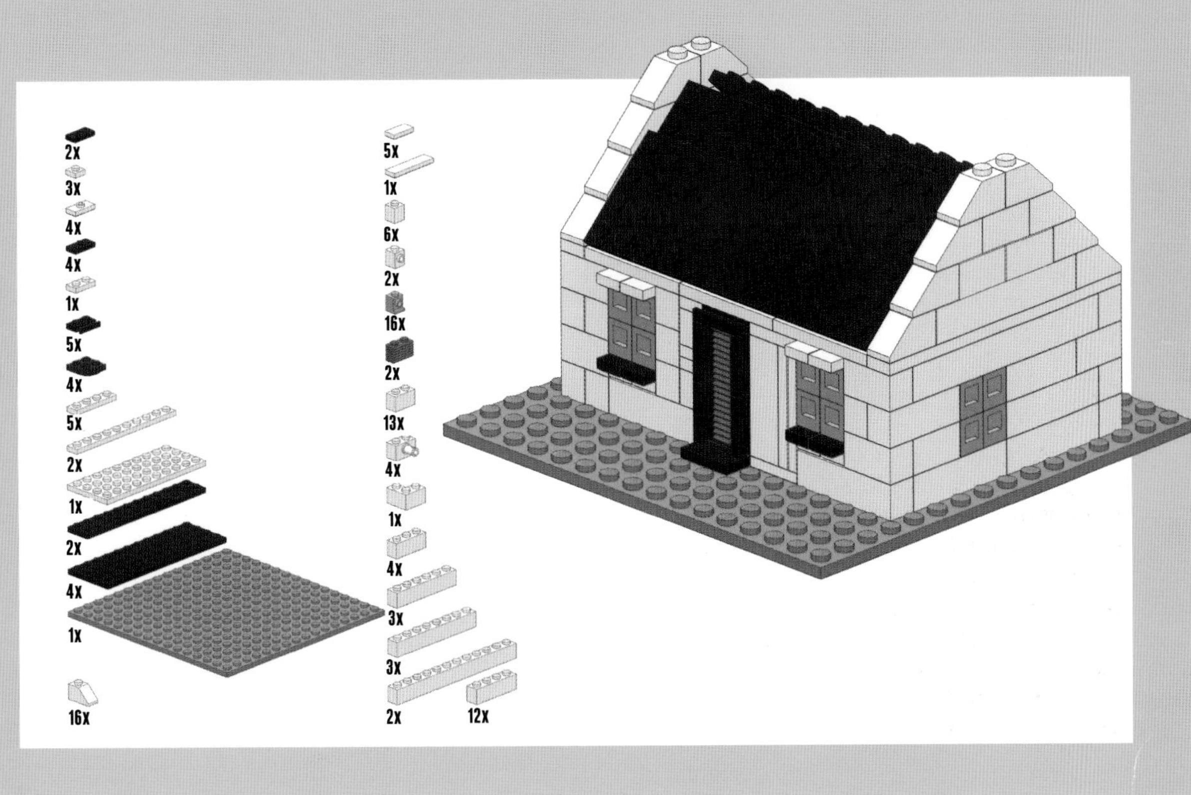
2x
3x
4x
4x
1x
5x
4x
5x
2x
1x
2x
4x
1x
16x
5x
1x
6x
2x
16x
2x
13x
4x
1x
4x
3x
3x
2x
12x

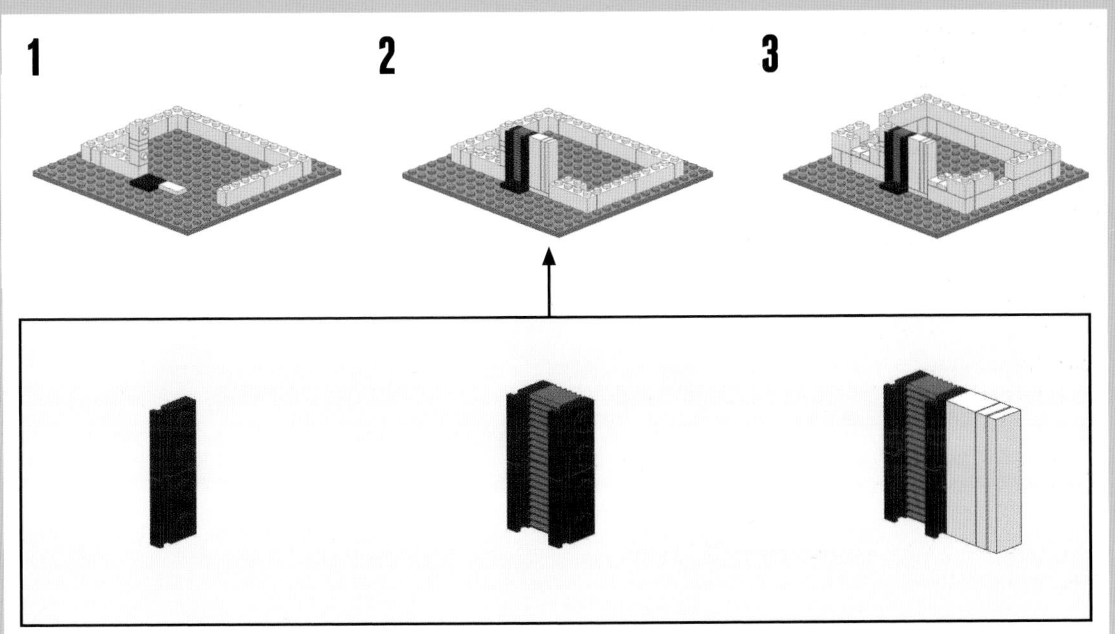
1
2
3

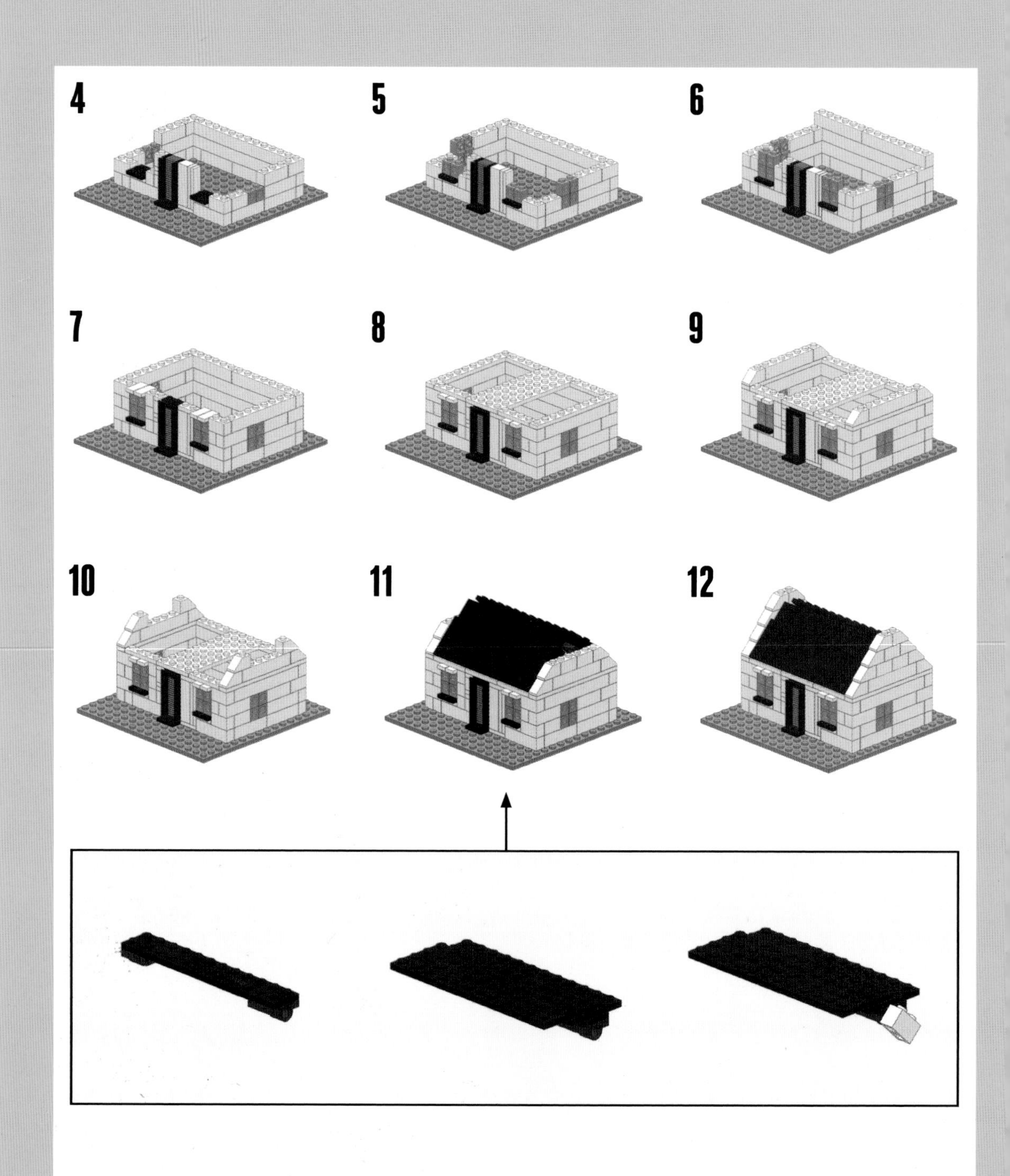
4
5
6
7
8
9
10
11
12

MOSAIC TECHNIQUES

LEGO® mosaics are, in principle, very straightforward. There are a limited number of LEGO colours, but thankfully more than enough to create a good picture. So the difficulties you may encounter will be related to the choice of image and how best to bring that out in LEGO tiles. There are a few tips that we can use to help us along the way.

Choosing your mosaic picture is the first challenge. You may be creating a mosaic of yourself, your favourite cartoon character or any other image you like. To create a mosaic with maximum impact, try to stay away from images that are particularly complex. The more shades or fine detail an image has, the harder it will be to convert that into a recognisable LEGO mosaic – at least without making it absolutely enormous! So if you can, stick to a simple image, with bold colours and features. I'm going to assume from here that you have this image on your computer.

There are many ways of converting your image into a LEGO mosaic. Really, a LEGO mosaic is just a low-resolution version of the image. You can try reducing the definition of the picture on your computer until it starts to become pixelated, as though it's made from LEGO tiles. However, this doesn't always work: you will often find that the image becomes unrecognisable, or that there are too many colours in it. This is where LEGO mosaic software comes in handy.

There are lots of software programs that will let you turn your image into a LEGO mosaic by reducing the colours and size down automatically. I've used Pictobrick (*pictobrick.de*) and Photobricks (*photobricksapp.com*) to help me create the mosaics in this book. Both are fairly simple to use and will ask you how large you'd like the mosaic to be and what method to use to cut down the number of colours. Once finished, you'll get an output of what bricks go where, and you can just copy the image down using LEGO.

Anything is possible with a LEGO mosaic. World records are toppling all the time, with mosaics regularly being built from more than a million bricks. So if you have the desire to build it, it can be done.

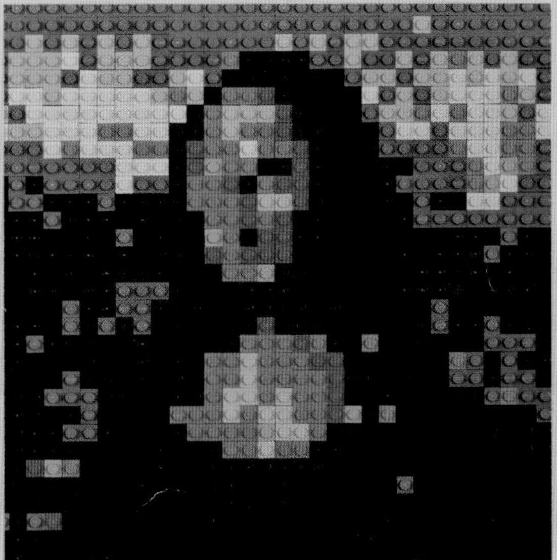

BRICK PICK

With an entire globe of landmarks to re-create in LEGO® bricks, where to begin? Here's a quick guide to all the buildable projects featured in this book – each includes a bill of materials listing all the parts you'll need, and step-by-step instructions demonstrating each step in the model's construction.

The models below are colour-coded by city: see below opposite for the key. Starting in San Francisco, we'll be travelling from West to East – not strictly as the crow flies, but leaving everywhere we stop a lot smaller than it was when we found it!

Cable Car, p.31

Excalibur Hotel, p.37

Luxor Hotel, p.38

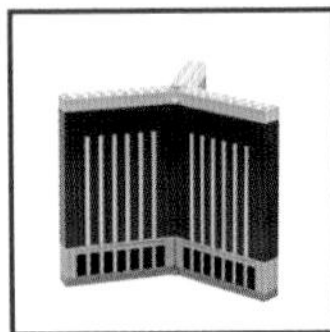
Mandalay Bay Hotel, p.39

New York-New York, p.40

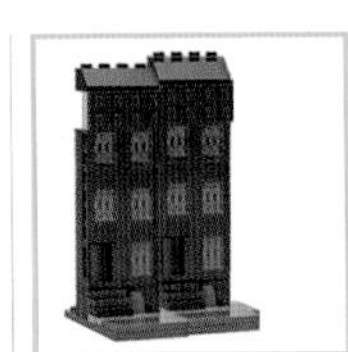
Brownstone, p.48

New York Taxi, p.50

Hot Dog, p.60

Hot Dog Stand, p.61

Marilyn Monroe, p.62

Fire Hydrant, p.63

Flatiron Building, p.63

White House, p.70

Capitol Building, p.71

Washington Monument, p.72

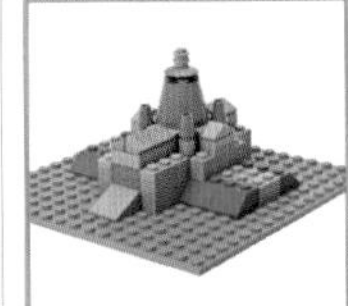
St. Joseph's Oratory, p.74

Chac Mool, p.76

Bica Funicular, p.86

Mons Meg, p.91

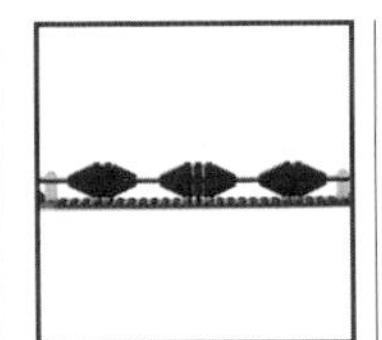
Forth Bridge, p.92

Red Phone Box, p.100

Mini Westminster Abbey, p.108

O_2 Arena (Millennium Dome), p.109

Canary Wharf, p.109

Buckingham Palace, p.110

St. Paul's Cathedral, p.120

National Gallery, p.121

Nelson's Column, p.122

Sagrada Família, p.128

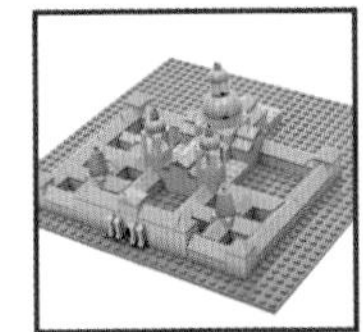
El Escorial, p.133

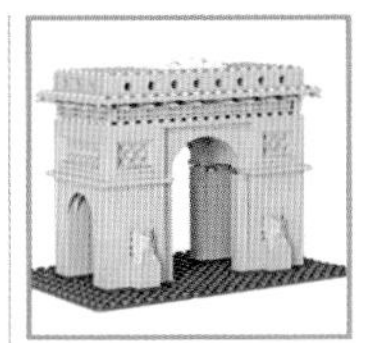
Arc de Triomphe, p.136

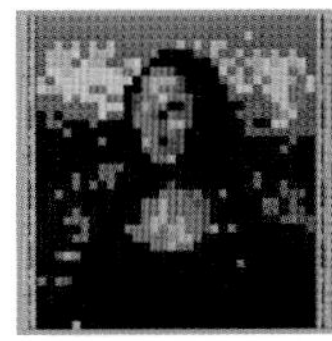
Mona Lisa, p.142

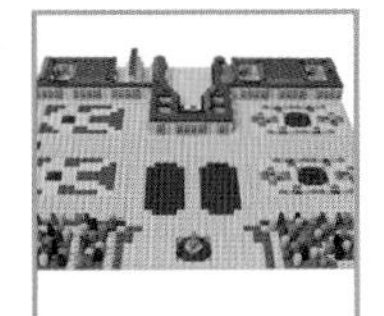
Versailles, p.148

Parisian Café, p.152

Windmill, p.157

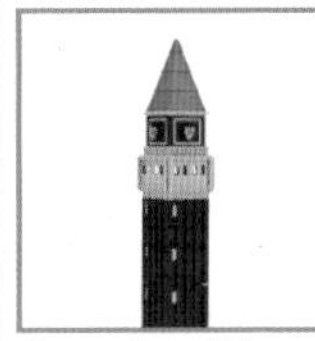
Campanile, p.160

Trevi Fountain, p.166

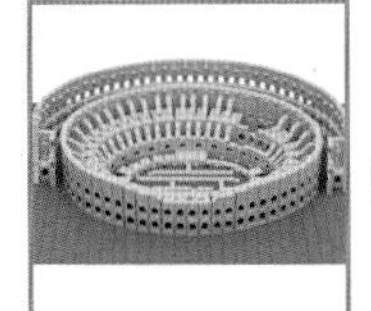
Colosseum, p.172

Rundetaarn, p.185

Christiansborg Palace, p.186

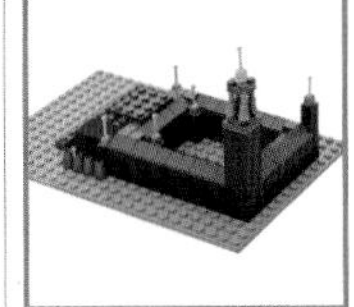
Stadshuset, p.188

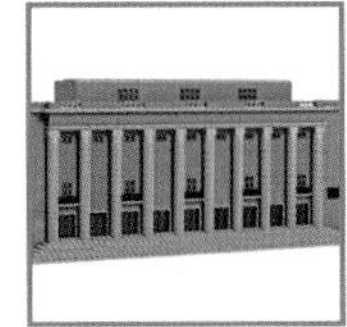
Tengboms Koncerthuset, p.190

Ampelmann, p.194

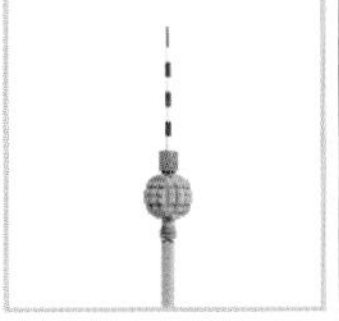
TV Tower, p.196

Charles Bridge, p.198

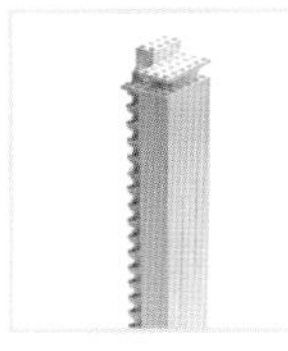
Olympic Stadium Tower, p.200

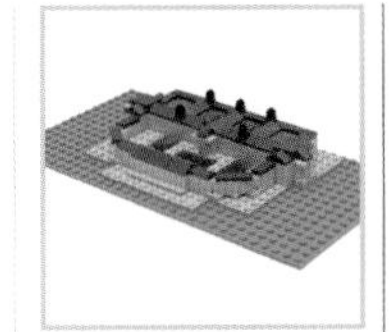
Szechenyi Baths, p.202

Krakow Cathedral, p.204

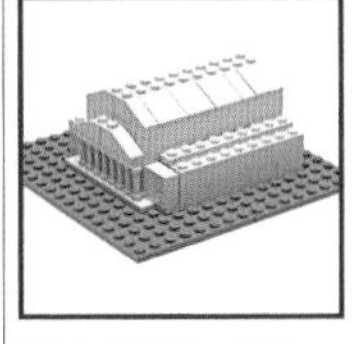
Bolshoi Ballet, p.208

Green Point Lighthouse, p.214

Penguin Colony, p. 217

Table Mountain Aerial Cableway, p.218

Petronas Towers, p.224

Marina Bay Sands, p.226

Junk Vessel, p.229

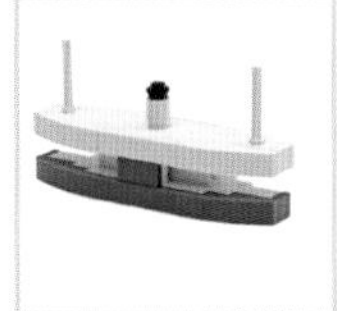
Star Ferry, p.230

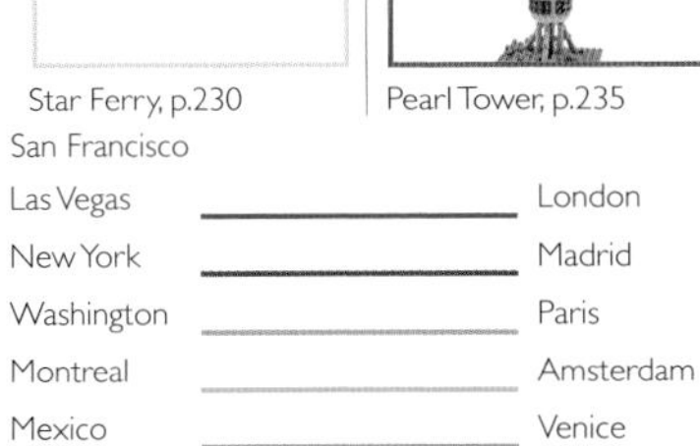
Pearl Tower, p.235

City Hall, p.240

Picnic Scene, p.242

________ San Francisco
________ Las Vegas
________ New York
________ Washington
________ Montreal
________ Mexico
________ Lisbon
________ Edinburgh

________ London
________ Madrid
________ Paris
________ Amsterdam
________ Venice
________ Rome
________ Copenhagen

________ Stockholm
________ Berlin
________ Prague
________ Helsinki
________ Budapest
________ Krakow
________ Moscow

________ Cape Town
________ Kuala Lumpur
________ Singapore
________ Hong Kong
________ Shanghai
________ Seoul
________ Tokyo

CUSTOMISING MINIFIGS

There are so many different minifigures created by LEGO® that it might seem fruitless to start creating your own, but actually you've probably already done it. Ever swap around some heads to create one that looks like you? Or how about putting hair on at a stylish angle to create a new 'haircut'? Creating customised minifigs doesn't need to involve paint, mouldable material or hacksaws. Some of the best ones are the simplest!

The best place to start when creating a customised figure is to think about 'who' you're making. If you want to create a cartoon character, chances are the LEGO head you need probably doesn't exist, so you're going to have to get creative. However, if it's something or somebody simpler, you might be able to use standard LEGO parts. Hundreds of different heads, hair and bodies have been created, and this is also the preferred way of LEGO purists.

One of the best places to browse for LEGO parts is Brickset (*brickset.com/parts/browse*). Their data is taken directly from LEGO, so names for parts and colours might not be completely intuitive, but it's useful for searching through lots of parts in one go and shows you which sets they appeared in, which allows you to check if you already have them. They also show whether the parts can be ordered directly from LEGO (green tick) or not (red cross).

If you've identified all the parts you need to create the minifig of your dreams, that's great; however, if not, we're going to have start breaking some LEGO rules!

If the colour you need doesn't exist yet in LEGO, there are a couple of options to try. One is painting the part. Acrylic paints are best (avoid enamels as they can eat into the plastic), and spray cans or guns will give you an even finish over a largish area, but can be awkward to use, requiring decent ventilation and quite a large amount even for a small piece of plastic.

You will be surprised what you can achieve with a paintbrush; the little paints that modellers use for army figures are ideal, but remember to use several thin coats instead of one or two thick ones. You'll get a better finish in the end.

Now on to the full customisation. There are various ways to customise torsos. The cheapest and easiest is to use regular inkjet printable stickers. Create the design on your computer (using Photoshop, Illustrator, GIMP, etc.), scale to size (you can readily find templates online) and then print it out. If you've done it on a white background, the sticker will almost certainly cover up the existing print on the LEGO minifig.

However, you might want to get fancier and use water slide decals. If so, you're probably going to have to remove the existing print on your minifig. The tried-and-tested way to do this is to use Brasso and a lot of elbow grease. Once you have made a minifig blank in this way, you can try out inkjet-printable water slide decals. As before, design the torso on the computer, print out, and follow the manufacturer's instructions (this normally means sealing your design with varnish before applying it). I prefer gloss varnish, but some prefer matt – the choice is yours.

Once the decal is applied, you'll want to seal it to the minifig – again, using either a spray or painted-on varnish is best. I tend to stick with water-based varnishes, but what you use is up to you. Custom heads can be created in the same way, though applying them to a curved surface can be challenging, and they might not be robust enough to withstand the hair being changed over and over.

Advanced Customisation

Some people (with a steadier hands than mine) paint their minifigs and create beautiful works of art. They also create custom parts, hair and headwear using mouldable clay, such as Sculpey or Fimo. There are online guides for how to do this, and it's an inexpensive way to create some outlandish figures.

Custom Parts

There are a few ways to create custom parts. One of the most accessible is to use polymer clay to sculpt the parts. The instructions for hardening the clay are on the packet, and your imagination and creativity are probably the only limiting factors. The likelihood is that you won't be able to create something that will actually lock into place with the LEGO part it's connecting to – so even though the tolerance of LEGO is extremely high, you can always use superglue to attach it.

More advanced techniques involve creating silicone moulds and casting parts in resin. This can create very detailed parts or can be used to create existing LEGO parts in new colours. 3-D printing is another option, although the current consensus is that their resolution isn't yet high enough to create acceptable parts.

Finally, there are the third-party sellers of custom parts. They make their parts in the same way LEGO does, with ABS plastic and expensive moulds. Their prices are reasonable, as they can make parts in large quantities. I'm particularly fond of BrickForge parts (*brickforge.com*), as they don't just focus on weapons and armor. But if that is not your thing, Tiny Tactical and Amazing Armory are also very well regarded.

There are also sellers, such as *minifigs.me*, who sell a range of ready-made minifig creations (e.g. for special occasions, or featuring celebrities), and also allow you to customise your very own personalised, made-to-order minifigure.

Caroline Savage,
minifigs.me

SAN FRANCISCO

TRANSAMERICA PYRAMID

Architect: William Pereira (1972)

LEGO® Edition by Arthur Gugick

Size: 53 cm (21 in) high, 20.5 cm (8 in) wide and deep

Bricks: 5,000

Scale: 1:485

The tallest skyscraper in the San Francisco skyline, the Transamerica Pyramid's pointed shape was designed to allow as much natural light and fresh air as possible to filter down to the street level. The greatest challenge posed during the construction of the LEGO model was approximating the building's sloped shape with incremental half steps using jumper plates. In essence it's nothing more than a series of nested, stacked squares, but it manages to convey the monolithic impressiveness of the original tower.

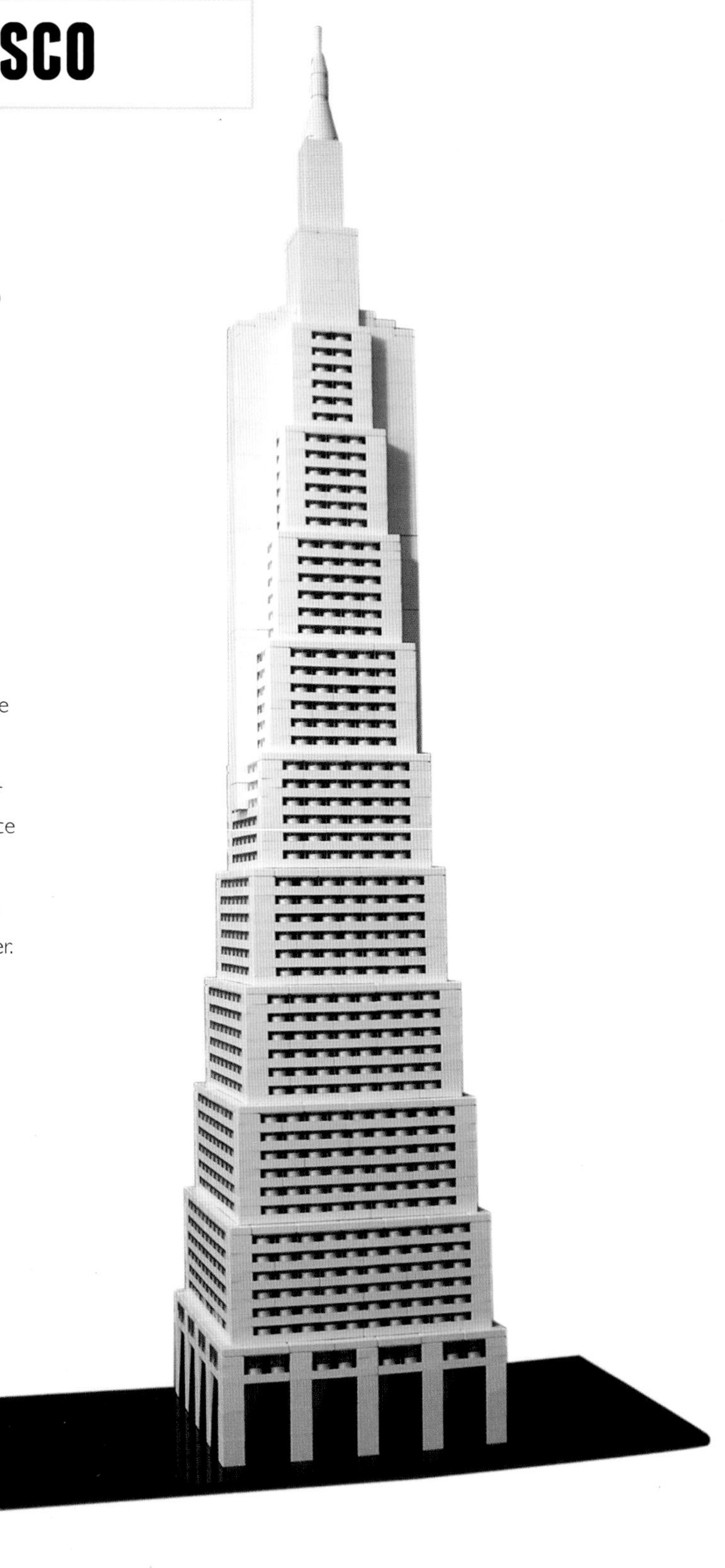

CABLE CAR

The famous San Francisco cable car is built to minifig scale. It is actually sitting on standard LEGO® train tracks, so it could move if there was a motor fitted to it. This model came out particularly well, and I'm very proud of it!

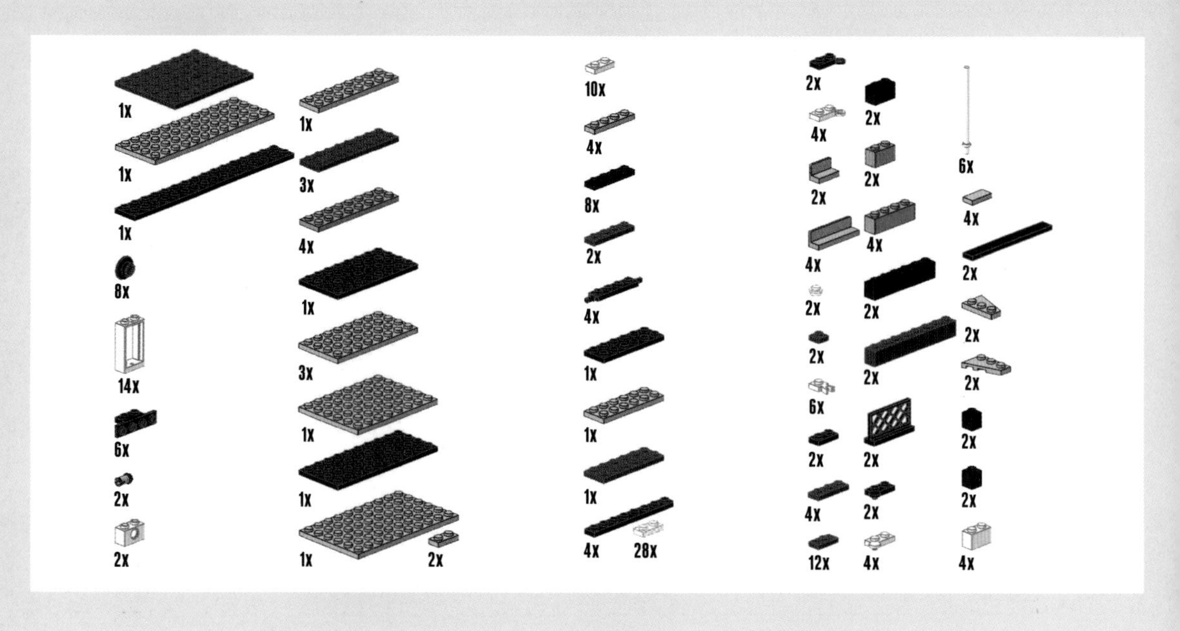
1x
1x
1x
8x
14x
6x
2x
2x
1x
3x
4x
1x
3x
1x
1x
1x
2x
10x
4x
8x
2x
4x
1x
1x
1x
4x
28x
2x
4x
2x
4x
2x
2x
6x
2x
4x
12x
2x
2x
4x
2x
2x
2x
2x
2x
4x
6x
4x
2x
2x
2x
2x
2x
4x

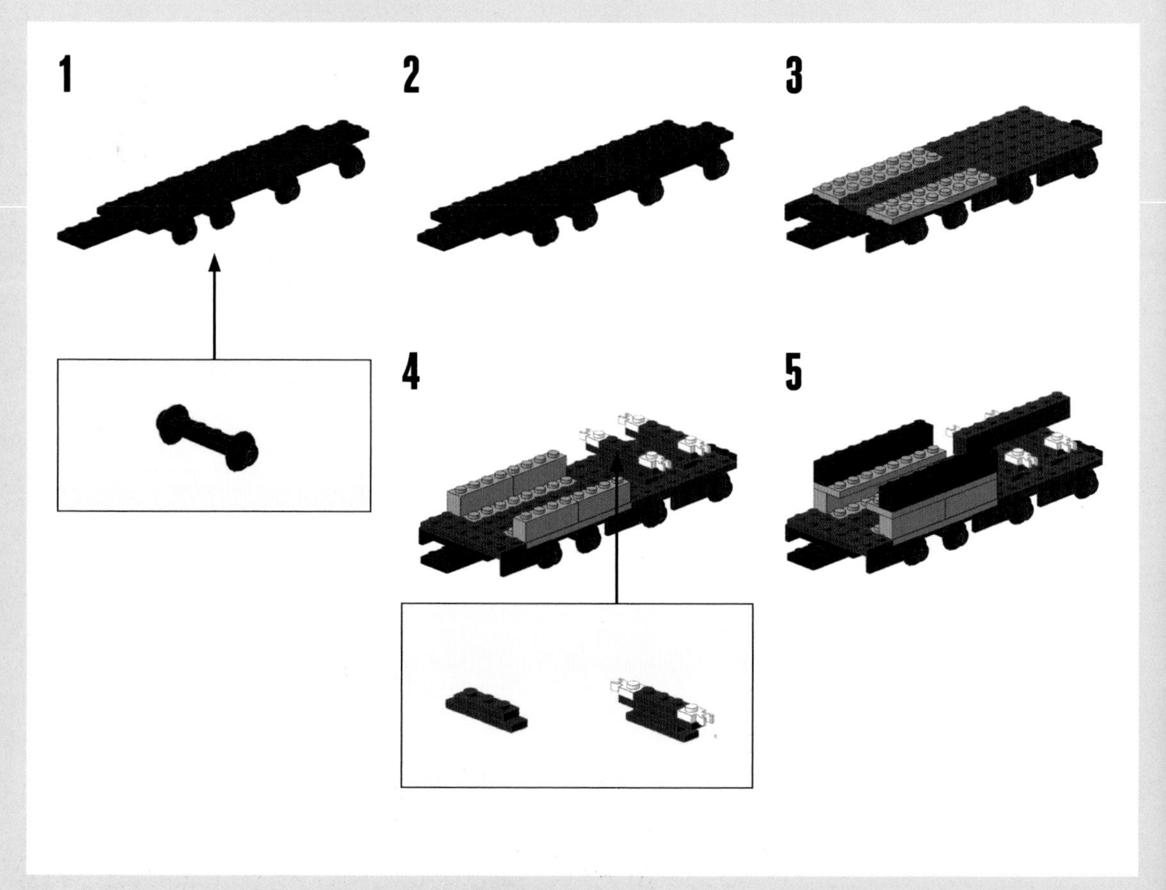
1
2
3
4
5

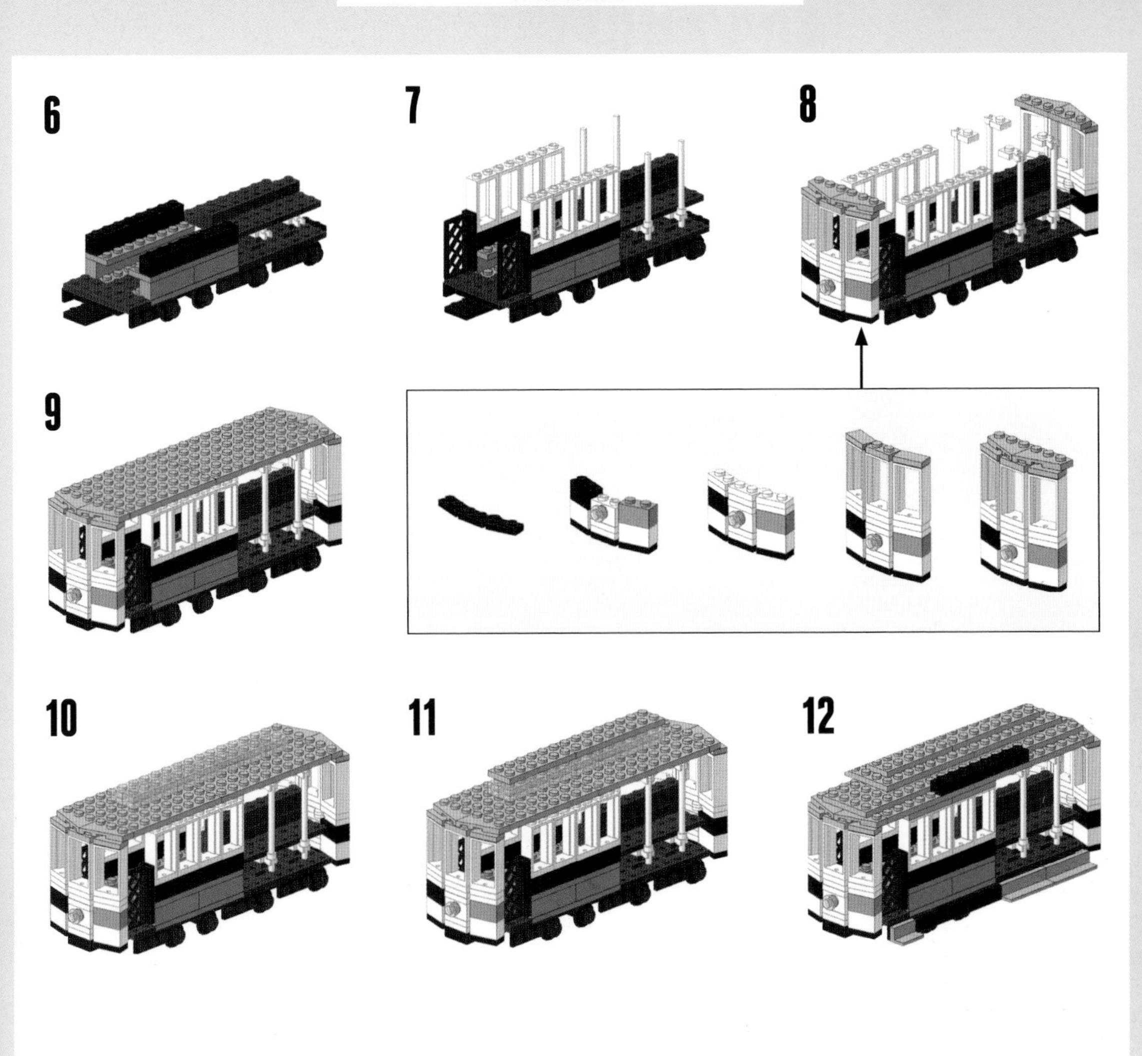
6
7
8
9
10
11
12

LOS ANGELES

OSCAR NIGHT RED CARPET

LEGO® Edition by Warren Elsmore
Size: 25 cm (4 in) long and wide
Bricks: 300
Scale: Minifig scale

This model is easier to achieve now than it ever would have been before, thanks to a new range called LEGO Friends which includes many more female figures, allowing for more variation in their clothes and hairstyles. This model is a pastiche of the red carpet outside the Oscar ceremony, with all the recognisable elements, such as actors posing for photographers. The limo in this scene is a LEGO release from 2010.

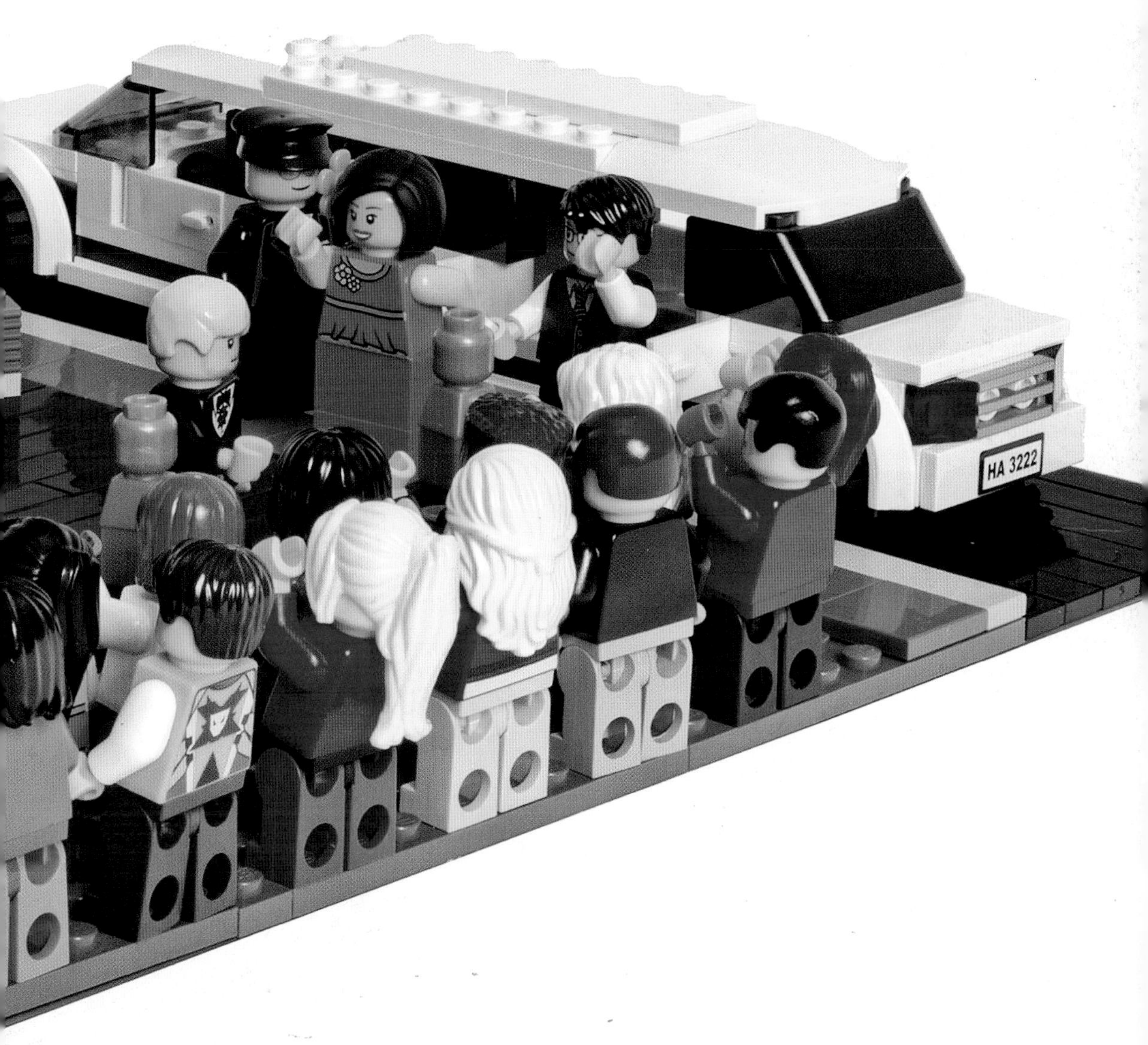

LAS VEGAS SIGN

Designer: Betty Willis (1959)
LEGO® Edition by Warren Elsmore
Size: 100 cm (39 in) high, 200 cm (79 in) wide
Bricks: 4,000
Scale: 1:2

The famously flashy Vegas sign, which features in many movies, is re-created in mosaic. It posed many difficulties in getting it to look good – the model is enormous at over 2 metres (6 feet 6 inches) wide, with all the elements painstakingly constructed from LEGO. The real sign itself is just over 4 metres (13 feet 1 inch) wide, so the model is half the size of the real thing. It is not only one of the biggest models in the whole book, but surely the one that is closest to being life-size.

EXCALIBUR

The Excalibur Hotel is built on an Arthurian theme, and when it was opened in 1990 it was the largest hotel in the world.

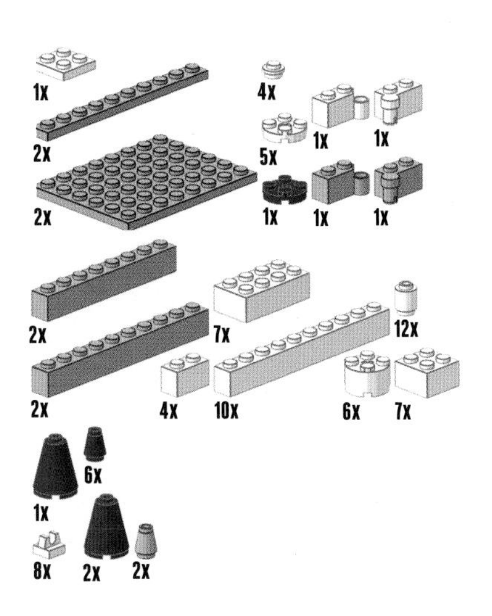

1

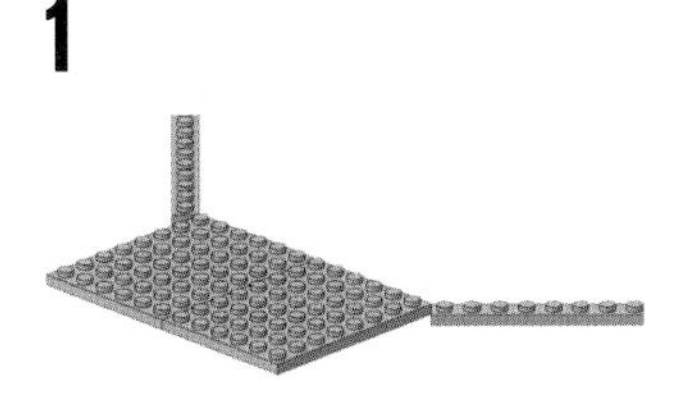

2

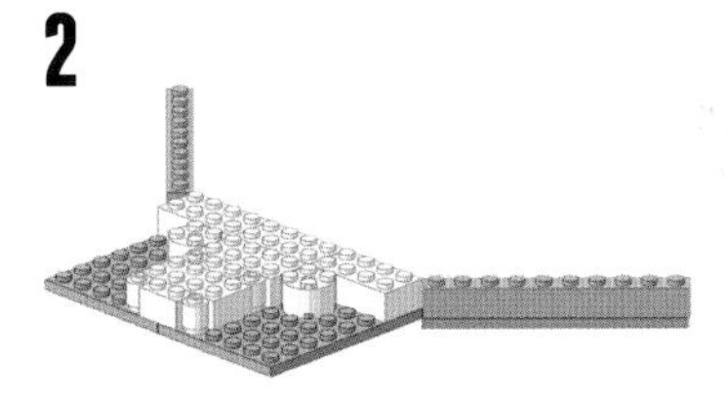

3

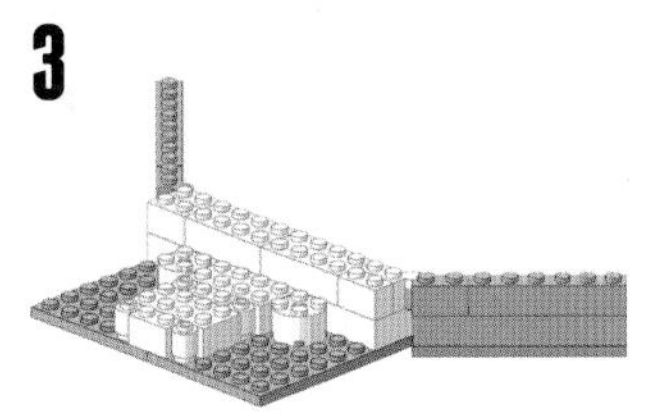

4

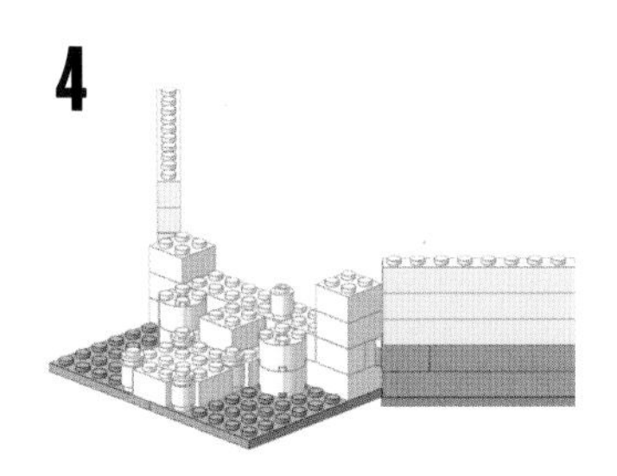

5

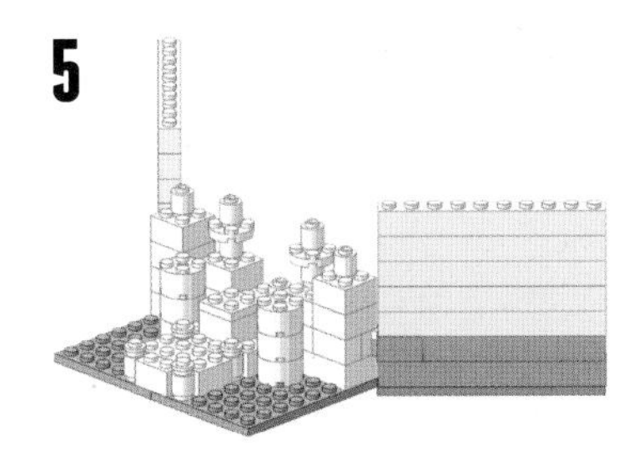

6

LUXOR

The Luxor Hotel is modelled on Khafre's Pyramid, the second largest of the ancient pyramids of Giza in Egypt.

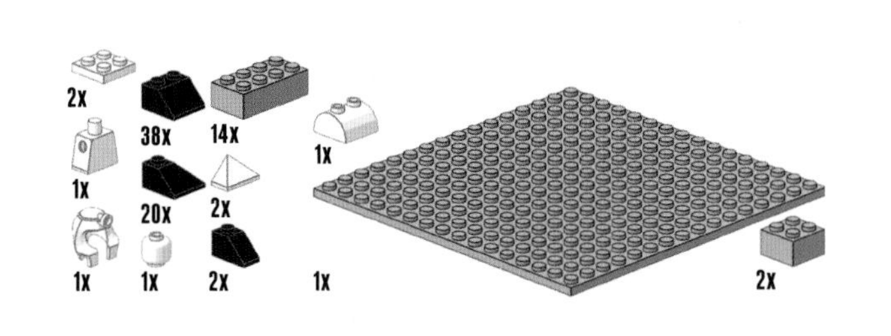

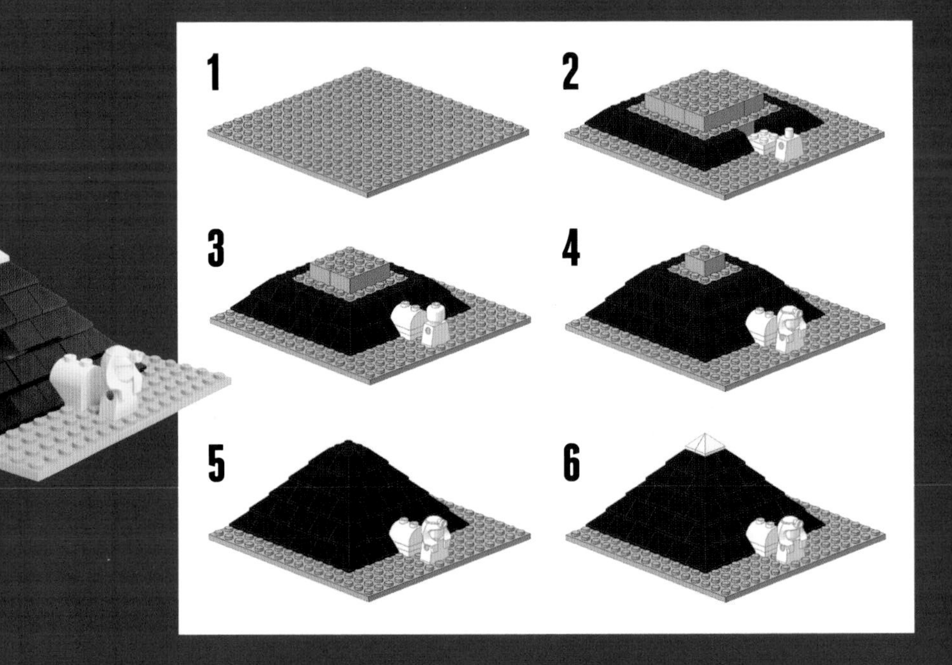

MANDALAY BAY

When the Mandalay Bay Hotel opened in 1999, Dan Aykroyd, Jim Belushi and John Goodman celebrated its opening by riding through the door on Harley-Davidsons.

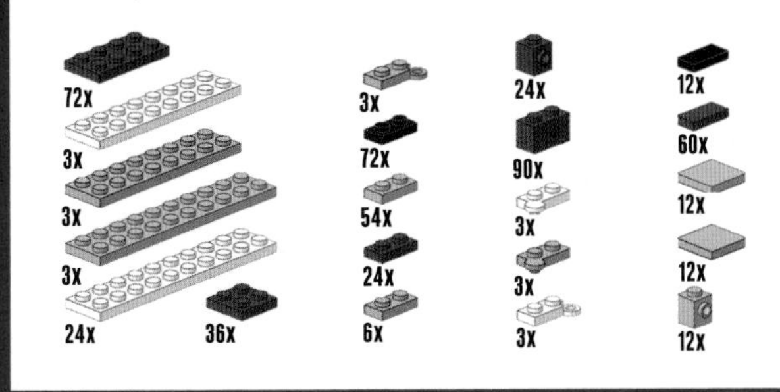

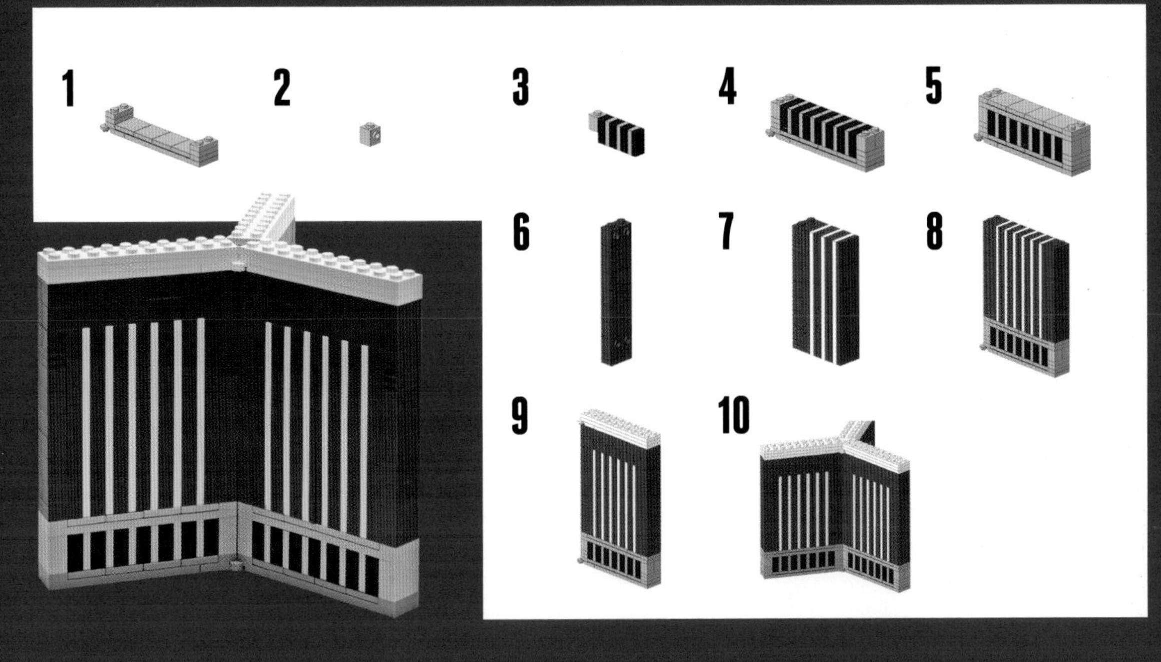

NEW YORK–NEW YORK

Of course one should not get confused between this model of the hotel and an actual model of New York City!

LAS VEGAS

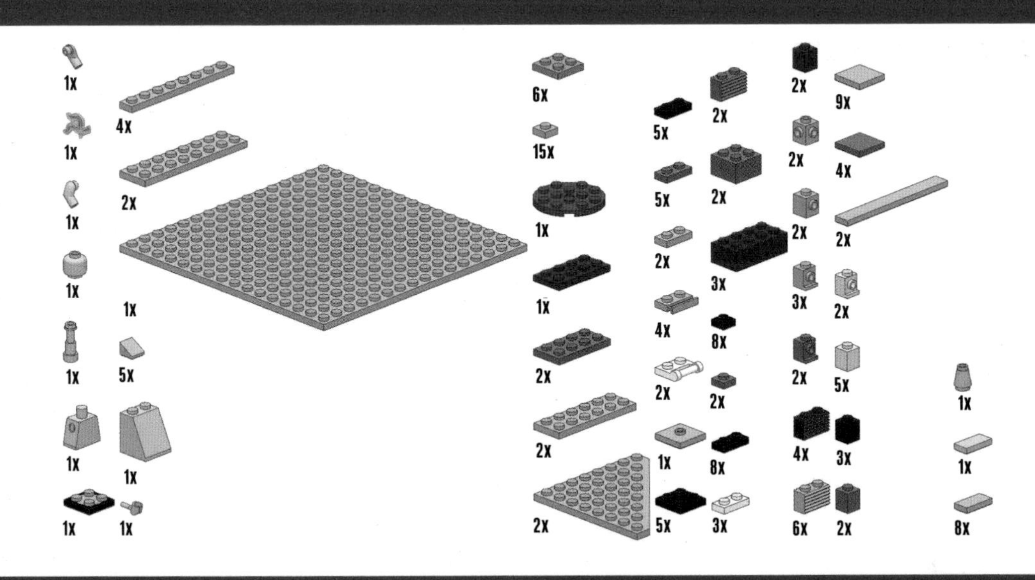
1X
1X
1X
1X
1X
1X
1X
4X
2X
1X
5X
1X
1X
6X
15X
1X
1X
2X
2X
2X
5X
5X
2X
4X
2X
1X
5X
2X
2X
3X
8X
2X
8X
3X
2X
2X
2X
3X
2X
4X
6X
9X
4X
2X
2X
5X
3X
2X
1X
1X
8X

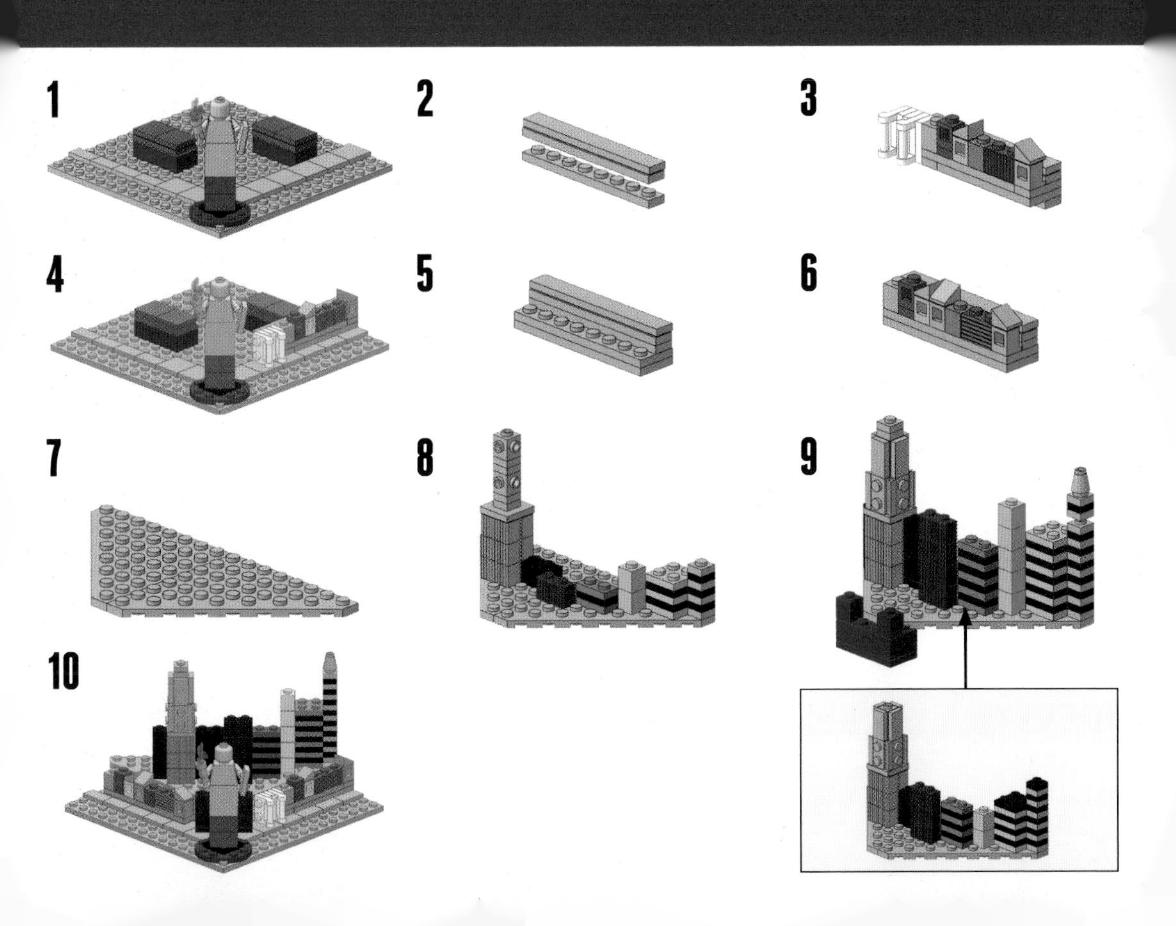
1
2
3
4
5
6
7
8
9
10

TRIBUNE TOWER

Architect: Raymond Hood & John Mead Howells (1925)

LEGO® Edition by Sean Kenney

Size: 122 cm (48 in) high, 81.5 cm (32 in) wide, 61 cm (24 in) deep

Bricks: 27,000

Scale: 1:116

This 1925 neo-Gothic building, home of the *Chicago Tribune* newspaper, was designed after an international open competition intending to find 'the most beautiful and distinctive office building in the world'. Many of the greatest architects of the day applied, and the winner was a firm of architects called Howells & Hood from New York.

CHICAGO

Photography by Sean Kenney, www.seankenney.com

NEW YORK CITY

As one of the greatest (and most photographed) cities of the world, New York City needs little introduction – and is not short of iconic imagery. Its skyscrapers are, of course, renowned worldwide, as are its bustling streets. Capturing the spirit of many of the towers with LEGO® bricks is easy because of the city's rectangular grid system. But some of New York's key buildings that I've replicated in LEGO break out of that mould.

One of the original skyscrapers of New York, the Flatiron Building, was a natural icon to create, and the LEGO model shows the key shape of the building in a minimal number of parts. As the floors repeat, it is possible to use the same LEGO construction for each floor – stacking up the bricks as the building grows. The distinctive angled corner of the building presented its own challenge. Too shallow to be created from any LEGO roof piece, the sharp point of the building still had to be re-created. The answer was to use hinges to fix the whole building into the correct angle.

One hugely recognisable feature of New York is Central Park, 843 acres of green in the middle of one of the world's most built-up cities – modelling this in LEGO was no simple feat. For instance, if the park was to include minifigs, it would have to be 88 metres (288 feet 9 inches) long. The answer was to drop the scale down as small as possible. At this tiny scale (1:2000), skyscrapers become single bricks and clumps of trees are represented by a single stacked plate. The one large building within the park, the Metropolitan Museum of Art, becomes a small thirteen-stud-wide building. But the iconic shape of the area is – I hope – still very recognisable. The trees and grassland fill the area with large swathes of green, pushing Manhattan back with the park's boundaries.

My models of New York also include the smaller, but no less memorable, sights: the brownstone buildings, row upon row of which cover the Upper West Side; the hot dog seller, pushing his street cart into prime position to provide a welcome snack; Marilyn Monroe simply walking down the street and being caught unaware by a ventilation grate! These models all provide a great opportunity to show how a city can be invoked by a small collection of bricks.

OPPOSITE: THE EMPIRE STATE BUILDING BY SEAN KENNEY

More than 1.2 metres (4 feet) tall and detailed with more than 13,000 tiny LEGO bricks, this sculpture of the Empire State Building was commissioned as the centrepiece for the Empire State Building's eightieth floor observatory gift shop – and it's the highest LEGO model in the world.

The model has a red, white and blue coloured top to emulate the building's nighttime lighting. The top of the real Empire State Building is lit up every night in different colours, and many U.S. holidays are commemorated with the familiar red, white and blue lighting scheme that most New Yorkers know well. It serves as a beacon in the centre of midtown Manhattan every night.

The building has a random pattern of drawn or open window shades, adding a bit of life to the model. And while buildings make interesting models, adding the human element really makes them come alive. Along with lots of microscale taxis, a street scene includes a New York City red double-decker tour bus, a small yellow taxi, a glass delivery truck and a three-wheeled traffic police vehicle about to give a parking ticket.

EMPIRE STATE BUILDING

William F. Lamb (1931)
LEGO® Edition by Sean Kenney
Size: 122 cm (4 ft) high
Bricks: 13,000
Scale: 1:363.5

Photography by Sean Kenney, www.seankenney.com

A King Kong's–eye view from the Empire State Building. The tiny people on the street are made from just two one-stud round plates, the top ones yellow and the bottom ones a darker colour.

BROWNSTONE

Instead of building with bricks pointing upwards, this brownstone model was built with LEGO® plates pointing sideways, which gives better definition and finer detail to the model. There are a few tricks to getting the sideways plates to attach to the upright bricks. The parts and instructions opposite are for building one of the three models below.

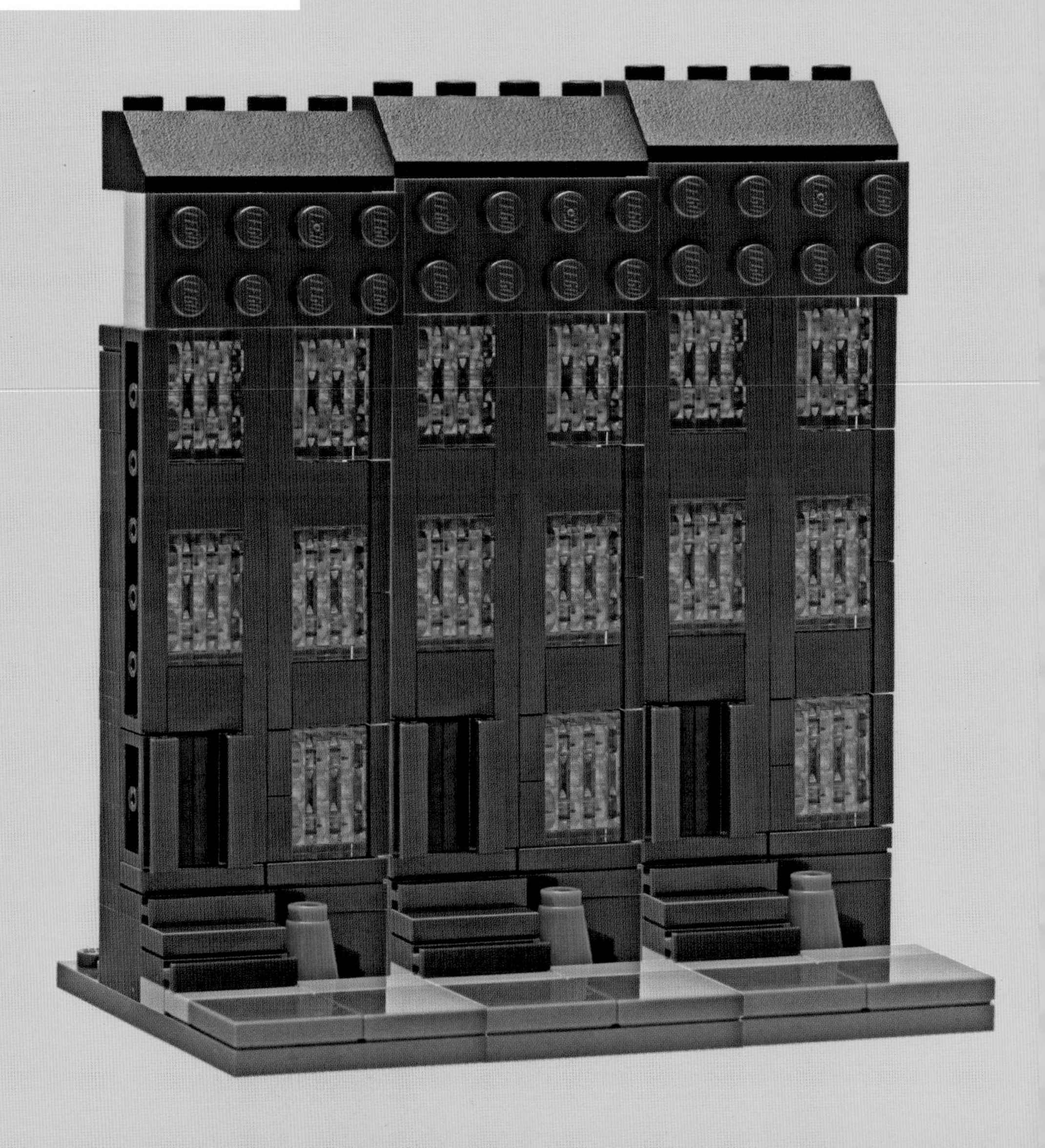

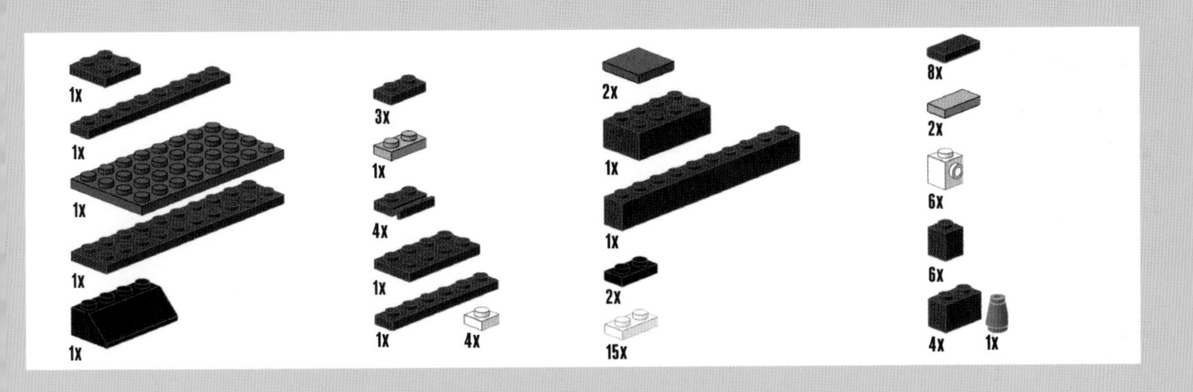
1x
1x
1x
1x
1x
3x
1x
4x
1x
1x
4x
2x
1x
1x
2x
15x
8x
2x
6x
6x
4x
1x

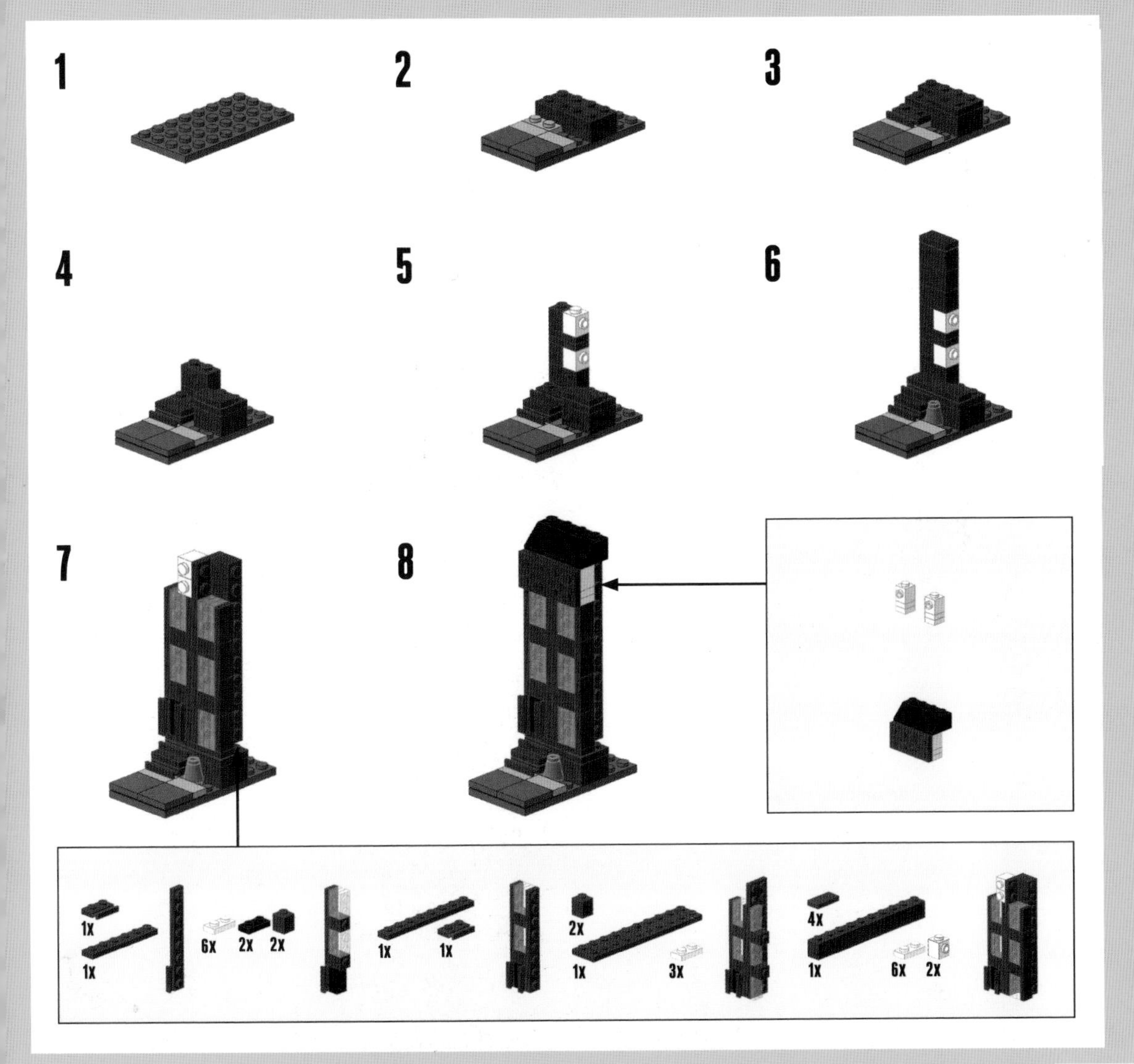
1
2
3
4
5
6
7
8
1x
1x
6x
2x
2x
1x
1x
2x
1x
3x
4x
1x
6x
2x

NEW YORK TAXI

The most common cab you'll see on New York's streets is a Ford Crown Victoria. But what makes these cabs iconic is the colour and, of course, the white advertising sign mounted on the roof. While a number of other models of car are used, the Crown Victoria still accounts for the bulk of the 13,000 taxis on the Big Apple's streets. But you better catch them while you can, as they're currently being phased out for larger hybrid vehicles.

This cab is built from a very small number of LEGO® parts, evoking the key features of the taxi. Wheels would be too large at this scale, so we've used four round LEGO plates to represent each wheel. Of course, the iconic advertising sign can't be overlooked, but at this scale there are no parts that would let us re-create this correctly. Instead, we've elicited the feel of this triangular shape by using some small 'cheese' slopes, so called because, well, imagine them in yellow.

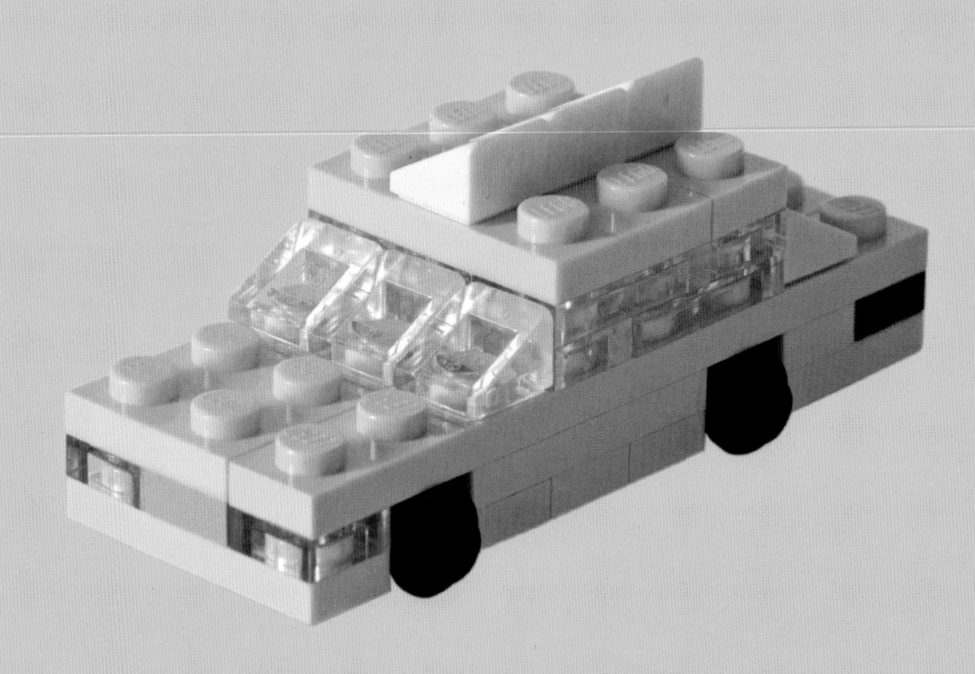

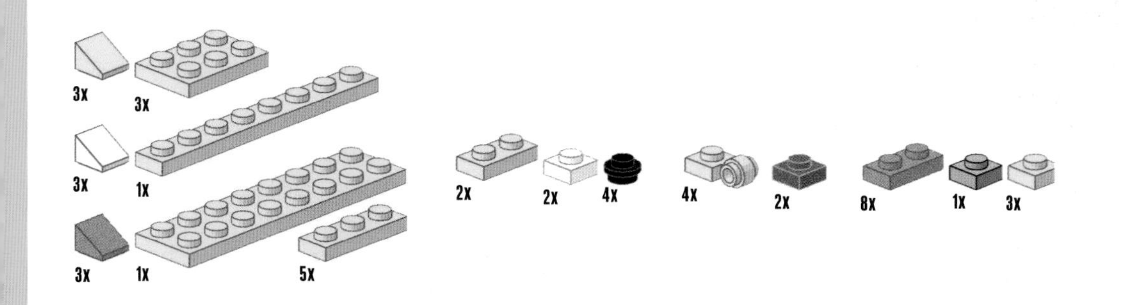
3x
3x
3x
1x
3x
1x
5x
2x
2x
4x
4x
2x
8x
1x
3x

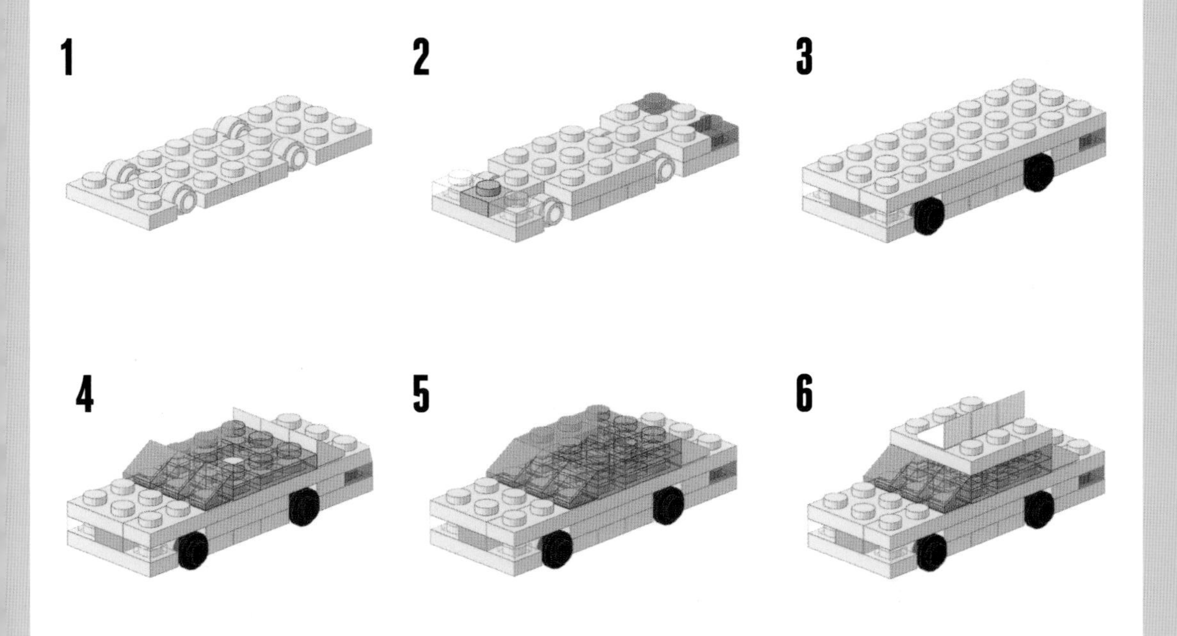
1
2
3
4
5
6

Photography by Alex Mandrilla

WORLD TRADE CENTER

Architects: Various

LEGO® Edition by Spencer Rezkalla

Size: 86 cm (34 in) high, 69 cm (27 in) wide, 56 cm (22 in) deep

Bricks: 20,373

Scale: approximately 1:650

The tallest building in the new World Trade Center, One World Trade Center (formerly known as the Freedom Tower), is due to be completed in 2013, and will be taller than the original Twin Towers.

These models of the complex comprise thousands of transparent elements to represent the reflective surfaces of the new buildings, and together they are made up of more than 20,000 pieces.

Using transparent LEGO® elements can give models realistic depth and a high level of detail.

Left: The World Trade Center's Port Authority Trans-Hudson (PATH) Transportation Hub by Santiago Calatrava, which will rival Grand Central Station in size.

Opposite: The finished complex will include a total of five high-rise office buildings, and a museum and memorial.

WALK SIGN

LEGO® Edition by Warren Elsmore
Size: 14 cm (5½ in) high and wide
Bricks: 2,300
Scale: 1:3.5

This is rather more complicated than it looks. To get a better resolution with the lettering, the whole sign was built side-on, and it was quite difficult to get the bricks to line up and attach so they don't fall apart.

THE CHRYSLER BUILDING

Architect: William Van Alen (1930)

LEGO® Edition by Spencer Rezkalla

Size: 49 cm (19¼ in) high, 18 cm (7 in) wide, 15 cm (6 in) deep

Bricks: 4,812

Scale: approximately 1:650

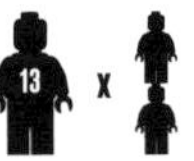

This model took nearly three months to design and build. The famous Art Deco crown is assembled from various rounded plates and tiles mounted sideways. Clip elements represent the four eagle heads perched high on the corners of the tower. Further down, metallic silver round plates suggest the building's hubcap-style decorative trim. The main body is clad in very light grey elements. This allows for a more striking colour contrast with the upper light grey crown. Small transparent plate elements form miniature windows. The interlocked solid coloured stud from the plate beneath helps create the visual illusion of multiple window panes within each element.

Photography by Alex Mandrilla

MACY'S DAY PARADE

Architects: Theodore W.E. De Lemos & August W. Cordes (1902)
LEGO® Construction by Warren Elsmore
Bricks: 12,000
Scale: Minifig scale

Inspiration for this model was a set called the LEGO® Grand Emporium released in 2010, which is made up of the corner of a large department store. I've expanded this so that it looks like Macy's and other stores in Manhattan. Instead of balloons, we've used large LEGO animals, and rather than being held up, they're connected to the wall behind them.

SHOP

HOT DOG

It's very strange and unusual to make a model that's life-size! It was fun to make, but I definitely wouldn't suggest trying to eat it. This model uses the plate technique mentioned in the introduction, in which LEGO® elements are fitted together on the inside with the flat surface showing all the way around, giving it the illusion of a rounded object.

Additional parts required for the sub-structure are listed separately in the box-outs below.

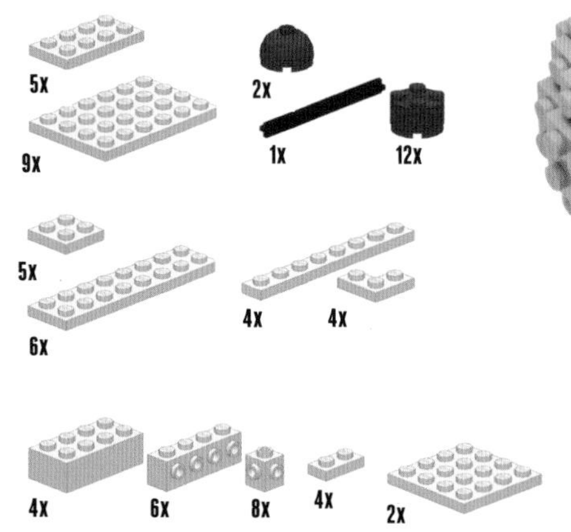

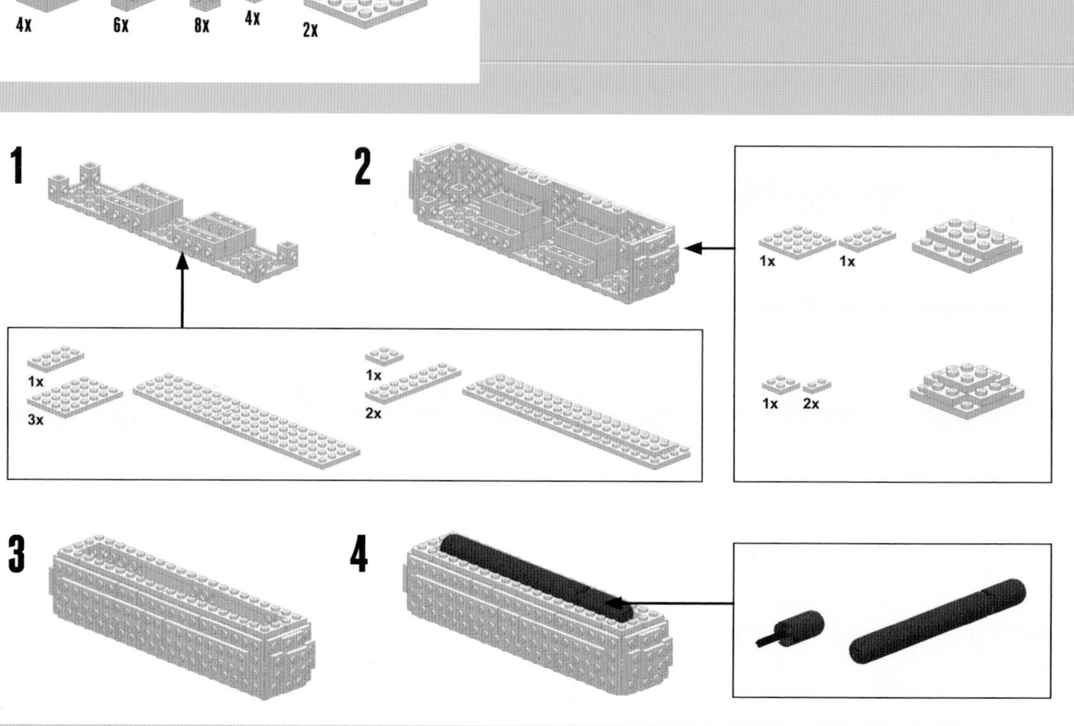

HOT DOG STAND

It wouldn't feel like New York without one of these guys, wearing their beanie hats and offering hot dogs to people on the street. Pretzels are an optional extra.

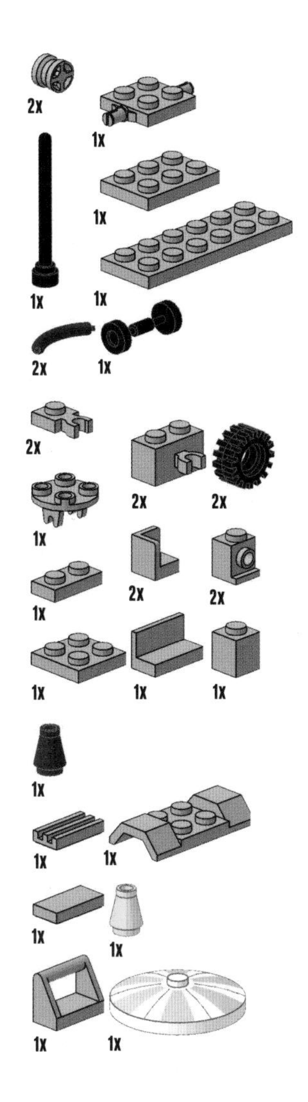

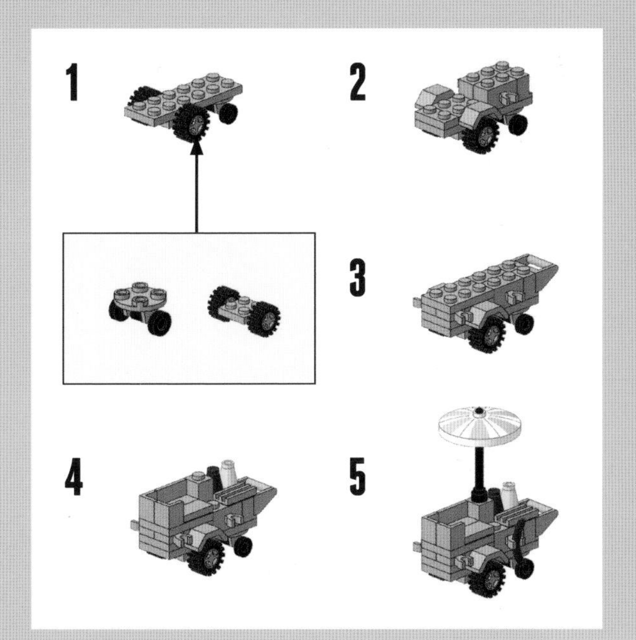

MARILYN MONROE ON SUBWAY GRATE

This is a re-creation of one of the most famous movie moments of all time – Marilyn Monroe surprised by a gust of subway wind coming up through a grate in Billy Wilder's classic *The Seven Year Itch*.

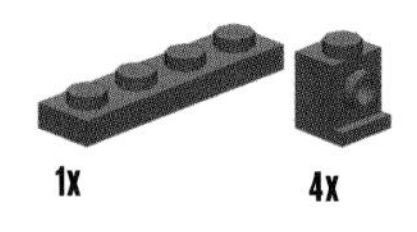

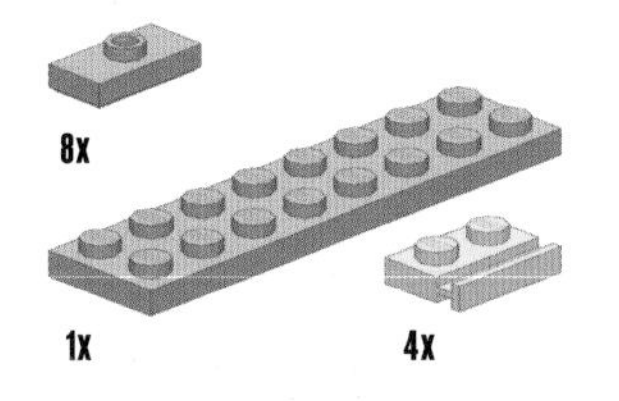

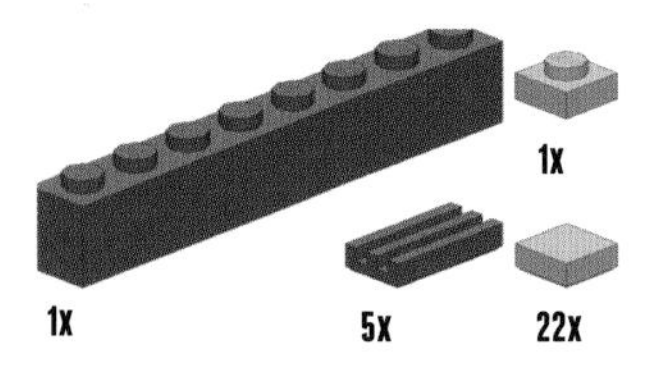

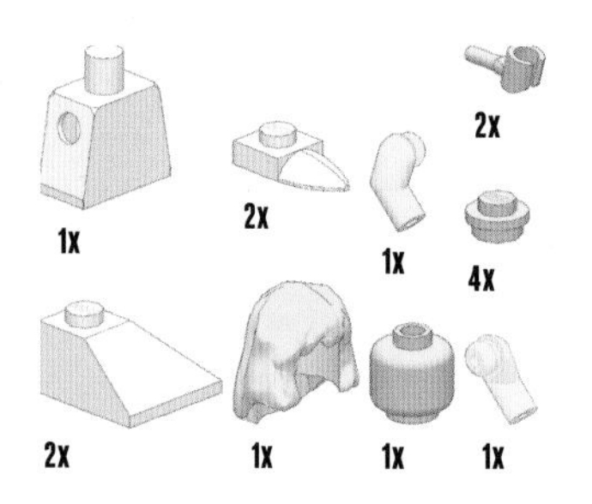

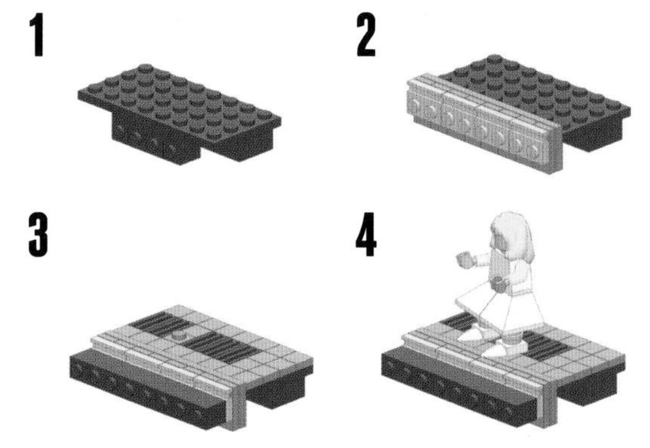

FIRE HYDRANT

Another iconic New York symbol, as seen in a hundred movies. We chose not to have this one spraying water!

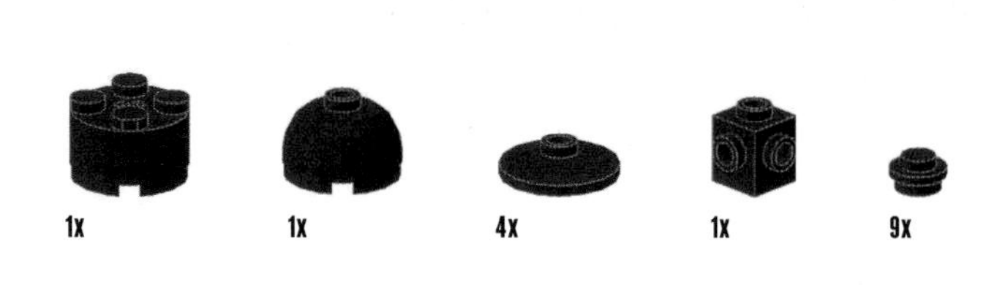

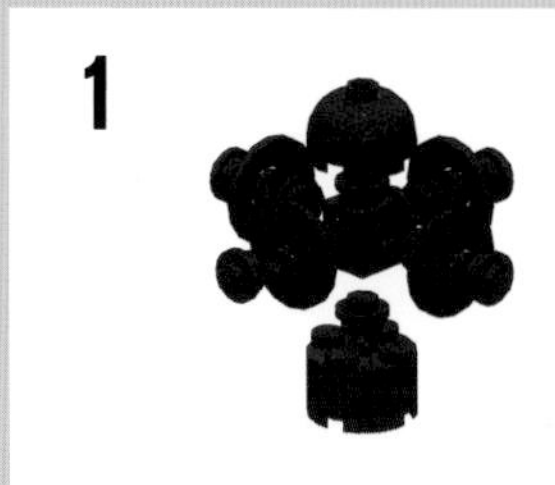

FLATIRON BUILDING

One of the most recognisable buildings in the world, the Flatiron Building is wedge-shaped and unusually narrow. You might remember it as where Spiderman's newspaper, the *Daily Bugle*, has its offices in the comics and films.

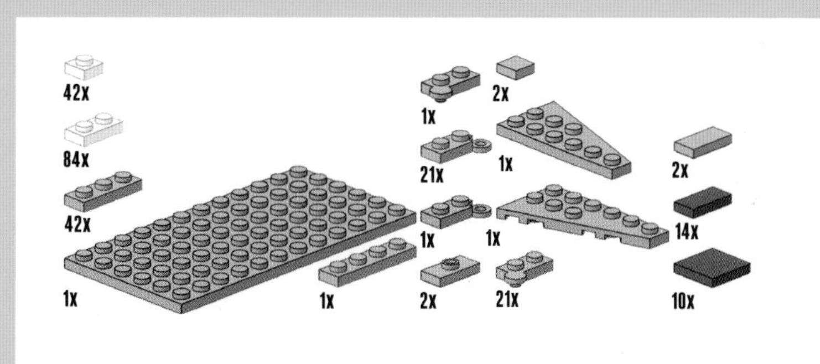

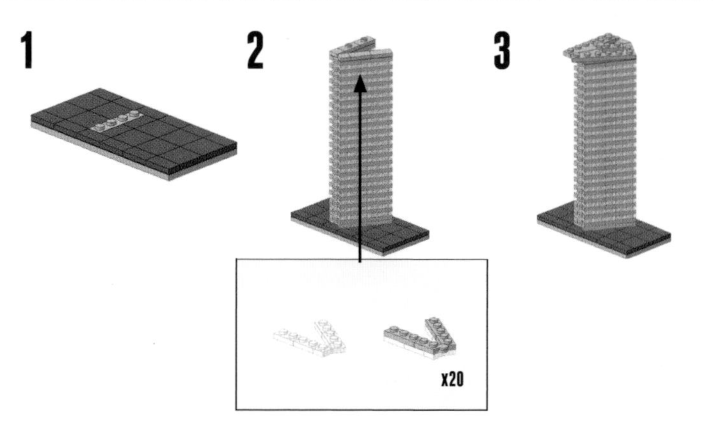

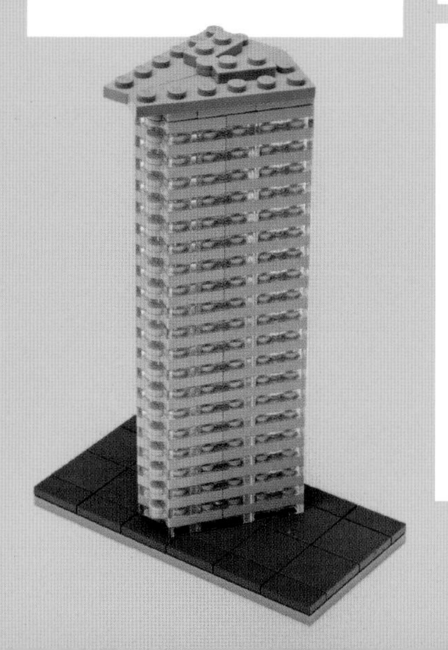

UN HEADQUARTERS AND FLAGS

Architect: Oscar Niemeyer (1952)

LEGO® Edition by Spencer Rezkalla

Size: 25 cm (10 in) high, 76 cm (30 in) long, 38 cm (15 in) wide

Bricks: 8,492

Scale: 1:650

This model took about five months to design and construct. The most innovative building technique was the use of thin panel elements mounted sideways on the slab-side of the building to form thin black spandrels. These horizontally delineate the individual floors of the 1950s international-style curtain wall facade. The individual blue-tinted windows are built by stacking a 1x2 tile and a 1x2 plate. Each of these assemblies is then wedged between the thin spandrel edges and held firmly in place by a friction fit. The collection of flags along the western edge of the complex introduces a splash of colour. Opposite are some larger examples of flags which can be easily constructed using the mosaic technique (see p.25).

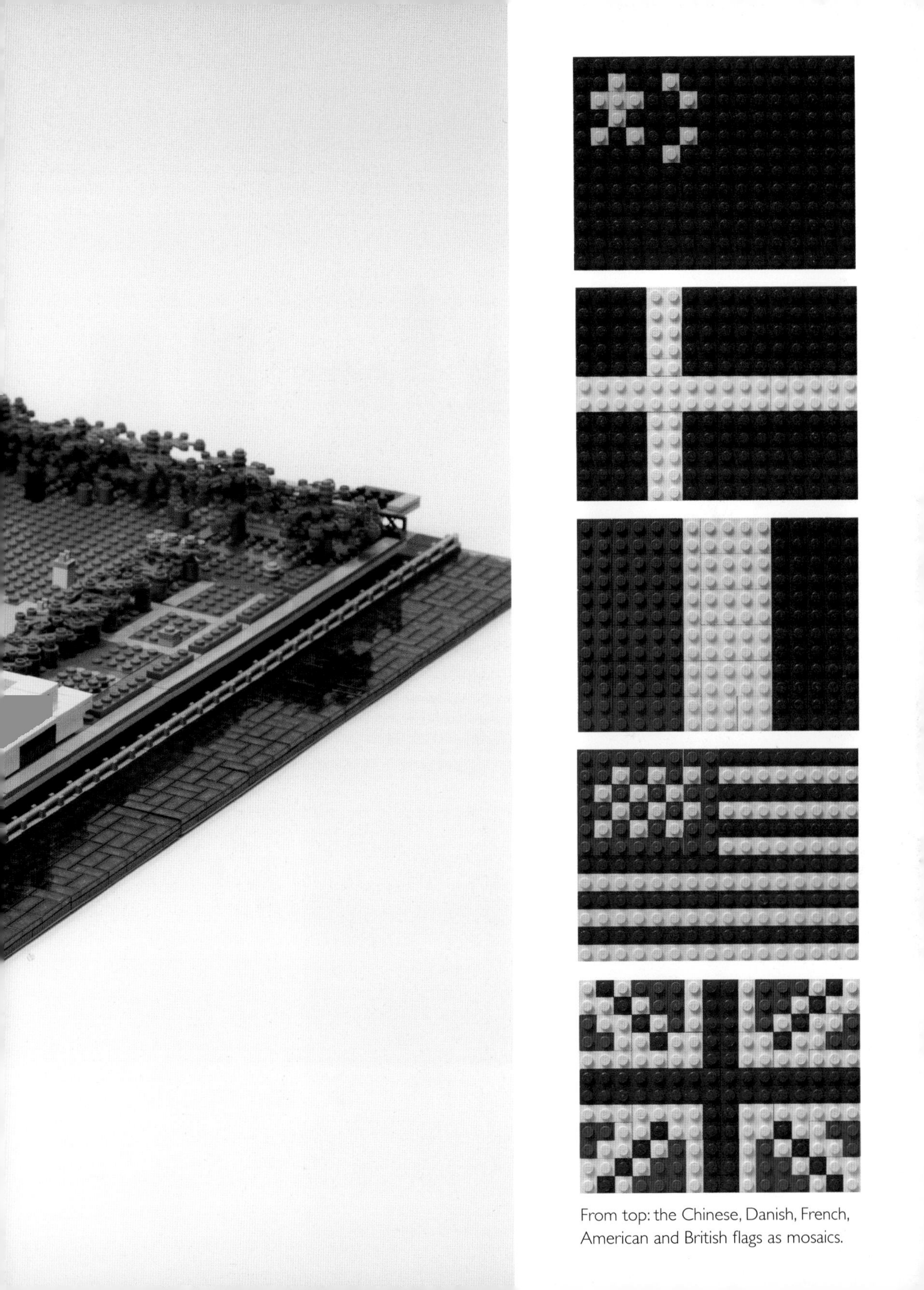

From top: the Chinese, Danish, French, American and British flags as mosaics.

CENTRAL PARK

Landscape designers: Frederick Law Olmsted & Calvert Vaux (1857)

LEGO® Edition by Warren Elsmore

Size: 102 cm (40 in) long, 51 cm (20 in) wide

Bricks: 16,000

Scale: approximately 1:2,000

This model is a combination of two techniques. First, I put a map through mosaic software (see the Mosaic section on p.25) to lay out the park, with its distinctive network of paths. After I laid it out, I used some microscale buildings for the skyscrapers, most of which are only one brick wide. It was a challenge to incorporate the number of trees required into the model as well.

WASHINGTON

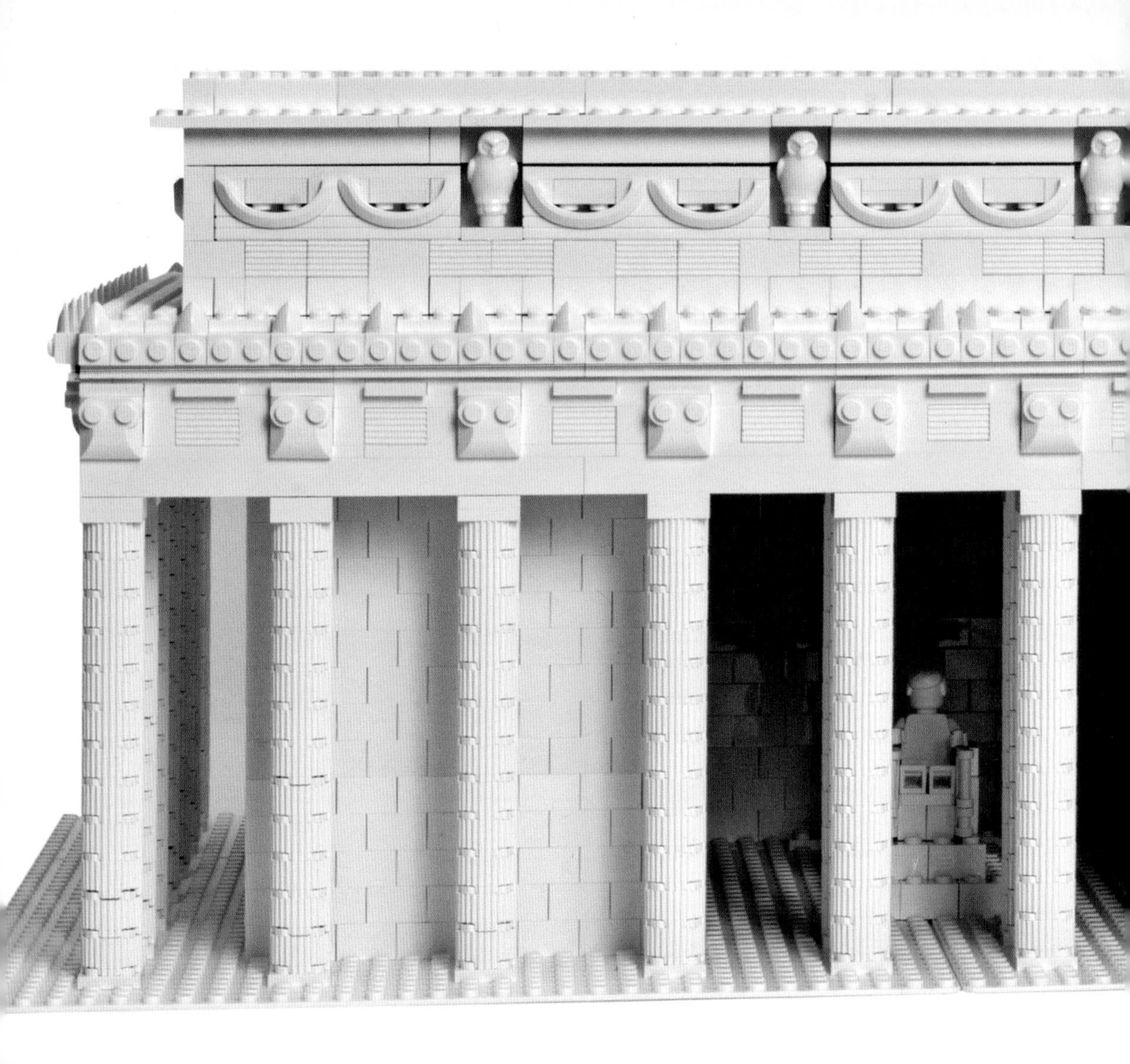

ABRAHAM LINCOLN MEMORIAL

Architect: Henry Bacon (1922)

Sculptor: Daniel Chester French (1920)

LEGO® Edition by Warren Elsmore

Size: 25 cm (9¾ in) high, 32 cm (12 in) deep, 46 cm (18 in) wide

Bricks: 2,000

Scale: 1:120

Around the top of the Lincoln Memorial is a frieze of eagles and swags, neither of which is available as LEGO parts. For the eagles in this model I used owls, and for the swags I used inverted wheel arches. President Lincoln himself is a LEGO minifig, and the marble books that make up his seat in the real Lincoln Memorial are in fact LEGO pieces with rounded sides in the model.

WHITE HOUSE

This is a very simple model with very few parts. By following these instructions you can create one of the most famous buildings in the world in under a minute!

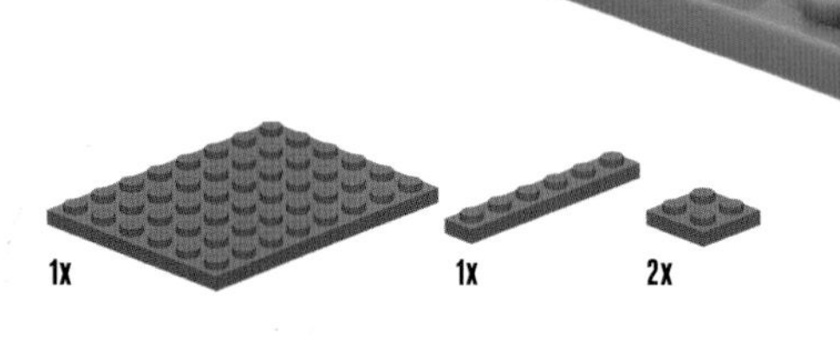

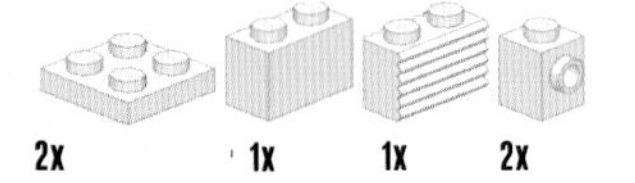

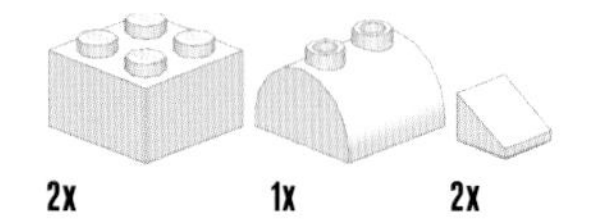

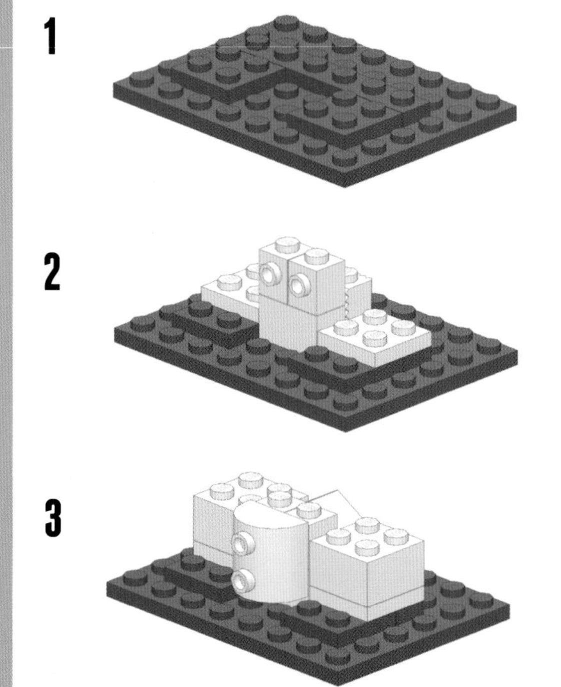

CAPITOL BUILDING

This is in the same mould as the White House model, but with the pieces rearranged to form the shape of the Capitol – a very famous, recognisable building, and an easy model for beginners to make and build their confidence.

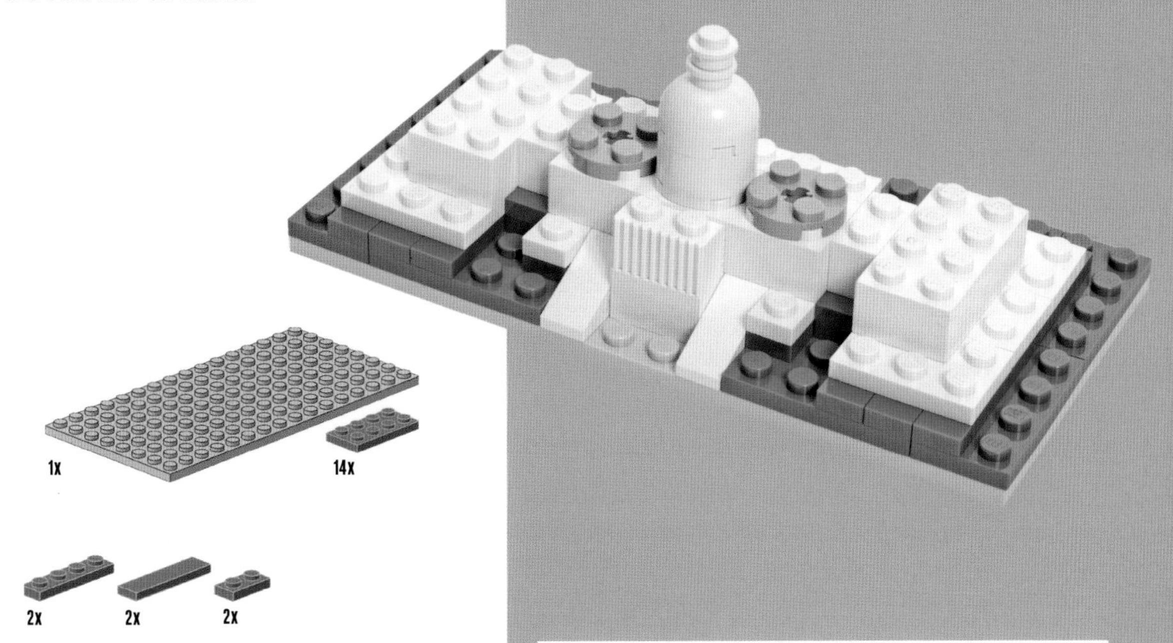

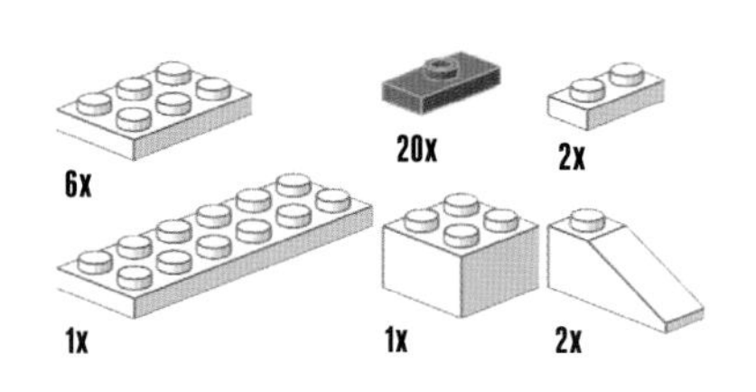

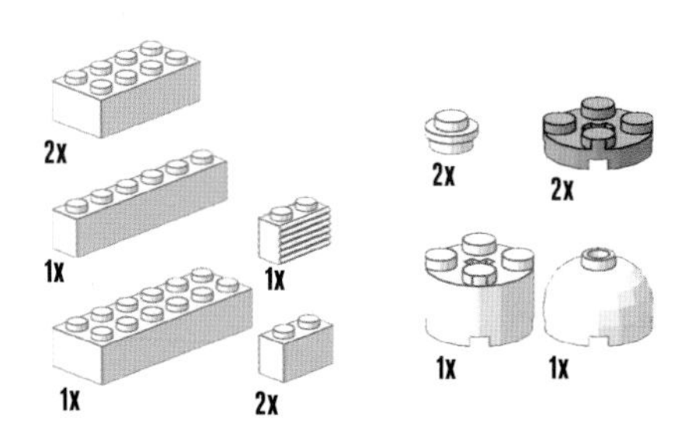

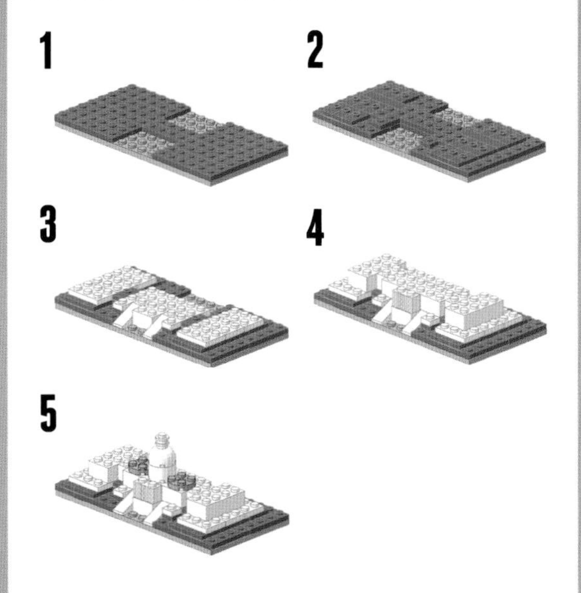

WASHINGTON MONUMENT

This great obelisk, the famous monument to commemorate George Washington, America's first president, is a quite straightforward model that a beginner could make. The flags are simply 'lamp holder' tiles attached to aerials, an easy but effective design. The reflecting pool is essentially a simple mosaic lined with regularly spaced trees, so the instructions below demonstrate how to construct just the basic monument.

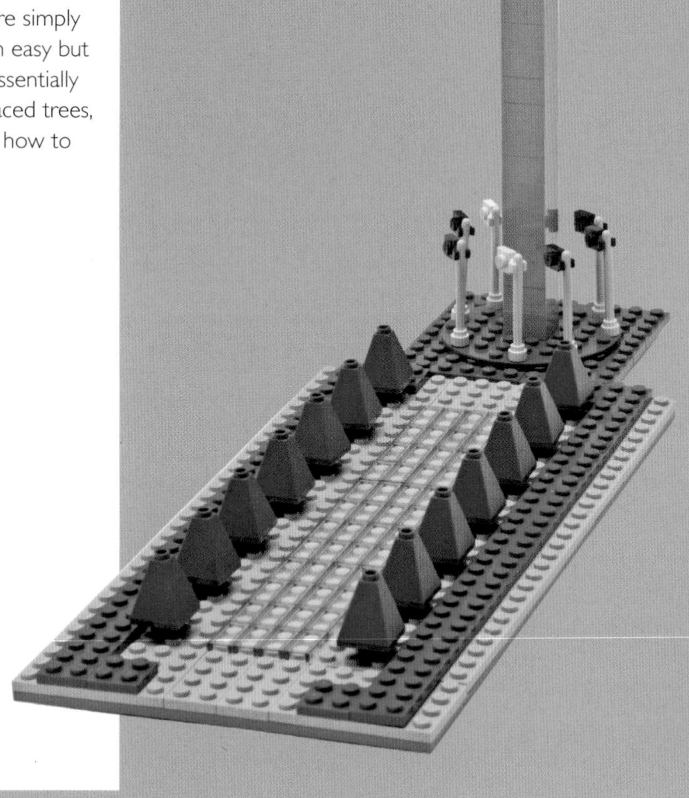

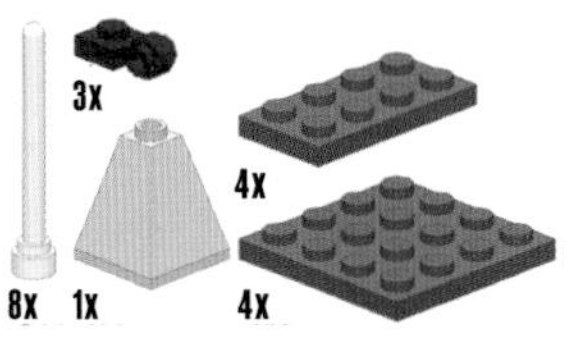

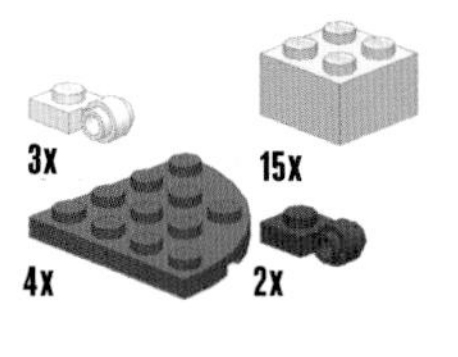

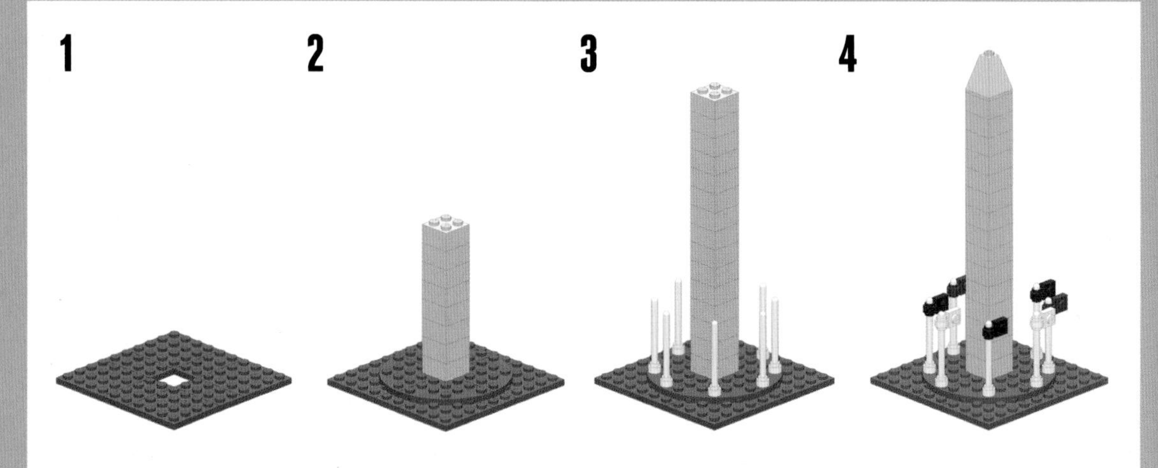

MONTREAL

MONTREAL BIODOME

Architect: Roger Taillibert (1976)

LEGO® Edition by Warren Elsmore

Size: 2 cm (¾ in) high, 42 cm (16½ in) long and wide

Bricks: 3,000

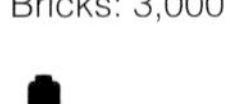

This building was originally built as the velodrome for the 1976 Montreal Olympics, and was later converted into a biodome which replicates four different ecosystems found in the Americas. It is a low-slung building and resembles a bird's footprint with three toes. The challenge when building the model was that the toes point out at different angles and meet in the centre. The model was made from five different wedge-shaped pieces joined together in the middle.

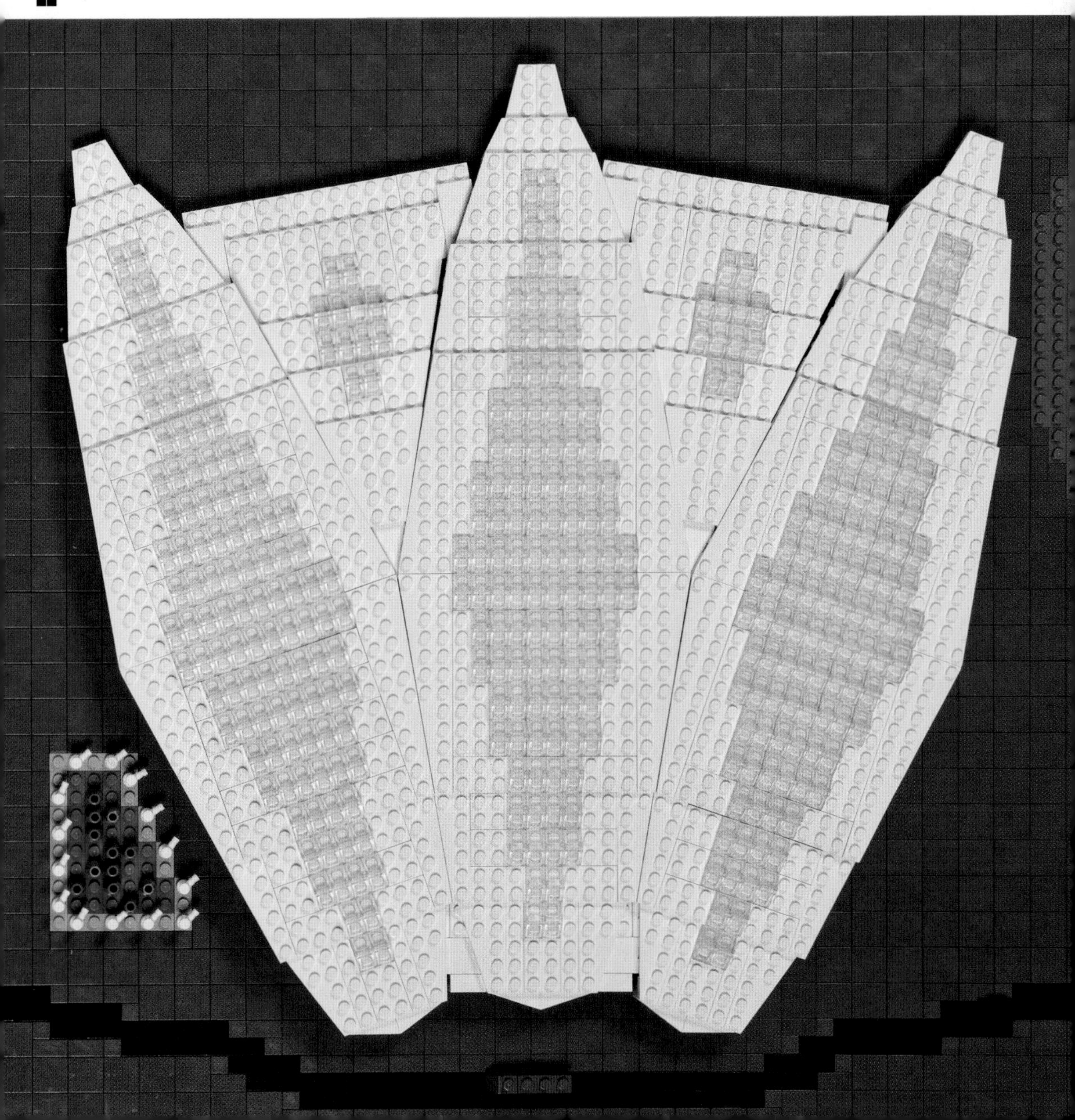

ST. JOSEPH'S ORATORY

This is one of the easier buildings in the book to re-create because the bricks are all studs up. There's a series of columns at the front, built using LEGO® profile bricks, which have grooves in them and are ideal to create the effect of columns.

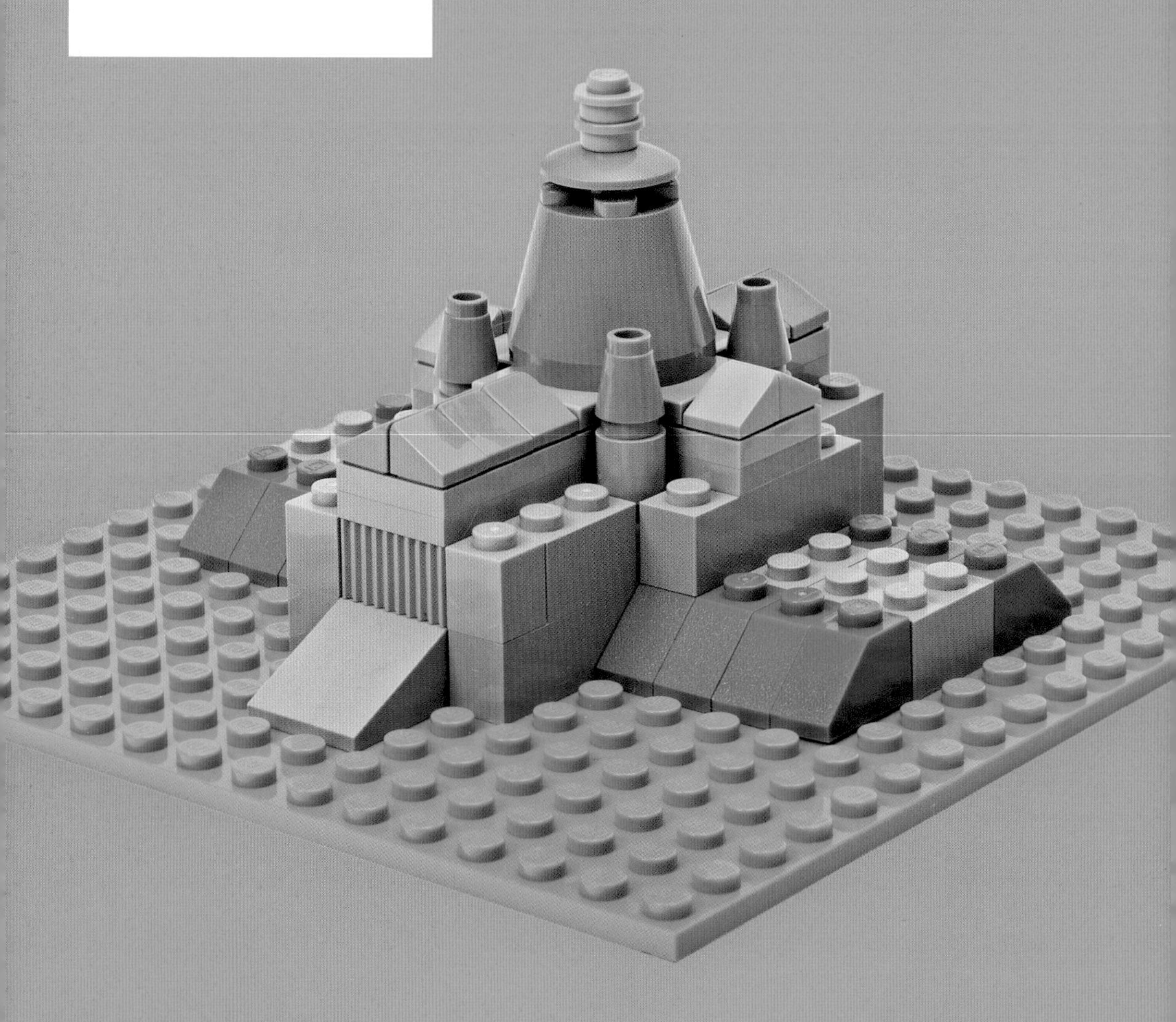

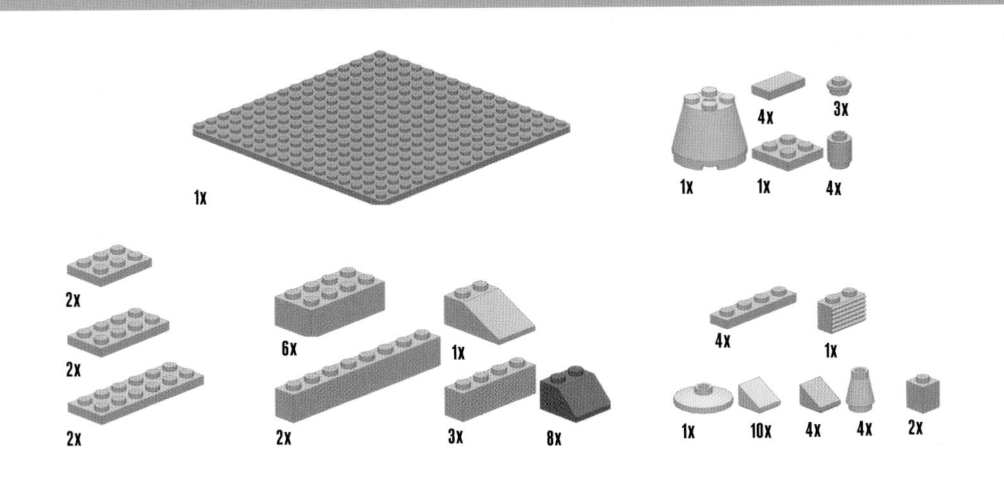
1X
4X
3X
1X
1X
4X
2X
2X
2X
6X
2X
1X
3X
8X
4X
1X
1X
10X
4X
4X
2X

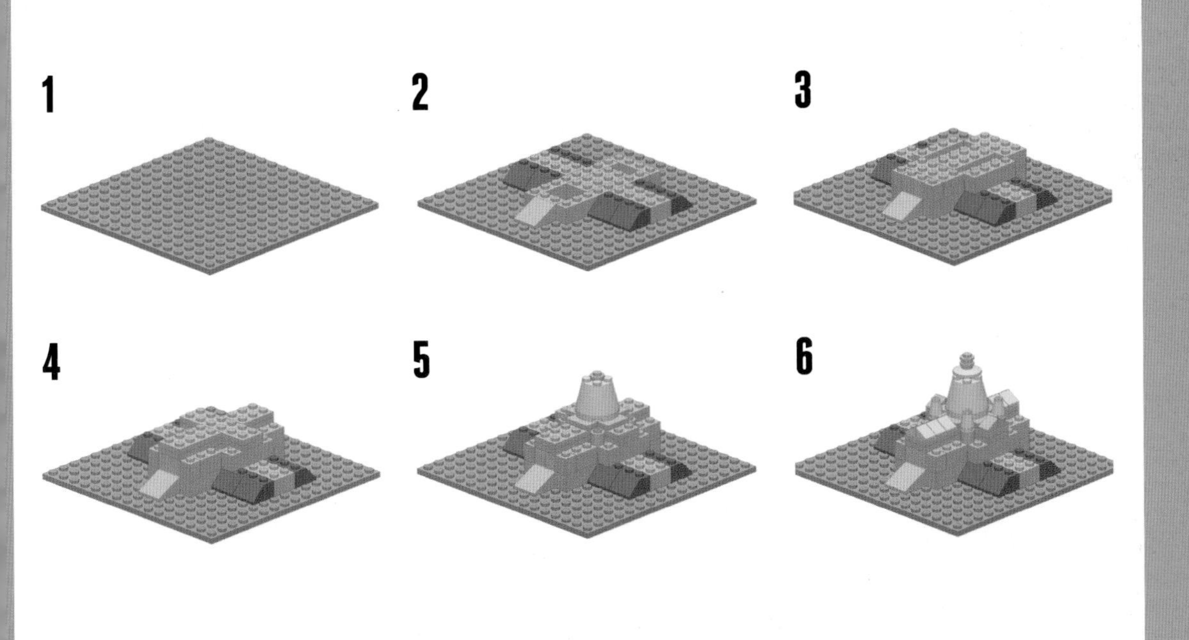
1
2
3
4
5
6

CHICHEN ITZA

CHAC MOOL

Chac Mool is a common type of statue found in many former sites of the Mayan civilisation. It is carved into the shape of a reclining figure with its knees up, its upper body leaning on its elbows and its head turned to one side. The meaning of the posture is not known, but it does leave a flat surface in the centre of the statue (the stomach), which may have been used as an altar – perhaps for sacrifices.

This type of statue was a huge influence on the great twentieth-century sculptor Henry Moore, and he made interpretations of it throughout his working life.

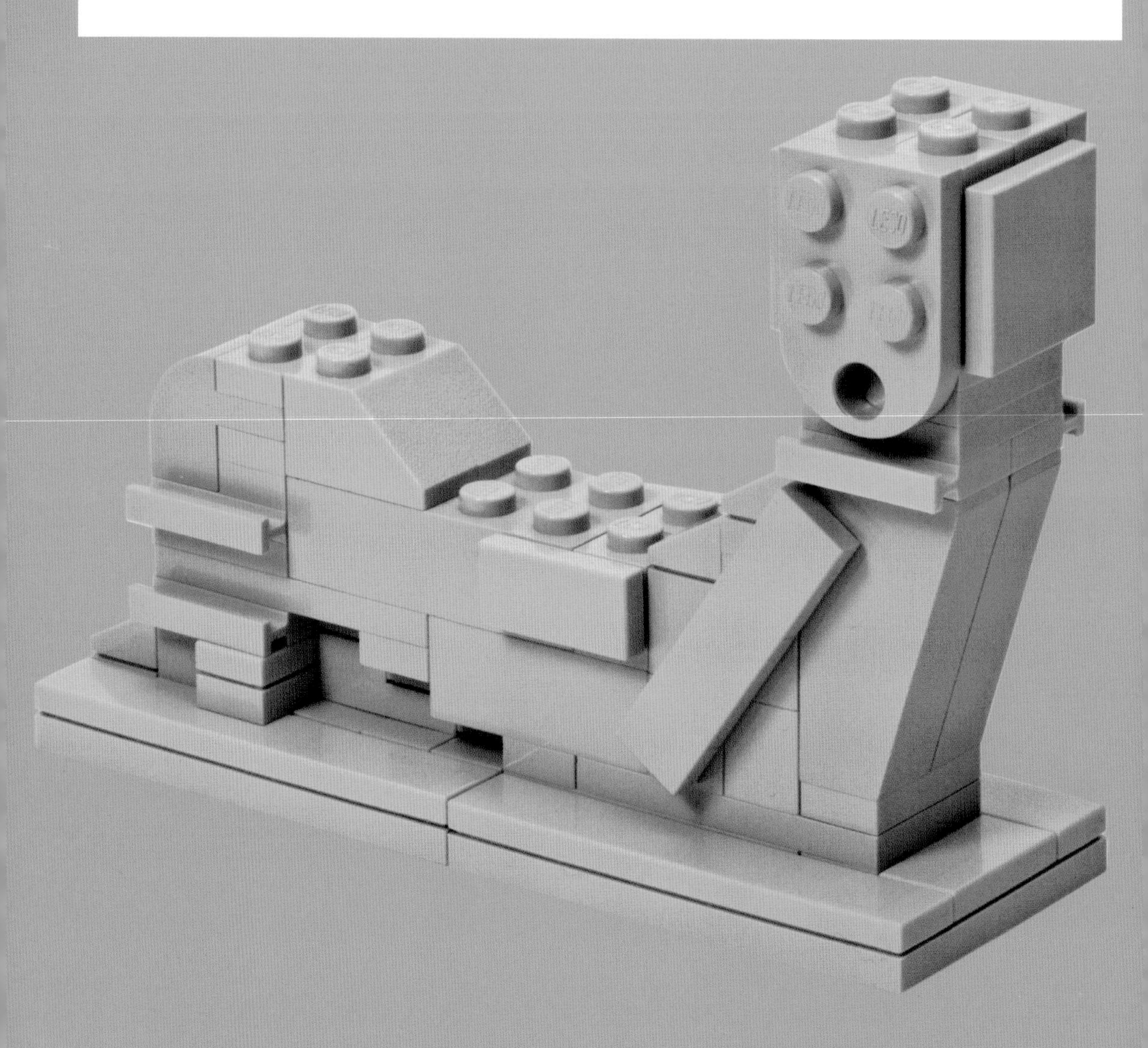

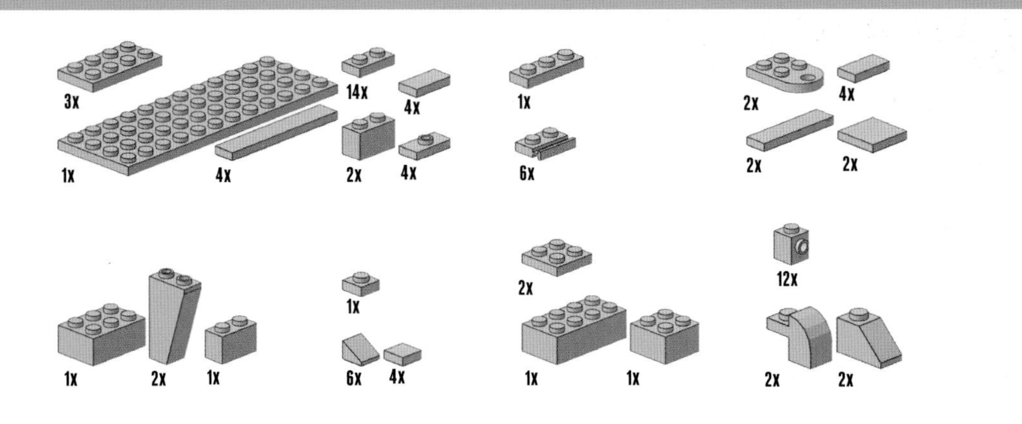
3x
14x
4x
1x
2x
4x
1x
4x
2x
4x
6x
2x
2x
2x
2x
12x
1x
2x
1x
1x
6x
4x
1x
1x
2x
2x

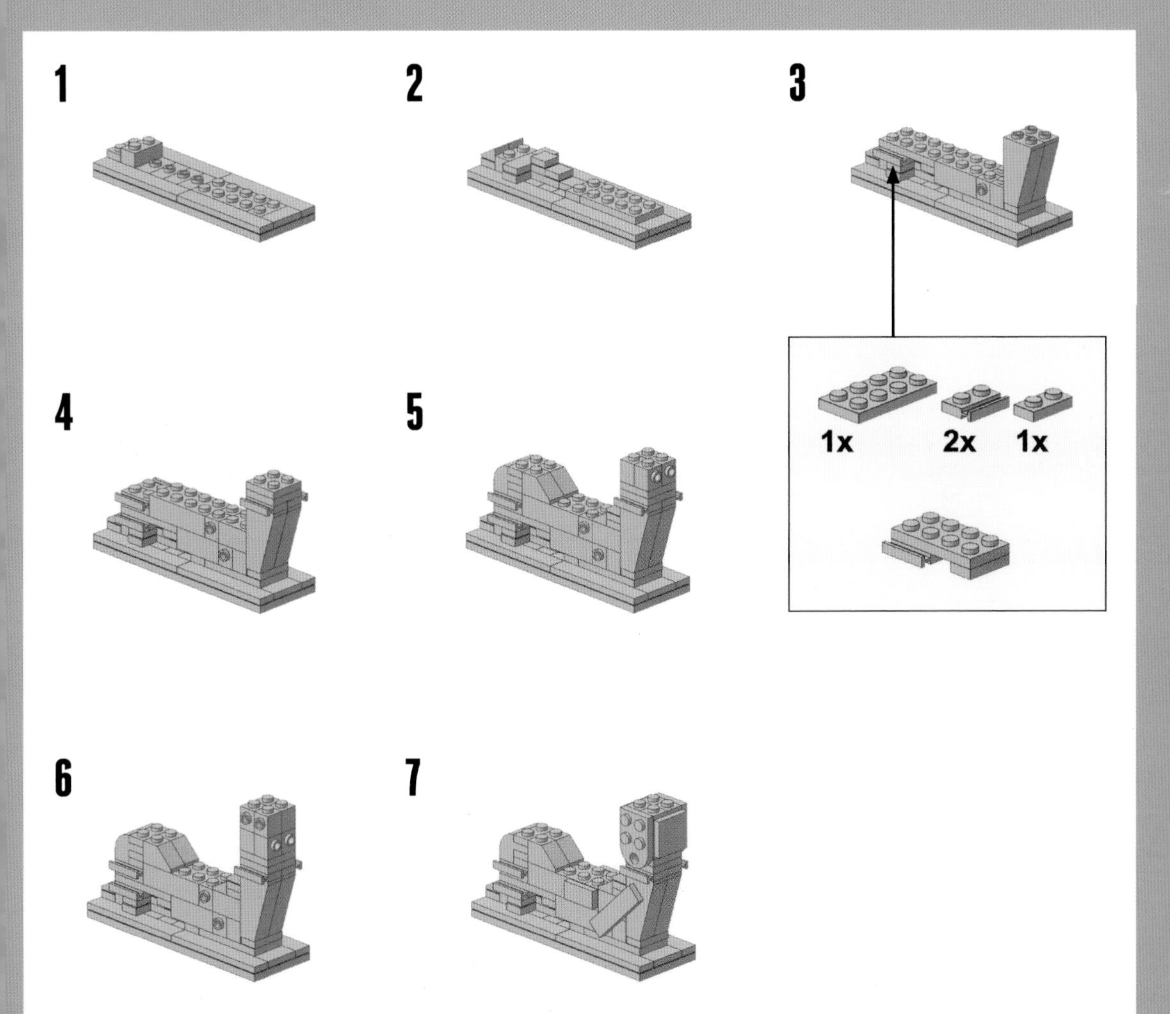
1
2
3
1x
2x
1x
4
5
6
7

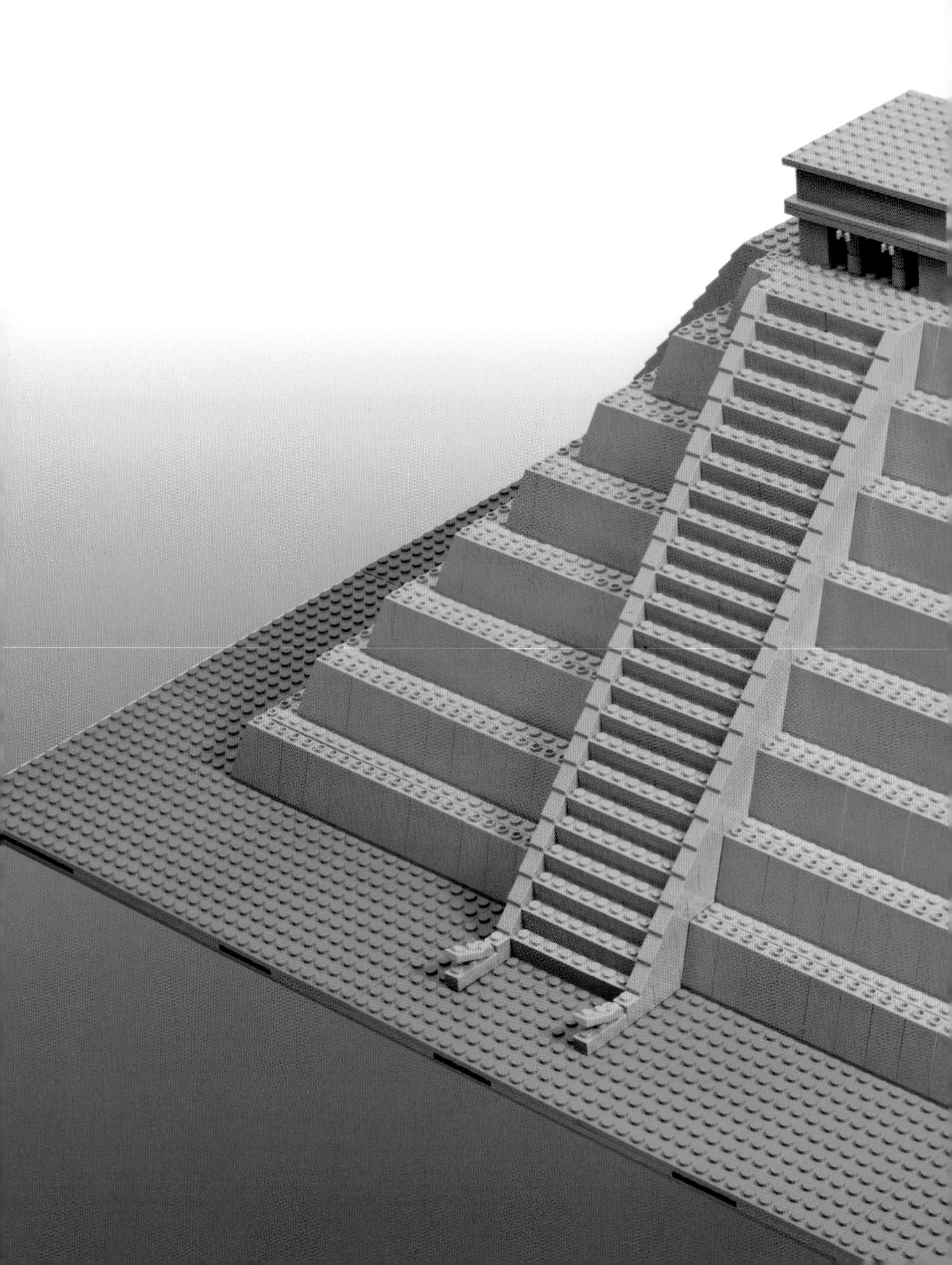

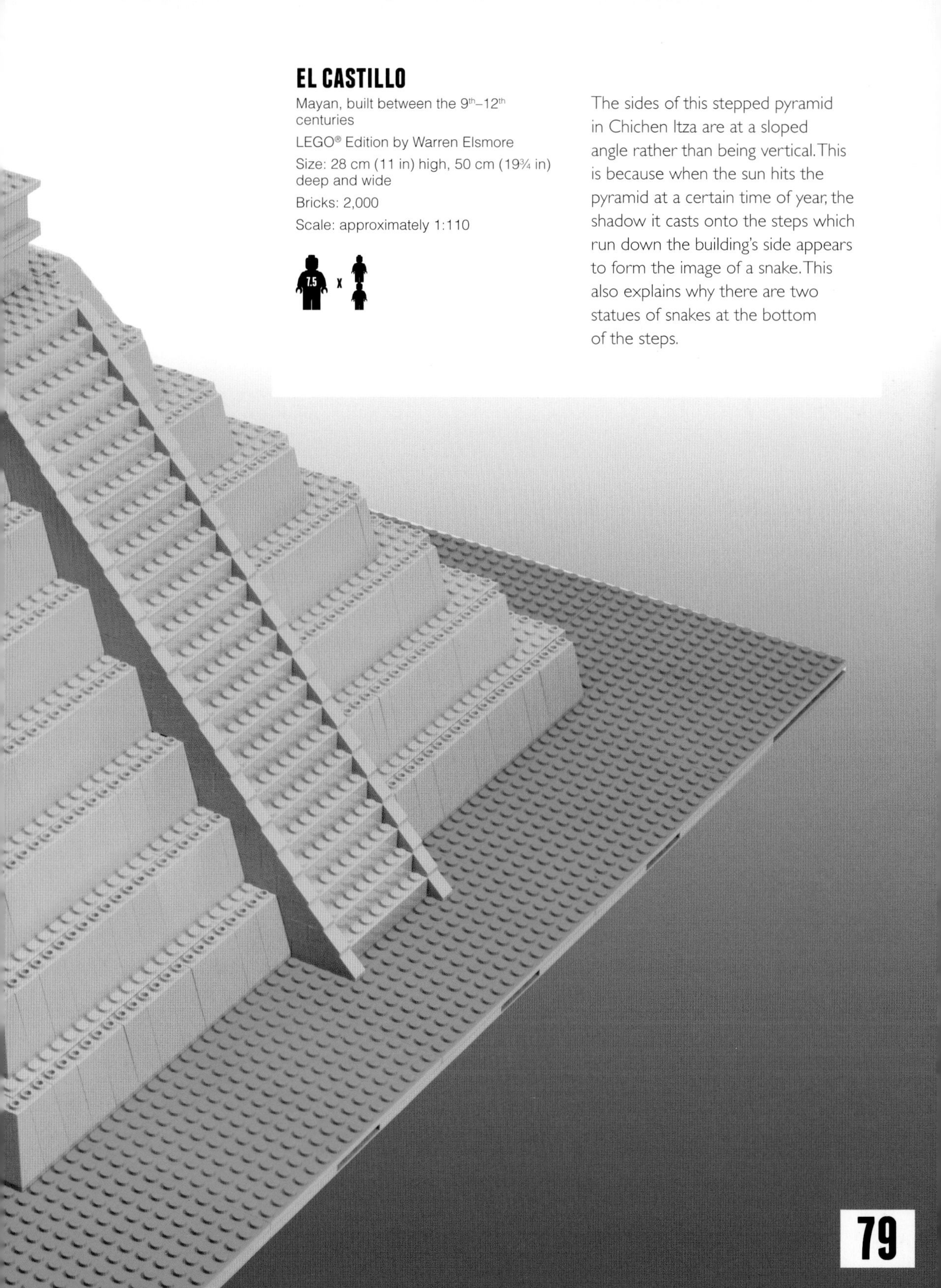

EL CASTILLO

Mayan, built between the 9th–12th centuries

LEGO® Edition by Warren Elsmore

Size: 28 cm (11 in) high, 50 cm (19¾ in) deep and wide

Bricks: 2,000

Scale: approximately 1:110

The sides of this stepped pyramid in Chichen Itza are at a sloped angle rather than being vertical. This is because when the sun hits the pyramid at a certain time of year, the shadow it casts onto the steps which run down the building's side appears to form the image of a snake. This also explains why there are two statues of snakes at the bottom of the steps.

RIO DE JANEIRO

BEACH VOLLEYBALL

It is not recommended to play this sport when there are LEGO® pieces around. Stepping on LEGO bricks by accident is painful enough without increasing the danger by playing volleyball!

CHRIST THE REDEEMER

Designer: Heitor da Silva Costa

Sculptor: Paul Landowski

LEGO® Edition by Warren Elsmore

Size: 33 cm (13 in) high, 9 cm (3½ in) deep, 35 cm (13¾ in) wide

Bricks: 1,500

Scale: 1:91

Rather than precisely copying the actual statue in Rio de Janeiro, I scaled up a LEGO minifig to six times its original size. The statue stands as a monument of religion over the city. It is made from soapstone and reinforced concrete and took nine years to build, from 1922 to 1931.

RIO CARNIVAL

LEGO® Construction by Warren & Teresa 'Kitty' Elsmore

Scale: Minifig scale

The LEGO minifig doesn't have many points of attachment for decoration, so we were trying to figure out how to make him or her wear a big carnival-type costume (see p.85). We came up with the idea of using what LEGO calls a 'tree limb', which allows for large decorations. I'd never normally put as much decoration onto minifigs as we did for the lead carnival dancers, but it really works here. The whole scene has an under-the-sea theme, and we'd originally tried to make the male carnival lead wear a squid costume, but that didn't work out. The real challenge for this model was trying to find a way of giving a minifig the biggest costume possible.

LISBON

BICA FUNICULAR

The Bica Funicular (or *Elevador da Bica*) is a Portuguese national icon that runs through the streets of Lisbon. It has been running for over a hundred years – it was opened in 1892.

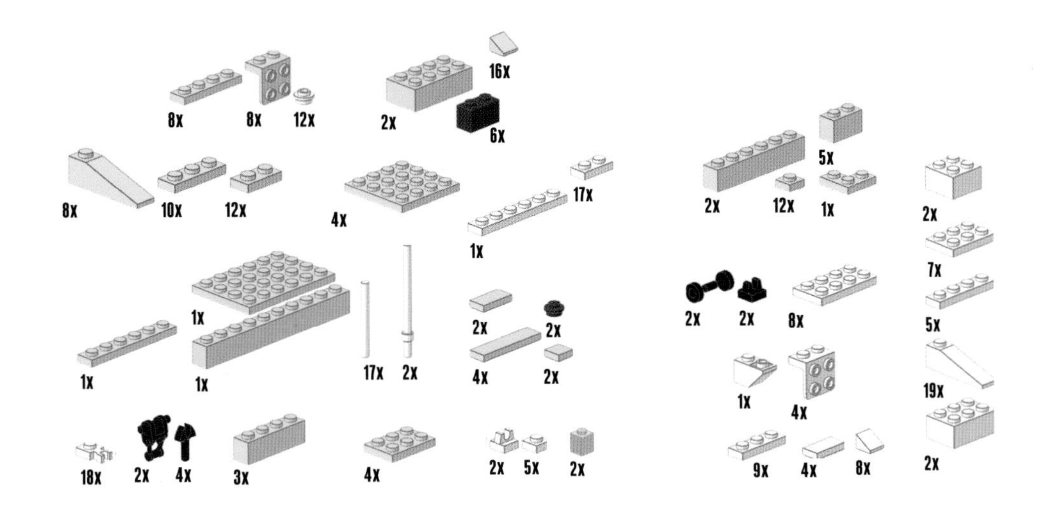
8x
8x
12x
2x
16x
6x
8x
10x
12x
4x
17x
1x
1x
1x
1x
17x
2x
2x
2x
4x
2x
18x
2x
4x
3x
4x
2x
5x
2x
5x
2x
12x
1x
2x
2x
2x
8x
7x
5x
1x
4x
19x
9x
4x
8x
2x

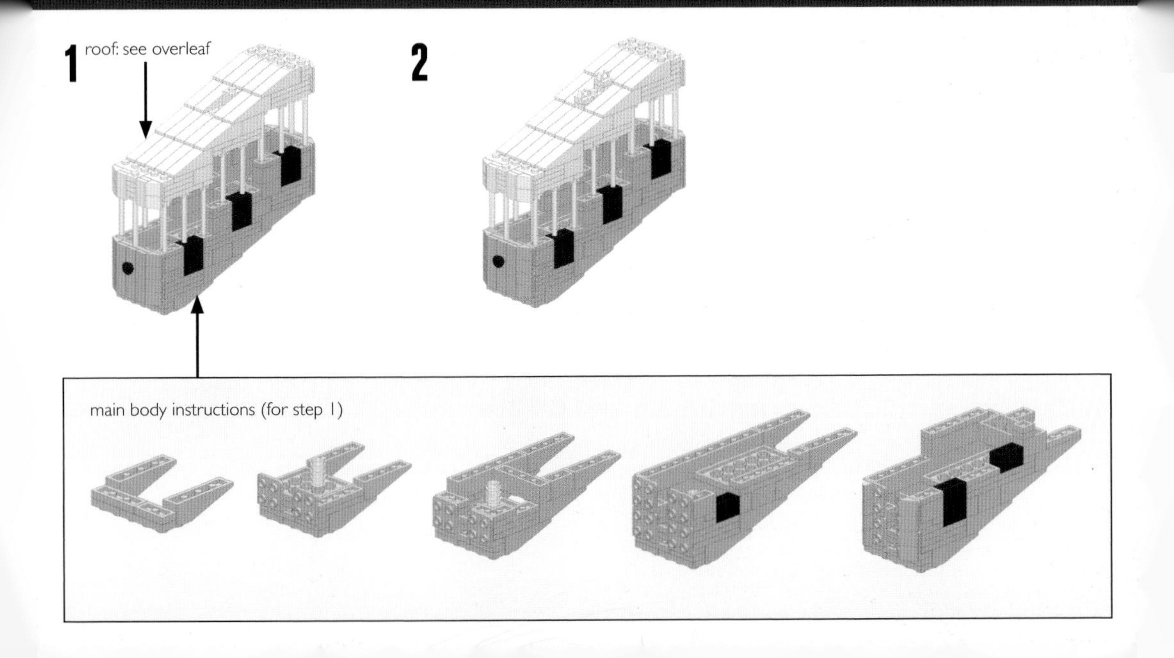
1
roof: see overleaf
2
main body instructions (for step 1)

continued from p.87

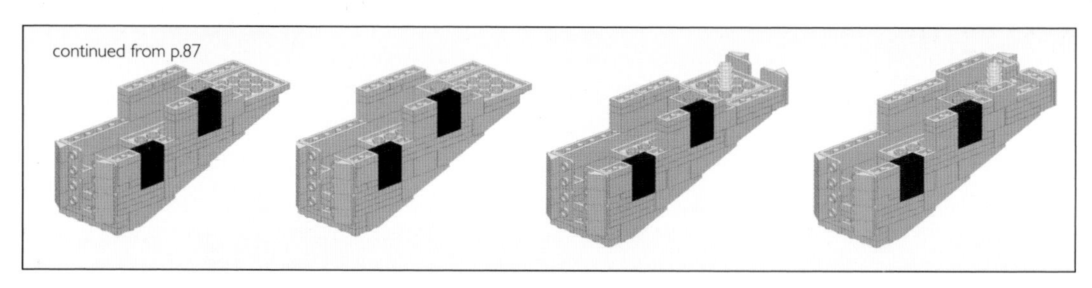

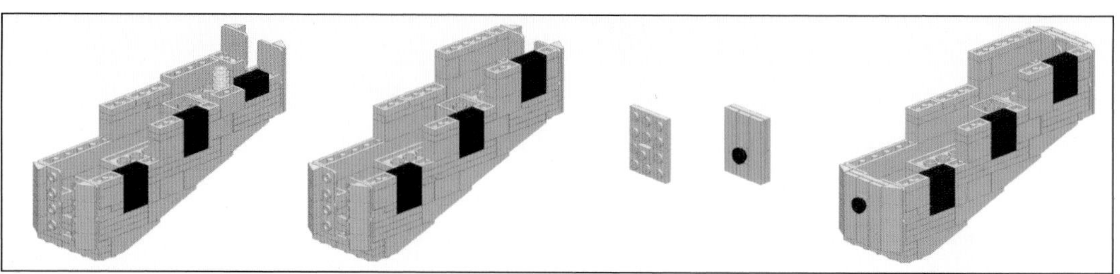

roof instructions (for step 1)

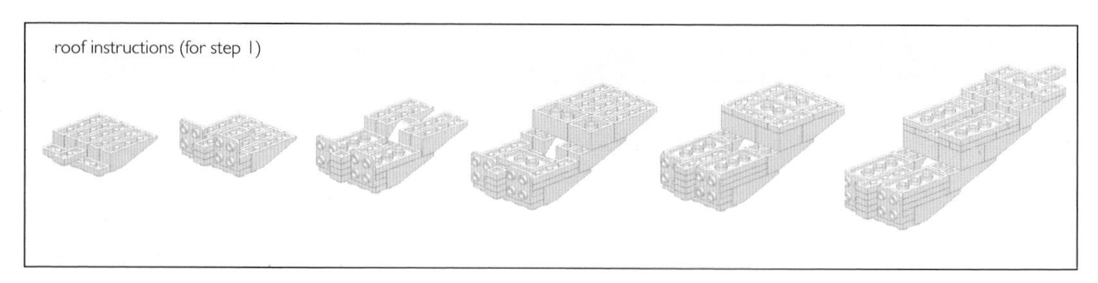

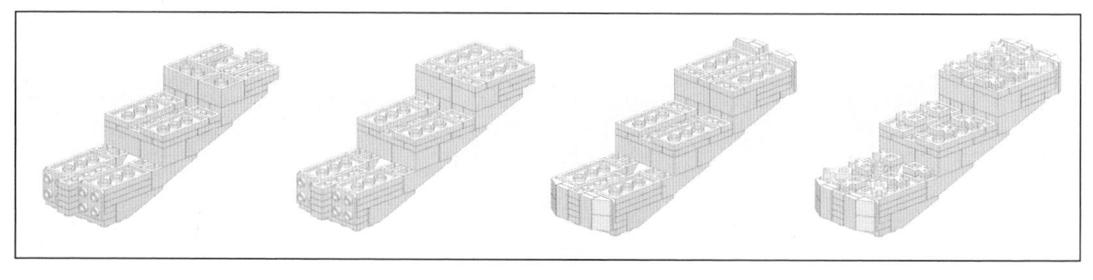

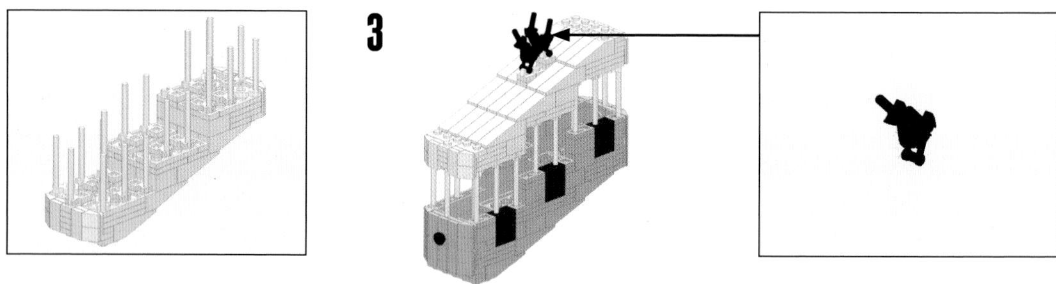

TORRE BELLEM

Architect: Francisco de Arruda (1519)

LEGO® Edition by Alastair Disley

Size: 26 cm (10¼ in) high, 17 cm (6¾ in) long, 29 cm (11½ in) wide

Bricks: 1,150

Scale: 1:133

Before building this model, Alastair collected many photographs of it from all angles, including from above. The model uses lots of the traditional 2x4 bricks, but also some 1x1 round tiles, one of LEGO's newest parts. The ornate round corner tower roofs were originally ice creams for Scala Figures, but they look just like the real decoration – sometimes you have to be imaginative when looking for the right piece.

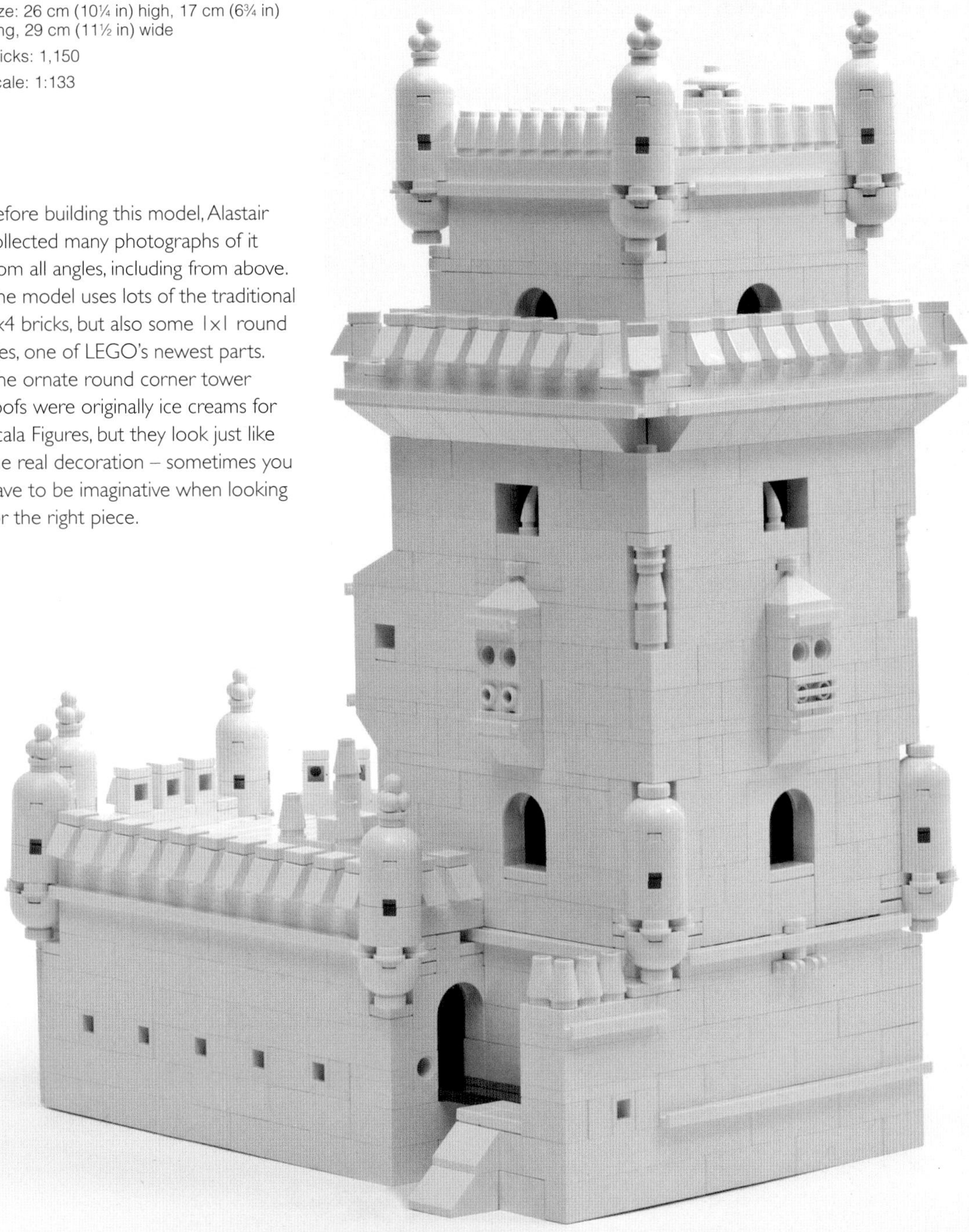

EDINBURGH

EDINBURGH TENEMENT

LEGO® Edition by Warren Elsmore

Size: 36 cm (14 in) high, 25 cm (9¾ in) long and wide

Bricks: 2,100

Scale: Minifig scale

This is a very traditional Edinburgh building, not unlike the ones near where I live. This building shows a Georgian architectural feature of unusually tall and large sash windows, which is common throughout Edinburgh. After living in the city for eight years, I should know the buildings well enough by now to re-create them in LEGO...

MONS MEG

This large medieval cannon, once capable of firing gunstones of 150 kg (330 lbs) over a distance of up to 3.2 km (2 miles), can be found at Edinburgh Castle. Unfortunately its barrel burst while firing a birthday salute to the future King Charles VII of Scotland and II of England in 1681, so it isn't such a lethal weapon today as it once was.

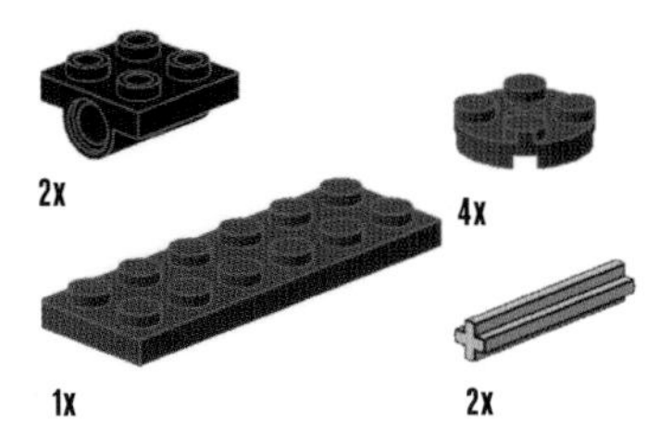

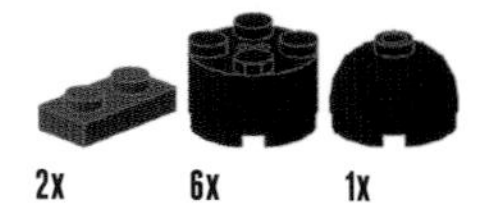

1

2

3

FORTH BRIDGE

This is one of my favourite structures in Edinburgh. Opened in 1890, this cantilevered rail bridge is now crossed by up to 200 trains a day. This LEGO® model is straightforward for anyone to build and keep as a souvenir.

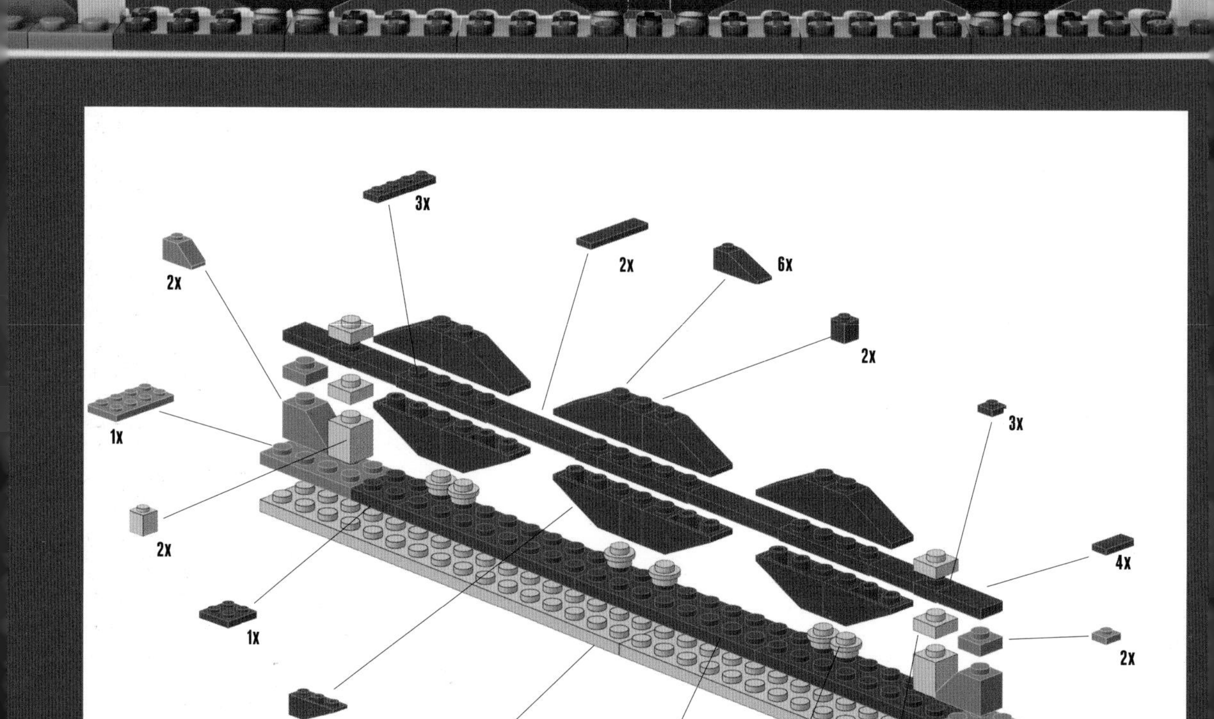

TERRACED HOUSES

These terraced houses are representative of Edinburgh's New Town area, which hasn't actually been 'new' since the late 18th century, but at the time was an unprecedented feat of elegant and spacious urban planning.

LONDON

London is full of beautiful and historical landmarks that are recognisable all over the world – and irresistible for a project like this. From the palatial (such as Buckingham Palace, p.110–15) to the snug (like the traditional pub on p.118–19), from the Victorian Gothic (St Pancras station, p.102–3) to the contemporary (the Olympic Park, pictured opposite), I have re-created many of the buildings and environments that every Londoner holds dear. Of course, no vision of the city would be complete without a Routemaster bus (p.126–7) and black cab (p.98–9).

Some of the models featured in this chapter are relatively easy to make with a few of the right pieces. The microscale St. Paul's Cathedral renders Sir Christopher Wren's seventeenth-century masterpiece all in white, with its world-famous dome represented by a single piece. You can, of course, represent any domed building with a similar single brick, and it would take only a few adjustments to the St. Paul's instructions to make a passable Hagia Sophia or Florentine Duomo.

I chose to build Nelson's Column (p. 124–5) to minifig scale, so that Horatio Lord Nelson himself could stand on top with a tricorn hat piece (3456703), making the hero of Trafalgar instantly recognisable. The lions may need a little more imagination, but, made together, this model is a perfect building block for your own central London scene. Unfortunately for authenticity's sake, minifig scale pigeons are not currently available!

Many of London's old buildings are heavy structures, built largely from stone and brick. Because this book's LEGO® models have to be structured to copy their real-life counterparts, my London models were some of the heaviest. For instance, a modern structure like the Burj Al Arab (p. 220–1) is made from lightweight materials, which means its LEGO model is quite light, too. A construction like the Battersea Power Station (p.116–17), however, is another story.

The Battersea Power Station, built in the 1930s, was once regarded as a red brick monstrosity. Now it is widely seen as one of London's proudest and most fascinating pieces of Art Deco architecture. The real building is, in fact, two power stations built alongside each other, which were only connected by brick walls in 1953. The distinctive shade of the London red brick is luckily very similar to a LEGO brick shade called dark tan. Although the design of the Power Station is easy to emulate (it took only two or three hours to complete), it is made up of a vast number of bricks, almost all of just one kind, and the result was an incredibly cumbersome model.

Perhaps my proudest ever LEGO moment came when the organisers of the London Paralympic Games asked for my Olympic Park model (opposite) to be displayed at the reception area where Great Britain's athletes met VIPs (including the Prime Minister) after finishing their events and receiving their medals – meaning that both the Prime Minister and all of the gold winners would have seen my creation. Considering that it took 300 hours to build over just three weeks, it was great to be able to show my model off!

LONDON OLYMPIC STADIUM

Architects: LOCOG (2012)

LEGO® Edition by Warren Elsmore

Size: 270 cm (106¼ in) wide, 300 cm (118 in) long

Bricks: 120,000

This model was, in fact, originally commissioned by LEGO and the Danish Tourist Board to go on display at their hospitality house for the four weeks of the Olympics. As you can see, it was a hugely complicated mixture of pieces and had to be completed incredibly fast to be ready for the Olympics.

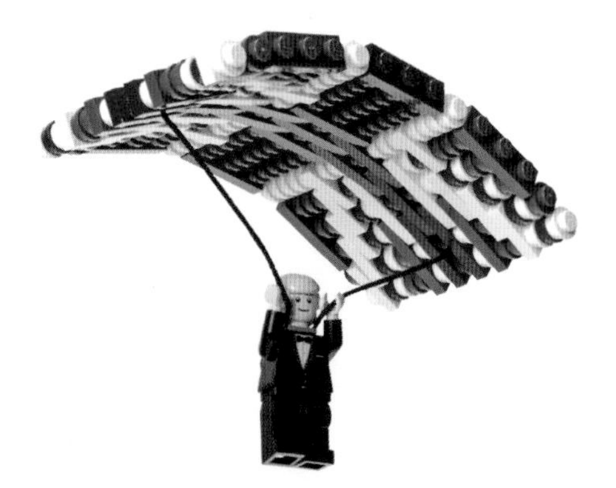

Main image: A game of hockey in the temporary Riverbank Arena, with the Basketball Arena and Olympic Village in the background.
Opposite top (and previous page): The main Olympic Stadium.
Opposite bottom: A rendering of Anish Kapoor's sculpture and observation tower, 'ArcelorMittal Orbit', outside the Olympic Park.

TAXI

Designer: Manganese Bronze Holdings
LEGO® Edition by Ralph Savelsburg
Size: 5.5 cm (2⅛ in) high, 12 cm (4¾ in) long, 4 cm (1⅝ in) wide
Bricks: 150

When Ralph built this, it was to go outside a curry house he had designed out of LEGO. He wanted to have a vehicle parked outside to make the whole scene look realistic, and decided a black cab was the best thing for it. The model isn't completely proportionate – it's a bit too tall and too long, but Ralph did his best to capture the look.

Finding enough space to put both driver and passenger inside turned out to be tricky, which is why the model turned out to be a bit bigger. The other thing with this model is that the doors open the wrong way for this type of cab – Ralph didn't initially realise that they're supposed to be hinged at the back, and instead made them open like modern cars.

These black cabs were introduced in the 1950s and were still in production in the 1990s, looking more or less the same for the entire production run. It was only because of new environmental laws that they were replaced with new designs.

RED PHONE BOX

A multifunctional model – once you've made it and shown it off, you can pop the lid off and use it as a pen holder! The red telephone box is an iconic image of London. The one we've re-created here in LEGO® bricks is known as a 'K2' box, and is the second revision of the public telephone box, though it was the first to be widely deployed throughout London. This phone box was actually designed in 1926 by Giles Gilbert Scott, the grandson of George Gilbert Scott, who designed St. Pancras Station, depicted on p.102–3.

Although fewer than 200 remain in use (of which many are listed buildings), these telephone boxes can now be seen on T-shirts, pencil cases, and many other souvenirs – and, of course, in LEGO bricks.

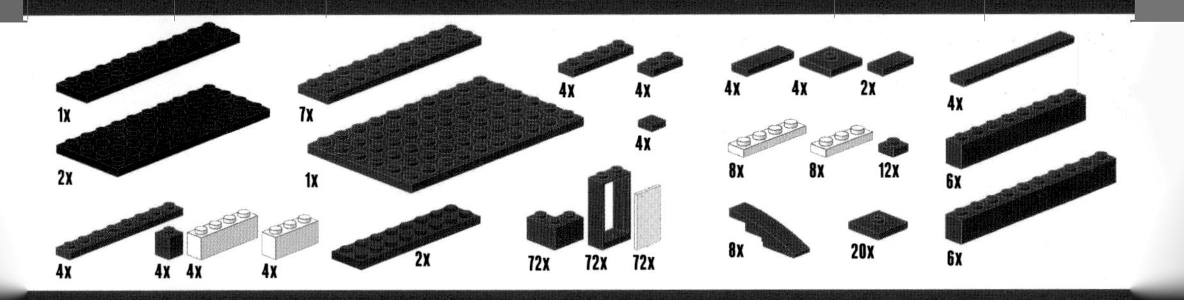
1x
2x
7x
1x
4x
4x
4x
4x
4x
2x
4x
8x
8x
12x
6x
4x
4x
4x
4x
2x
72x
72x
72x
8x
20x
6x

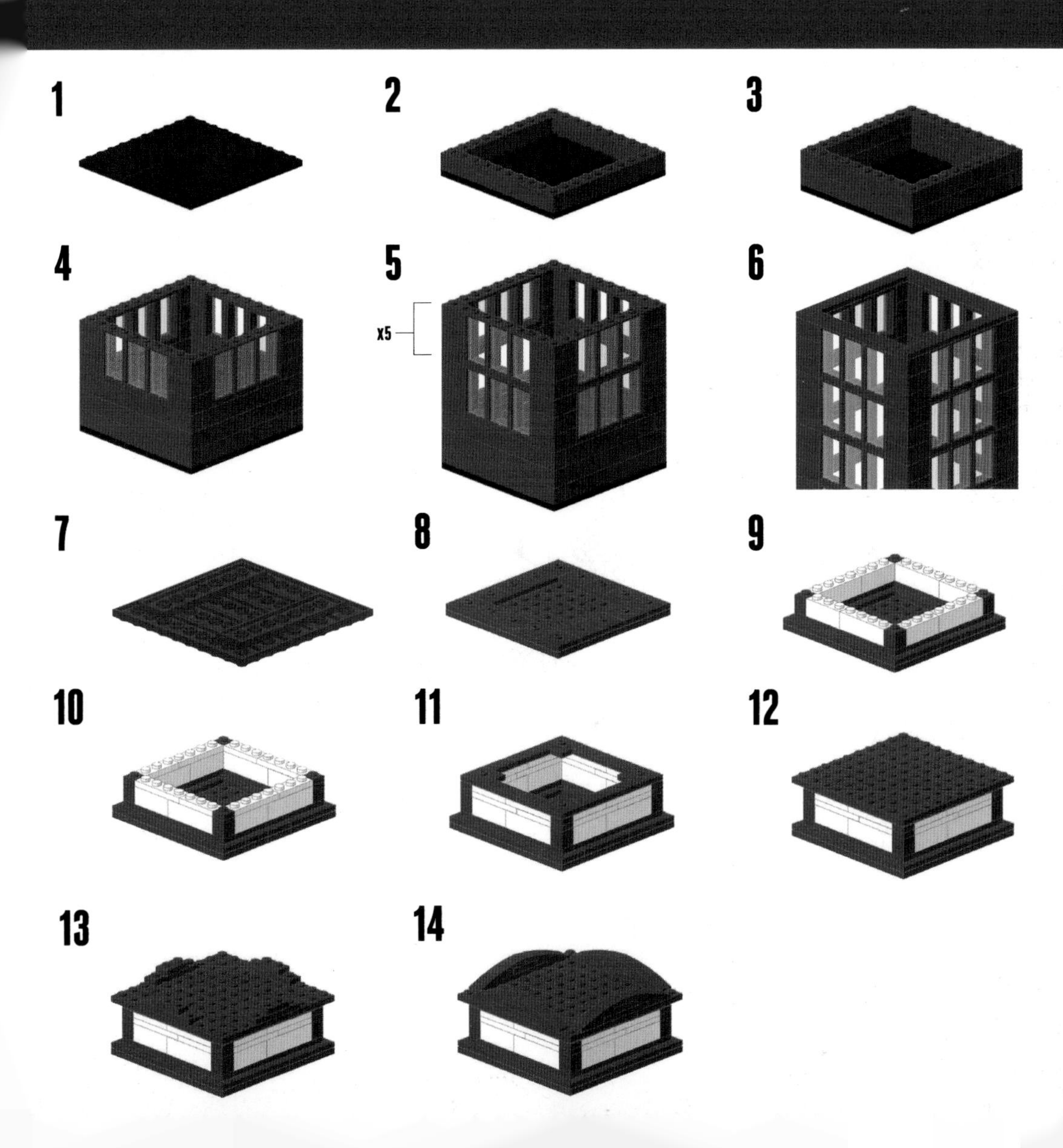
1
2
3
4
5
x5
6
7
8
9
10
11
12
13
14

ST. PANCRAS STATION

Architect: George Gilbert Scott (1868)
LEGO® Edition by Warren Elsmore
Eurostar trains by Carl Geatrix
Size: 140 cm (4 ft 7 in) high, 350 cm (11 ft 6 in) long, 150 cm (4 ft 11 in) wide
Scale: approximately 1:100
Bricks: 180,000

138 x

This huge model is built to minifig scale, almost 1.5 metres (5 feet) wide and 3.5 metres (11½ feet) long. It has six working platforms and hundreds of minifig passengers. In making this model, I had to use 'selective compression', which makes the upper floors slimmer than they are in real life. If the model was strictly 100% accurate in terms of scale, it would be much too big and heavy to move.

The arched roof in this model uses the same structural technique as the real building, with the walls being able to support the huge weight of the arch as tie beams attach them to the floor.

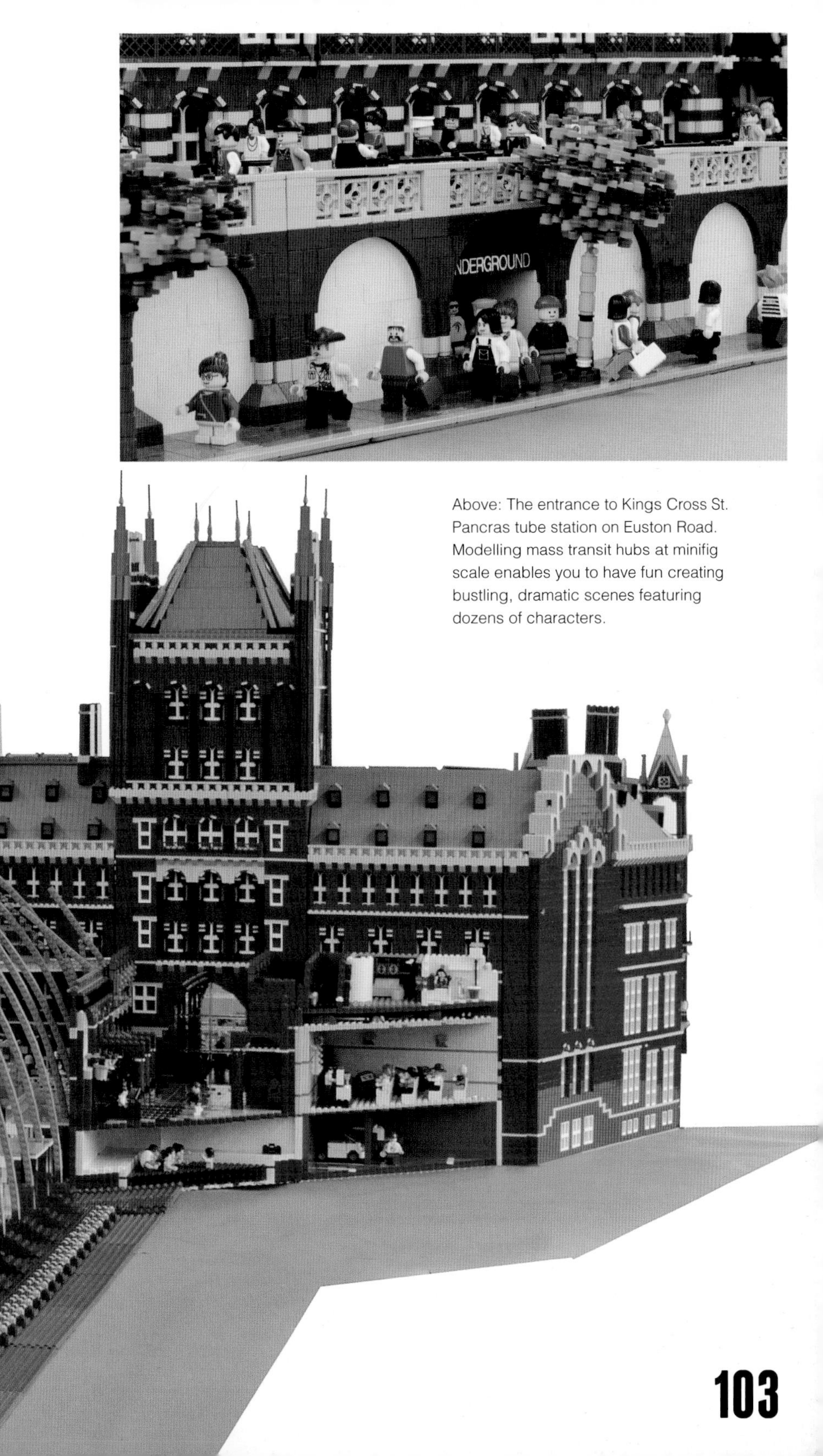

Above: The entrance to Kings Cross St. Pancras tube station on Euston Road. Modelling mass transit hubs at minifig scale enables you to have fun creating bustling, dramatic scenes featuring dozens of characters.

WESTMINSTER ABBEY

Architect: Various, 13th–16th centuries

LEGO® Edition by Ed Diment, Annie Diment, Naomi Farr, Stuart Crawshaw & Warren Elsmore

Size: 160 cm (63 in) high, 295 cm (116 in) long, 145 cm (57 in) wide

Bricks: 180,000

Scale: 1:43

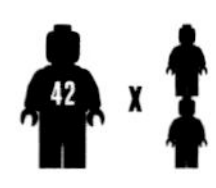

All the bricks used in this spectacular re-creation of Westminster Abbey are regular LEGO elements – it includes no specially commissioned bricks, no altered bricks, no glue and no non-LEGO parts.

There are huge quantities of the archetypal 2x4 LEGO brick in this model, as it is great for strength, for multiple connection combinations and for use in larger-size models. Inside, there are approximately 400 assorted minifigs in the congregation.

It took four people eight weeks to build. The time frame was short, as we were working to a deadline of the Royal Wedding in 2011, and for it to go on display afterwards at the 2011 LEGO Show in Manchester.

One of the bigger challenges was making it so that it came apart in sections to make it easily transportable. This always meant that the nave floor (made with an under-layer of LEGO pieces which allowed us to re-create the classic diagonal black-and-white-tiled floor) had to be put back together again at every event, and the tiles repositioned along on the section's seams.

And it was all trial and error – this model was not built from instructions!

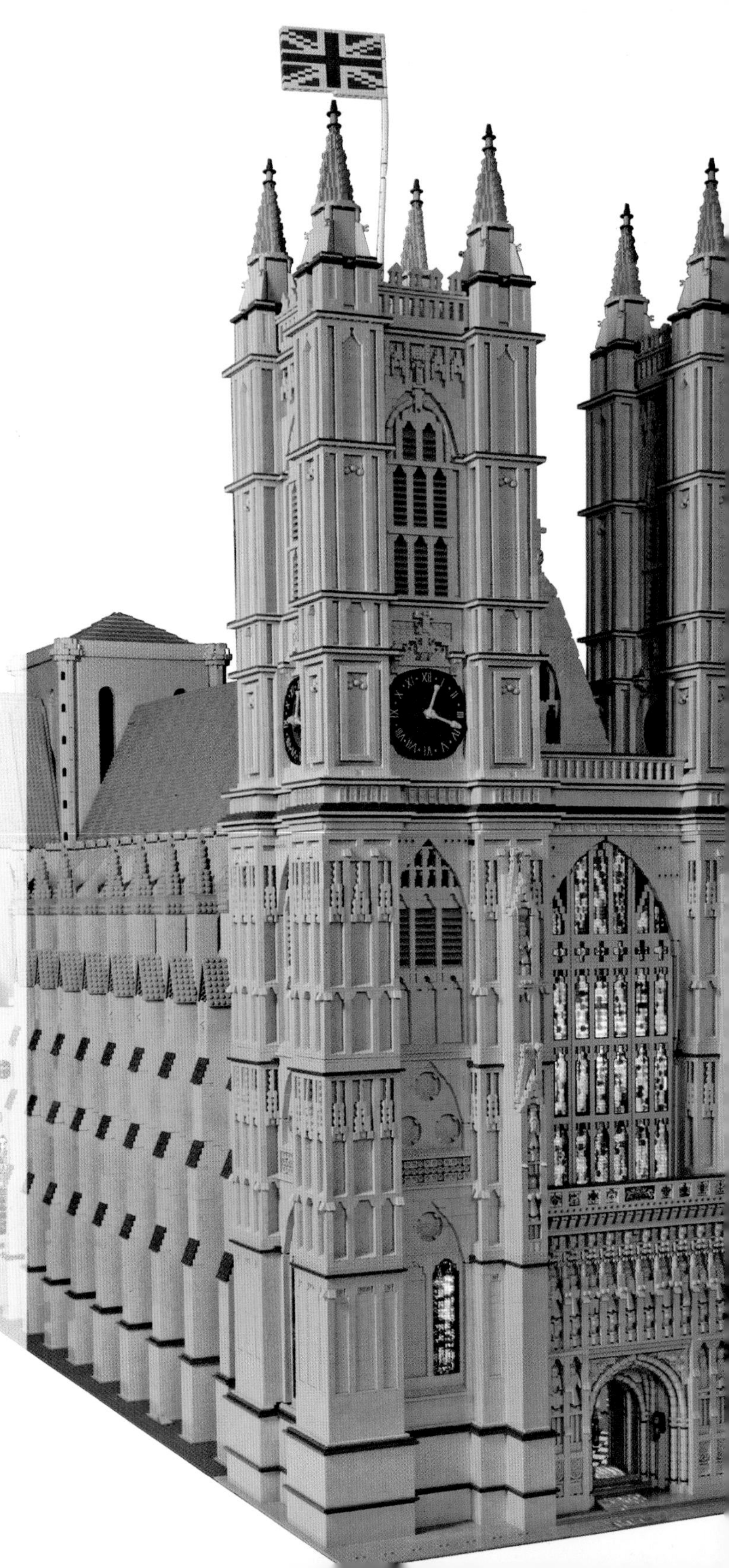

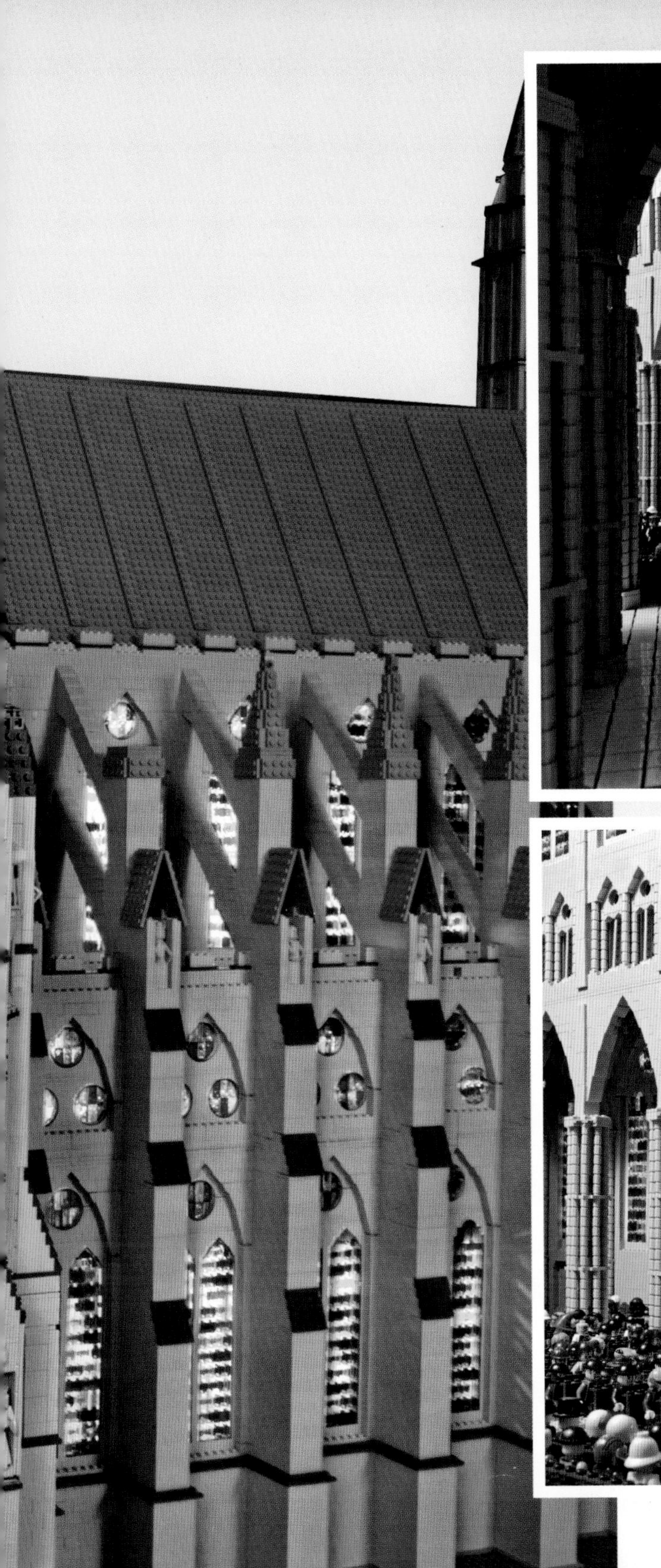

MINI WESTMINSTER ABBEY

This model is certainly a lot easier to build than the larger version! The walls on this model are all built sideways to allow the model to contain more detail in less space. Each of the stained glass windows is a single transparent LEGO® plate.

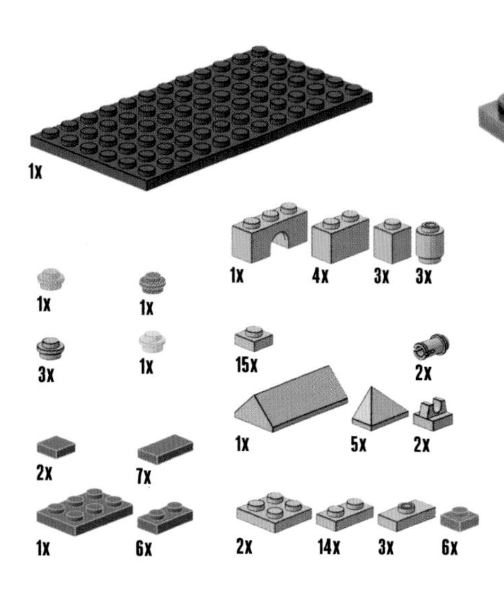

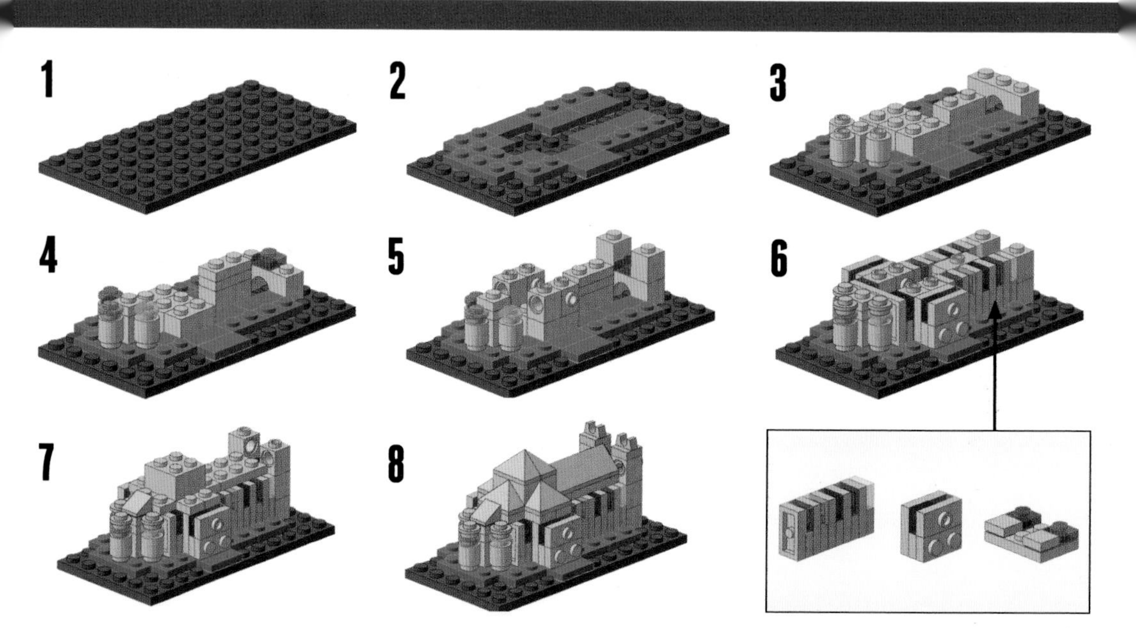

O_2 ARENA

There's a bit of trick perspective involved in this picture of the former Millennium Dome, which allows the yellow supporting struts to appear to come through the roof as they do in real life, when they don't in fact on the model – it's another good example of how cheating the eye is sometimes necessary, to make a LEGO® model work visually.

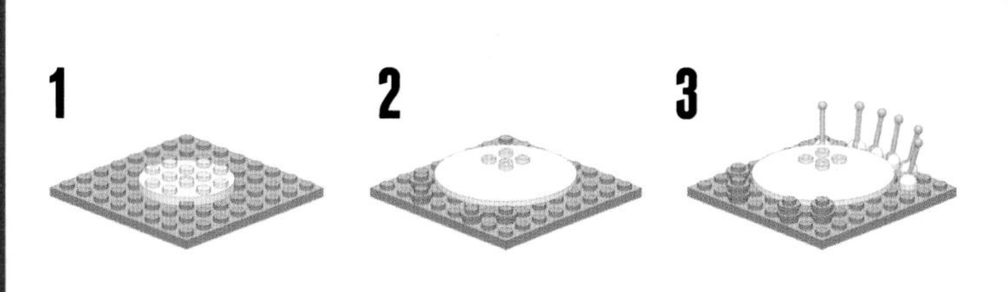

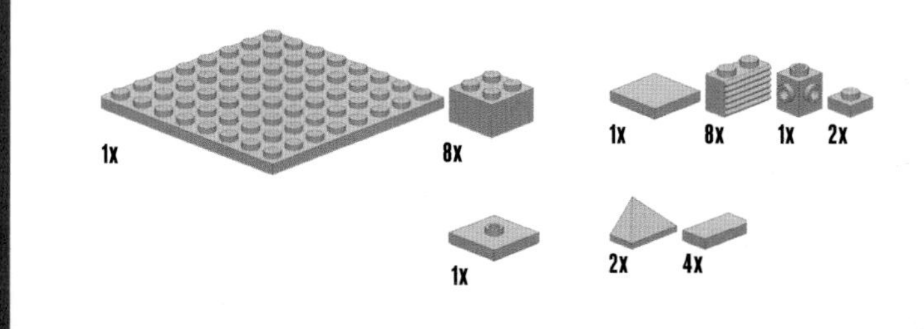

CANARY WHARF

The tower on the right-hand side of the picture is a good example of the right part working perfectly at the right scale. These flat 'grill' bricks emulate the light and dark of the front of an office tower block very well.

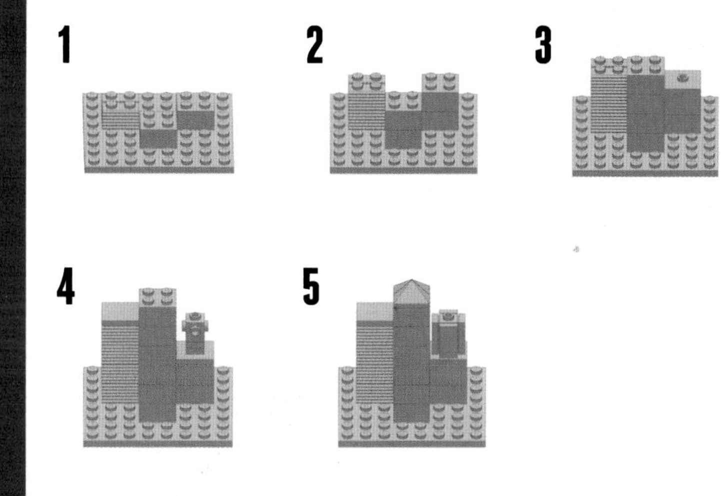

BUCKINGHAM PALACE

This was commissioned for the Royal Wedding between Prince William and Kate Middleton. The Royal Family is represented by bespoke minifigs, although unfortunately we didn't have space for Pippa in the end.

These custom minifigs were created through a combination of water slide decals, painting some parts (the Queen's hat was once a magician's top hat) and hacksawing others – Camilla's hat was a cowgirl's stetson with a braid that needed removing.

2x 2x 18x 6x 12x 6x 3x 1x 1x

16x 12x 10x 16x 14x 3x 3x 1x 4x 6x

1x 4x 3x 4x 6x 8x 6x 6x 2x 32x

2x 2x 4x 18x 18x 72x 14x 61x 44x 76x

2x 3x 14x 14x 18x

1x 26x 3x 21x 5x 2x 6x

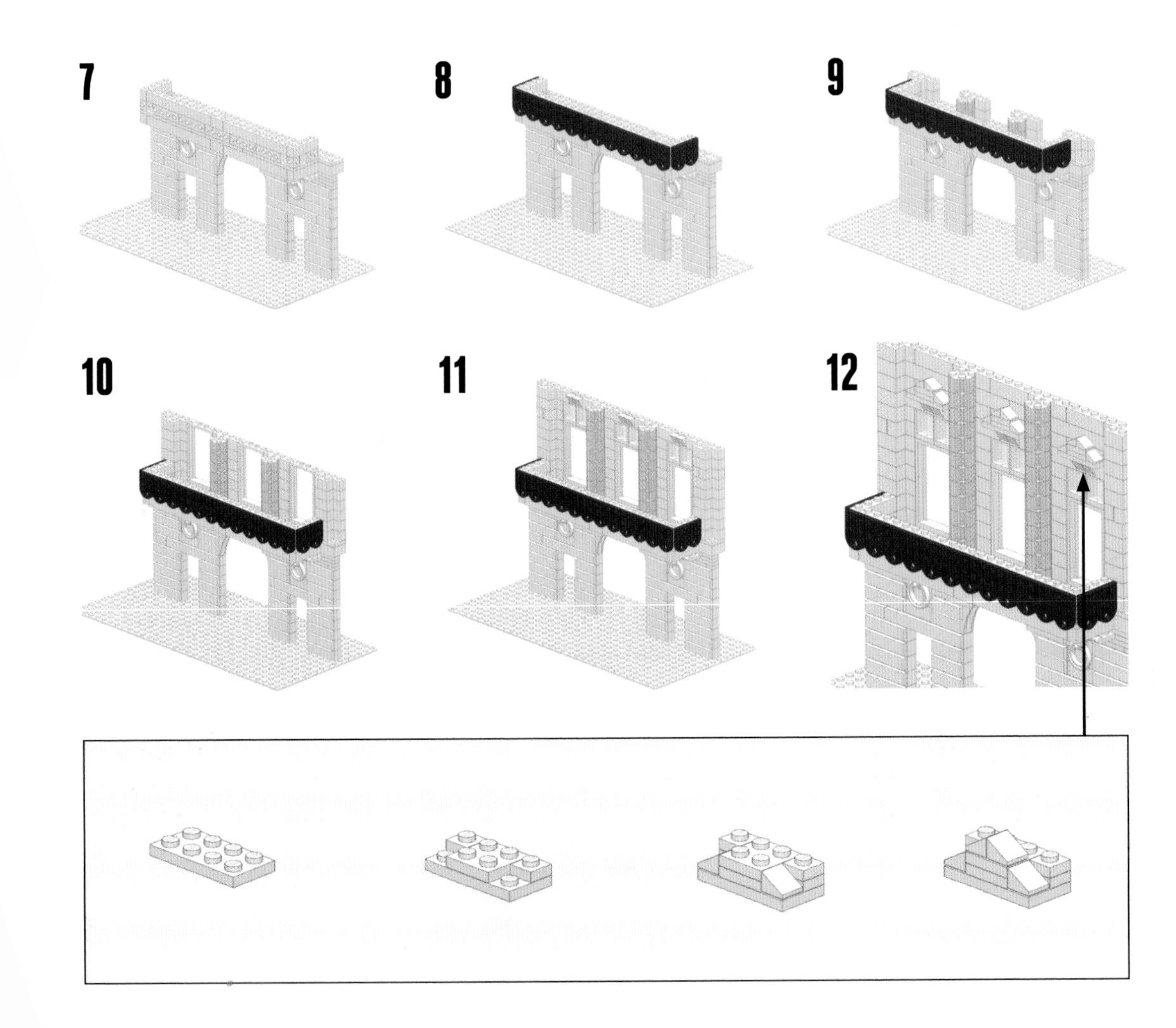
7
8
9
10
11
12

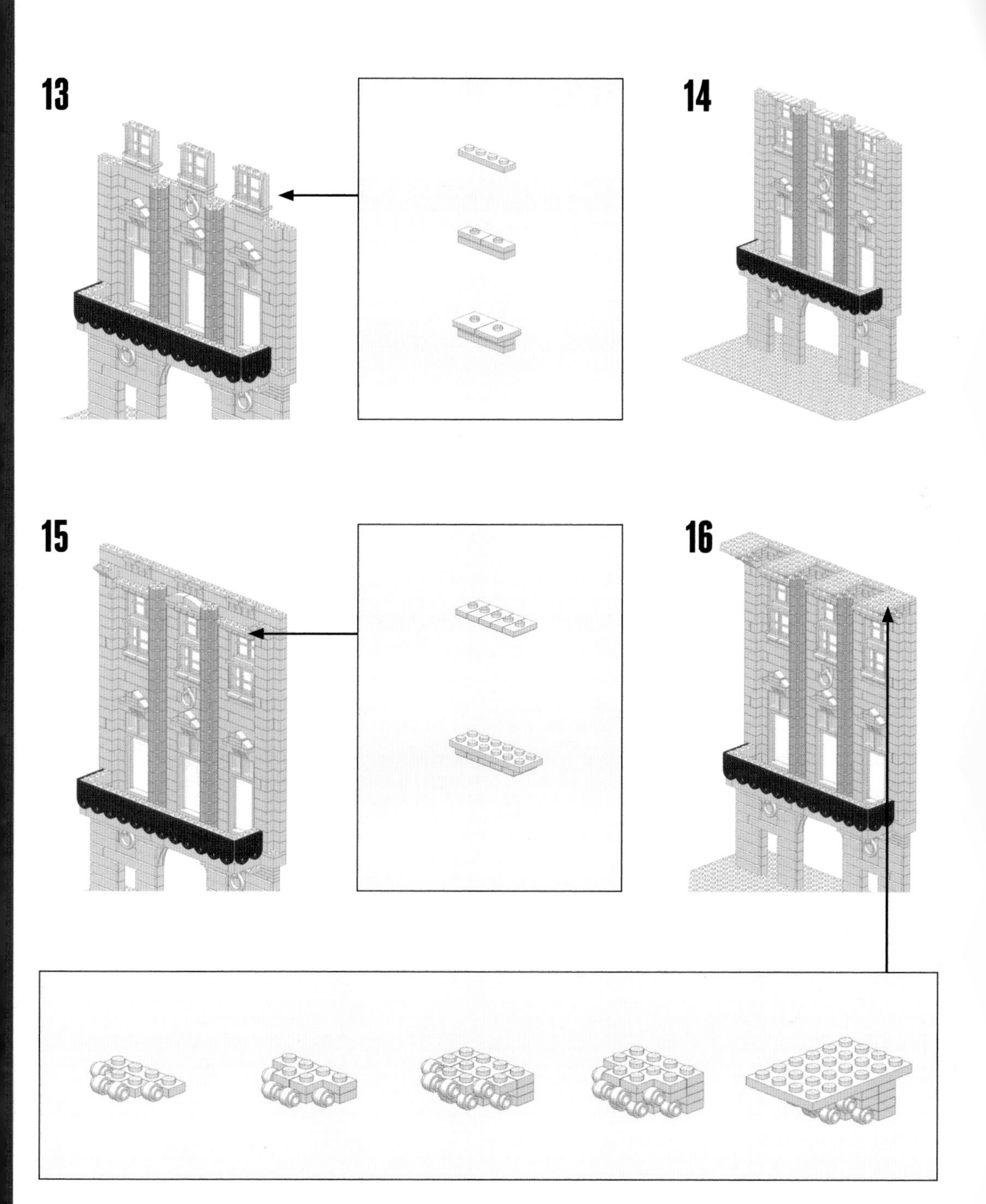
13
14
15
16

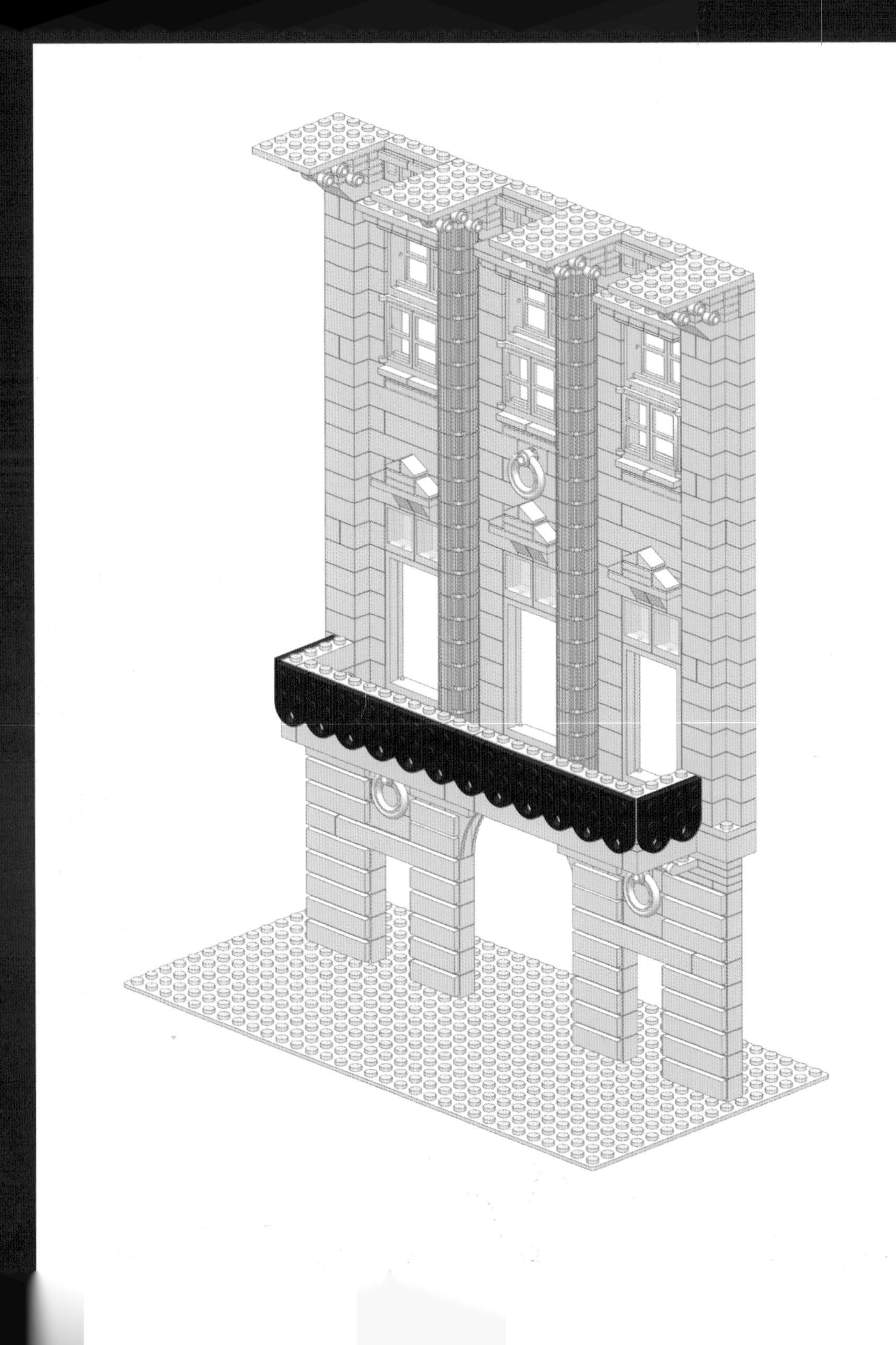

BATTERSEA POWER STATION

Architect: Sir Giles Gilbert Scott (1933–1955)

LEGO® Edition by Warren Elsmore

Size: 17 cm (6¾ in) high, 25 cm (9¾ in) long and wide

Bricks: 1,500

Scale: 1:530

9¾ x

Once thought of as a monstrosity, the Battersea Power Station, built in two phases starting in 1929 and 1945 respectively, is now a Grade II listed building and regarded as a great work of Art Deco architecture. This model was constructed using only two types of brick and took just a few hours to complete. The flying pig is a reference to the cover of Pink Floyd's 1977 album *Animals*, on which the pig was pictured floating above the power station.

LONDON PUB AND STREET SCENE

LEGO® Construction by Warren Elsmore

Size: 24 cm (9½ in) high, 50 cm (19½ in) long, 25 cm (9¾ in) wide

Bricks: 3,000

Scale: Minifig scale

This model represents the sort of English pub that tourists might expect to see when they visit London. It is in the style of the great coaching inns, many of which used to be found in the Southwark area on the south bank of the River Thames, on the way to London Bridge. The street around it is cobbled, which was done by randomly scattering around 1x1 round plates.

Above: some quintessential English activities – visiting the pie shop and carousing in the beer garden. The wood beam structure visible both in and outside the buildings is a traditional Tudor architectural style.

ST. PAUL'S CATHEDRAL

A quick and easy model of one of the great architectural masterpieces by Sir Christopher Wren.

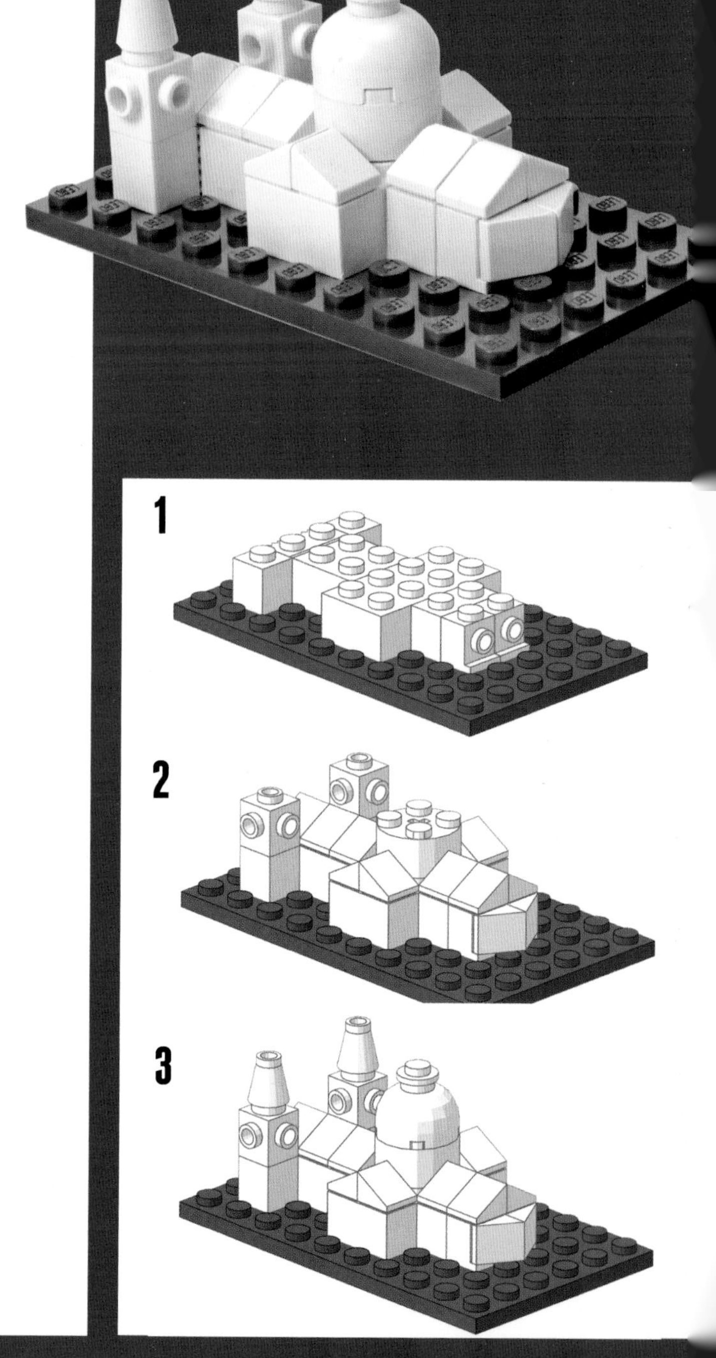

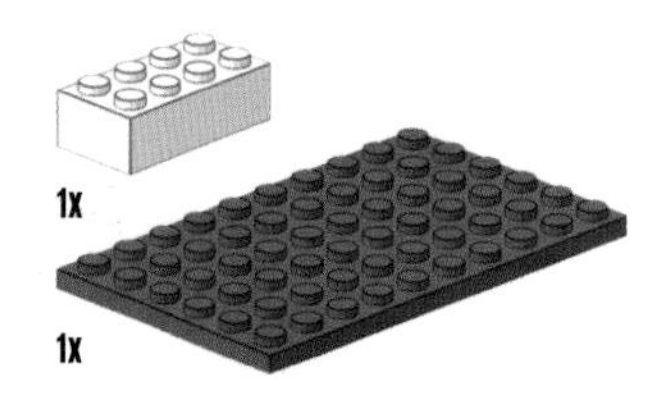

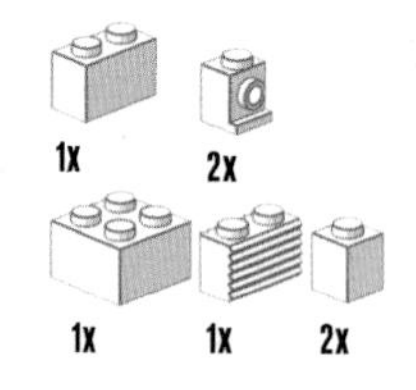

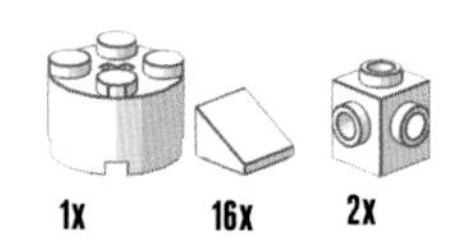

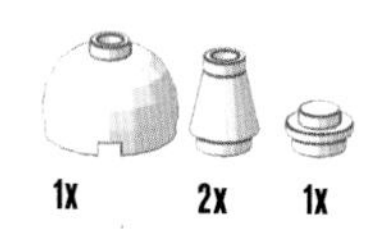

NATIONAL GALLERY

This simple model was made using the same bricks as St. Paul's, opposite. The National Gallery, situated in Trafalgar Square, is the fourth most visited art museum in the world.

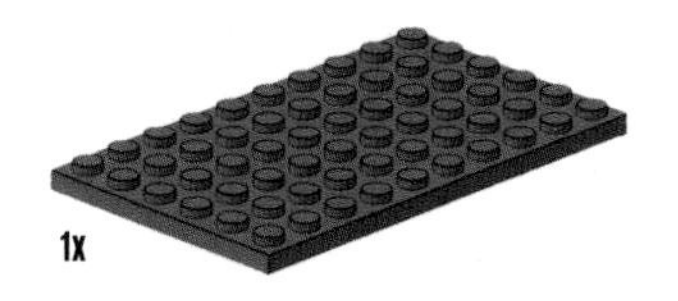

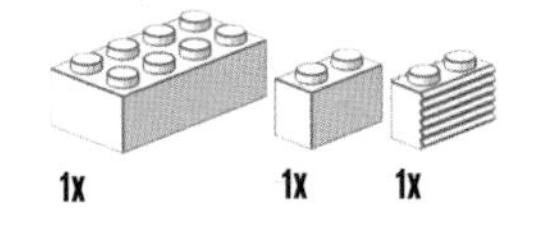

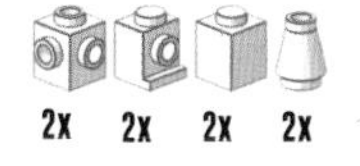

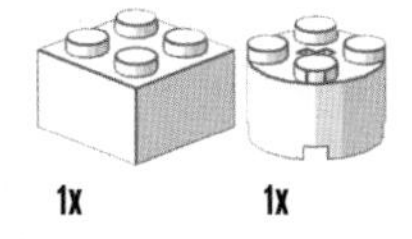

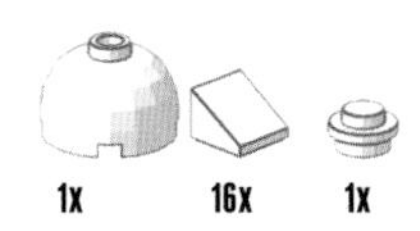

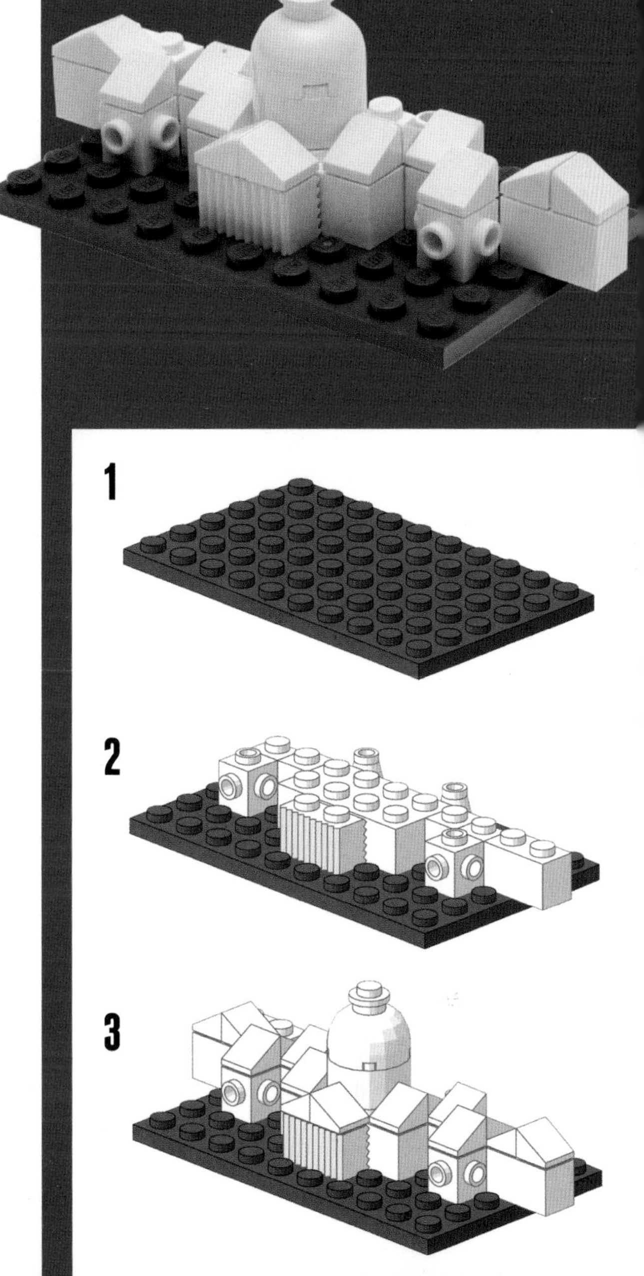

NELSON'S COLUMN

The lions on Nelson's Column were the tricky part – to make a recognisable lion at such a small scale required some ingenuity, and each of the features of the lion are represented by a different type of brick. I used plates with a rounded end to represent the paws and used rounded bricks for the back.

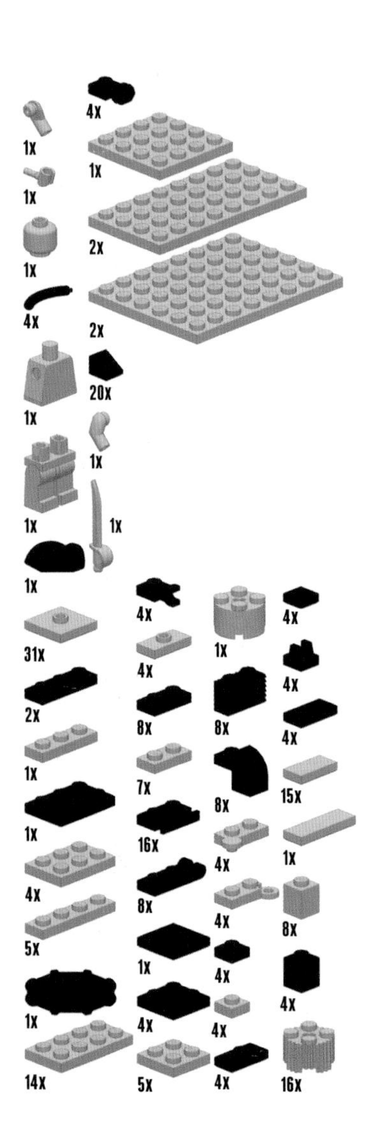

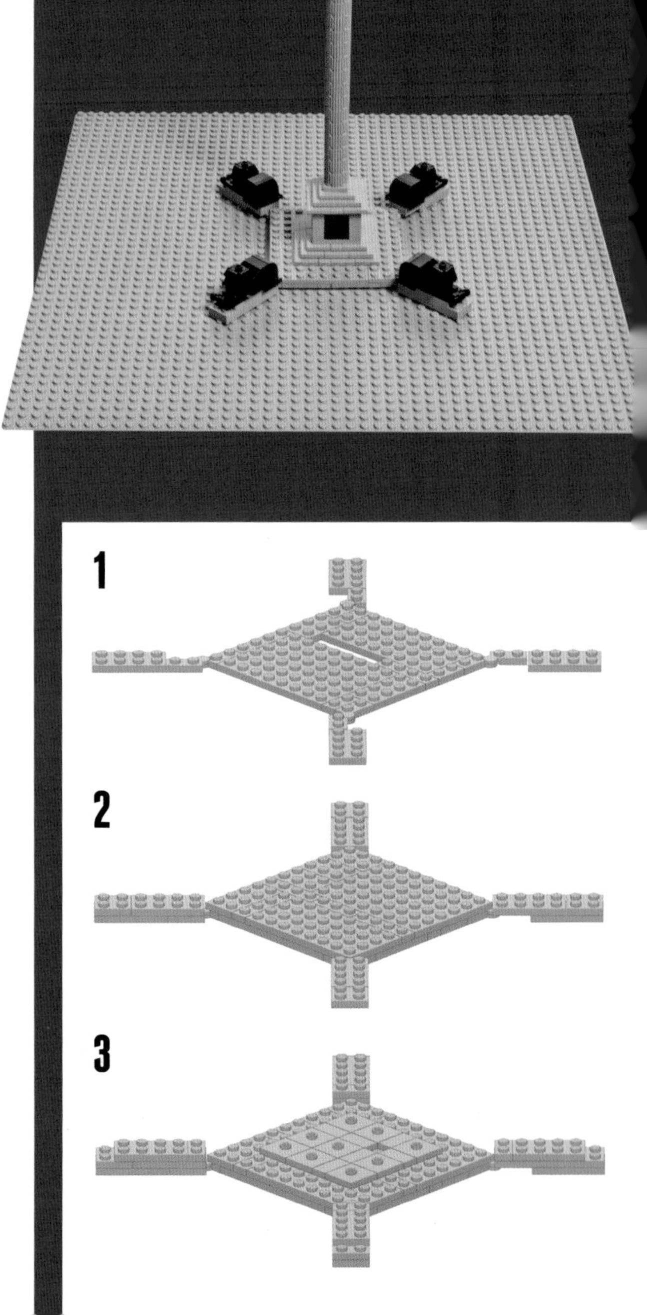

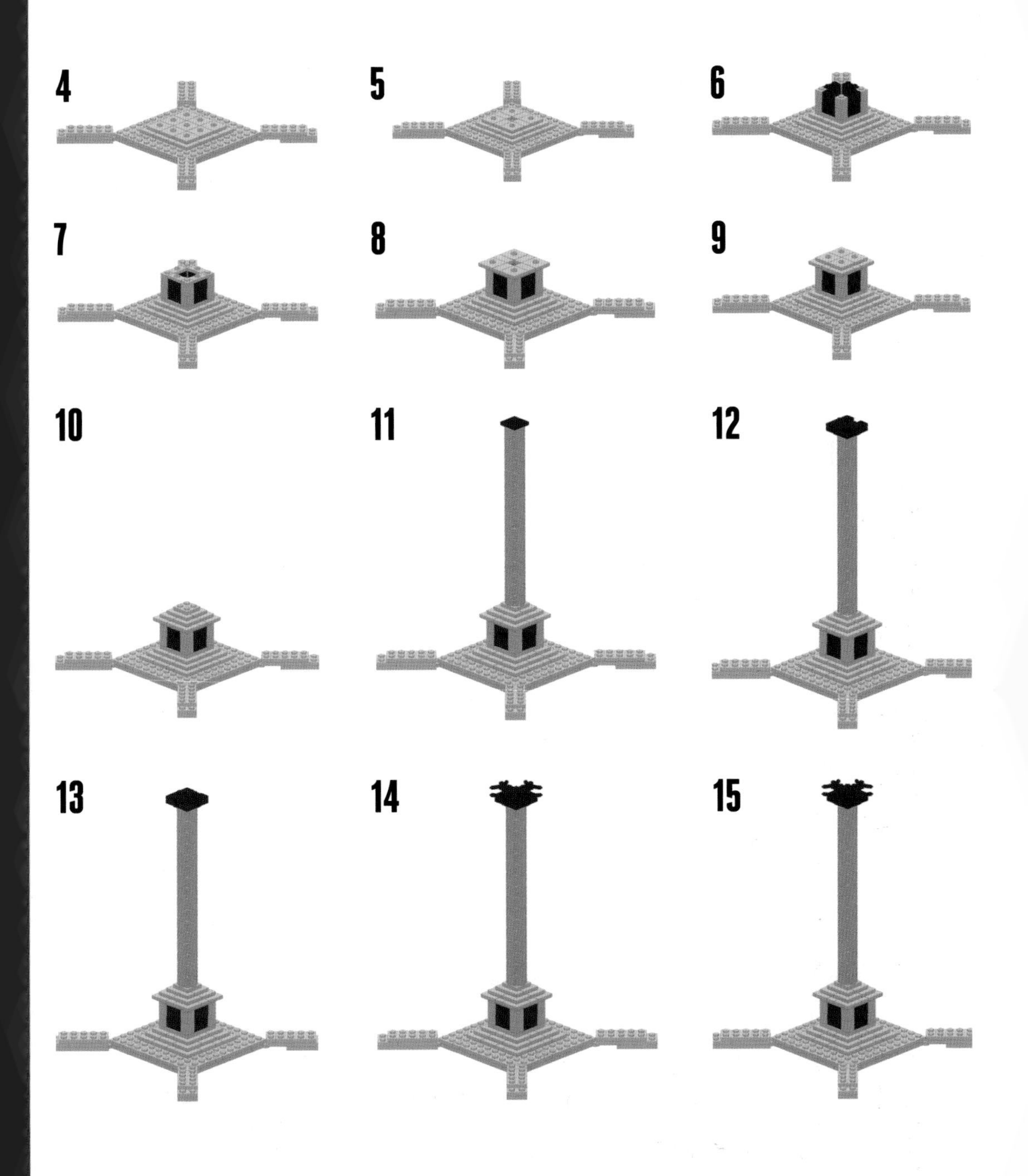
4
5
6
7
8
9
10
11
12
13
14
15

16

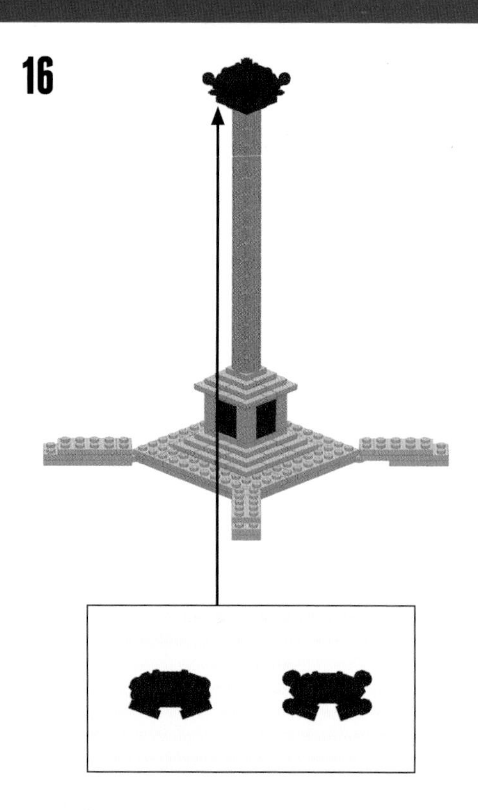

17

18

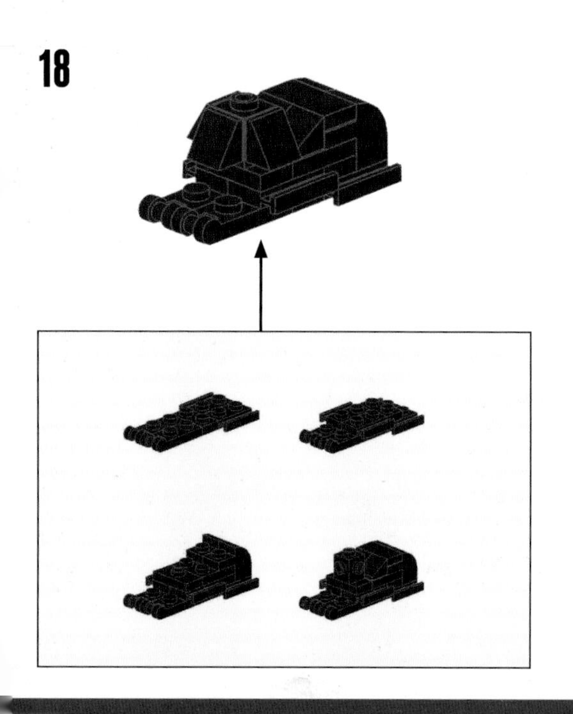

19

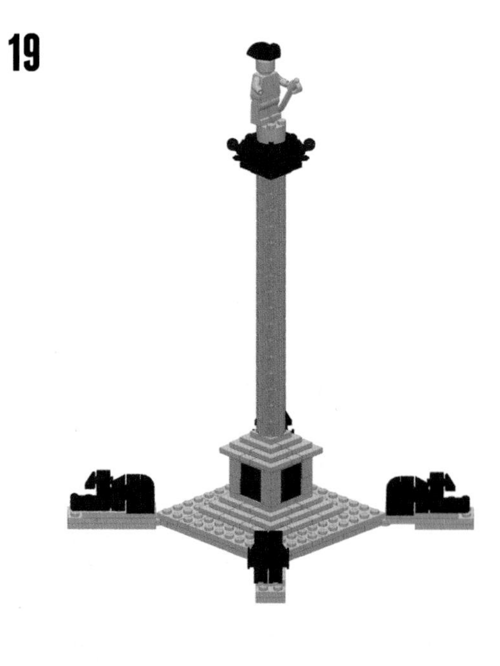

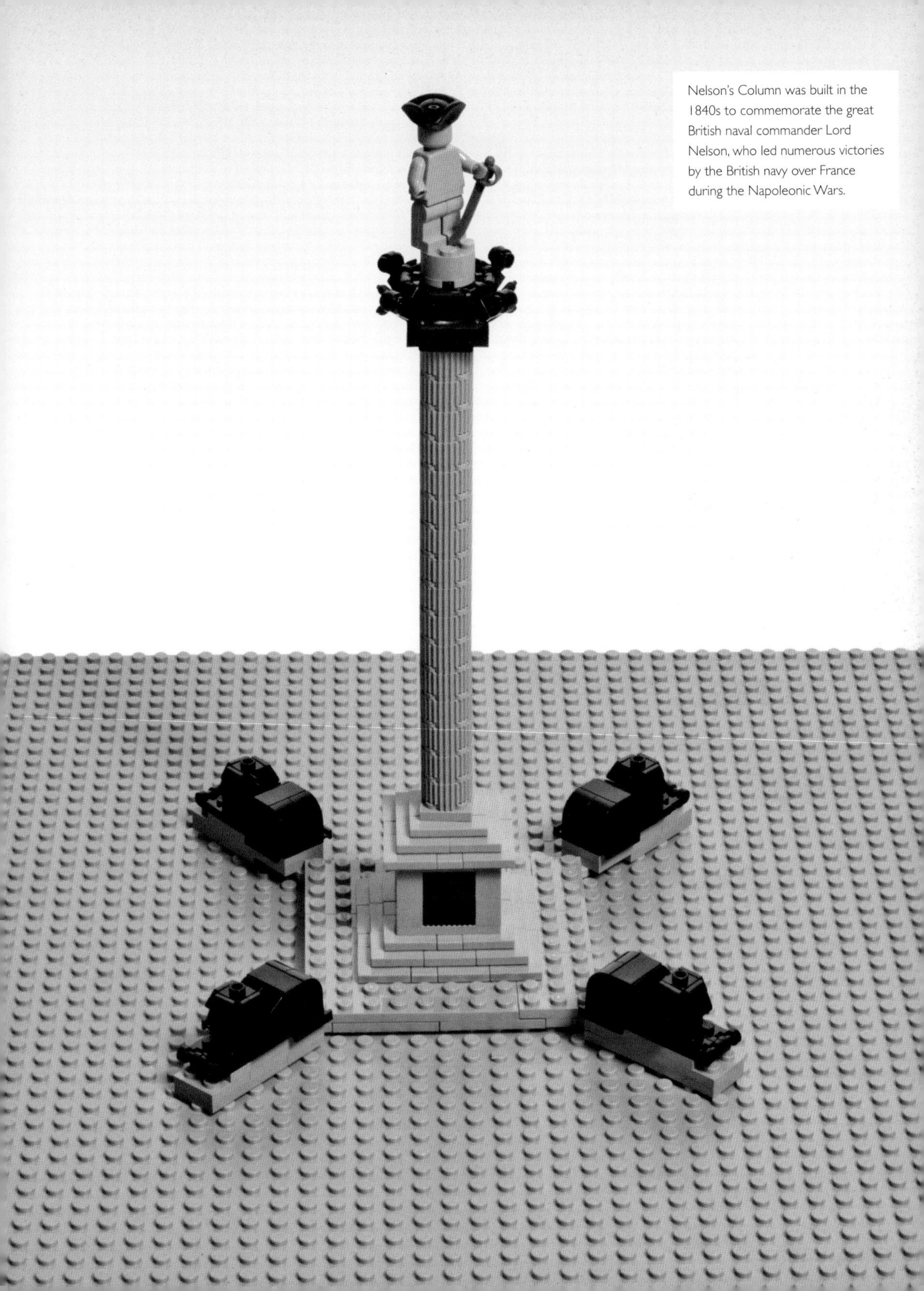

Nelson's Column was built in the 1840s to commemorate the great British naval commander Lord Nelson, who led numerous victories by the British navy over France during the Napoleonic Wars.

15
LEGO land
Regent St
Billund
The Brickish
Asso

LONDON BUS

Designer: London Transport

LEGO® Edition by Ralph Savelsburg

Size: 12 cm (4¾ in) high, 22 cm (8½ in) long, 6 cm (2⅜ in) wide

Bricks: 450

Scale: 1:43

Building vehicles for minifigs is very tricky because minifigs do not have the same proportions as humans – they're much shorter and stockier. In this bus, there is only enough space on each row for two passengers to sit, one on each side of the aisle, unlike a real bus, where there would be two on each side. Next to the minifigs on the pavement, this bus does look quite enormous – the scale ended up being 1:43. It's seven studs wide, which is quite difficult because pieces usually end up being made in even numbers. It has been on display in the famous Hamleys toy shop, which is served by the number 15 bus!

BARCELONA

SAGRADA FAMILIA

There are eighteen spires on Antoni Gaudí's famous cathedral, which represent important figures in the Catholic faith: in ascending order, the twelve apostles, the four evangelists, the Virgin Mary, and (tallest of all), Jesus Christ.

Aside from being one of the most striking pieces of architecture in the world, what is interesting about this cathedral is that it is not finished yet – in fact, it is now just over half built. Begun in 1883, it is not due for completion until 2026.

The pieces on the top are repurposed minifig paddles – the same as would be used for signalling on the tarmac at the airport. This model is very small for one so detailed, but it is one from this book that I'm most proud of!

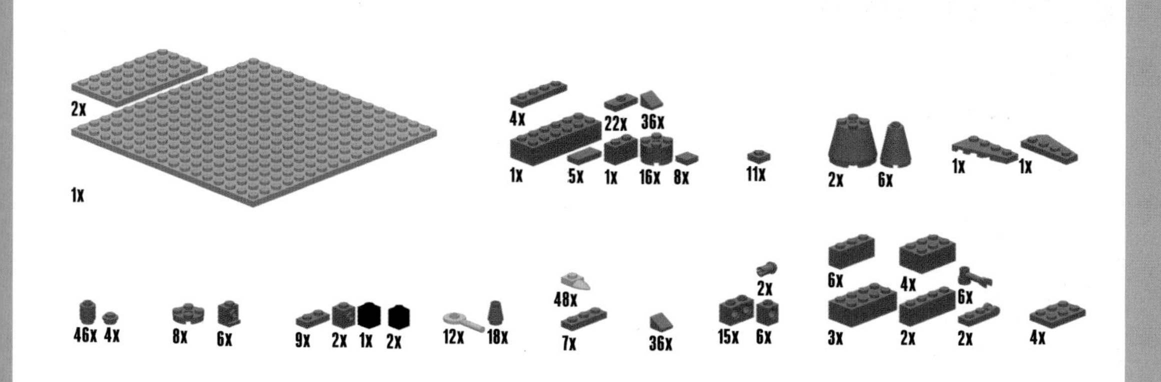
2x
1x
4x
22x
36x
1x
5x
1x
16x
8x
11x
2x
6x
1x
1x
46x
4x
8x
6x
9x
2x
1x
2x
12x
18x
48x
7x
36x
2x
15x
6x
6x
4x
6x
3x
2x
2x
4x

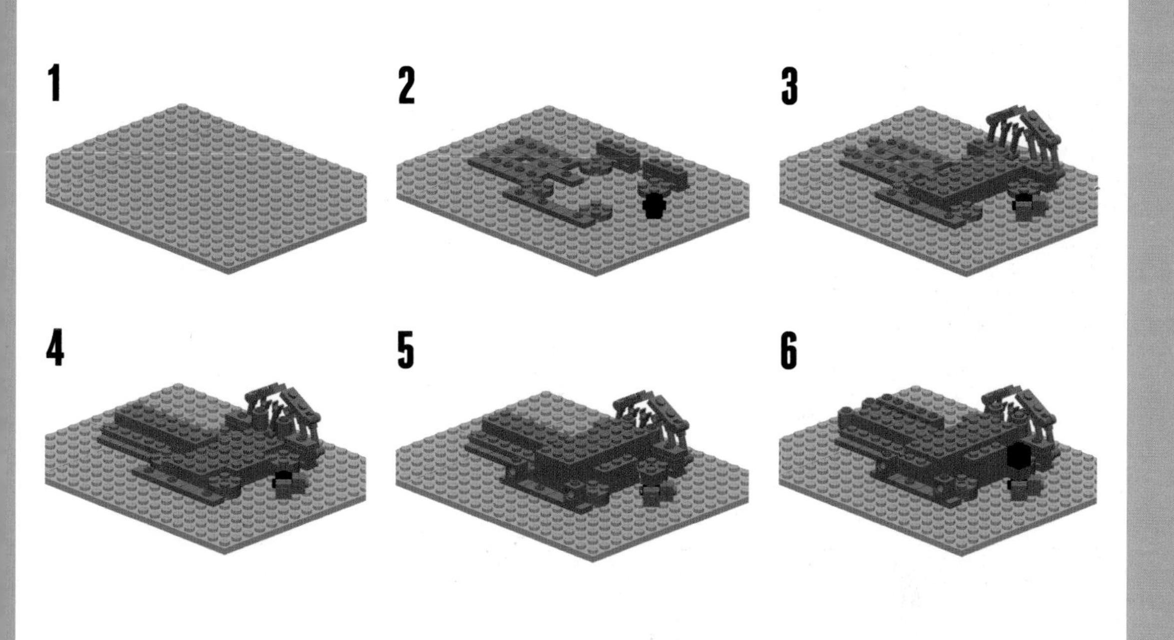
1
2
3
4
5
6

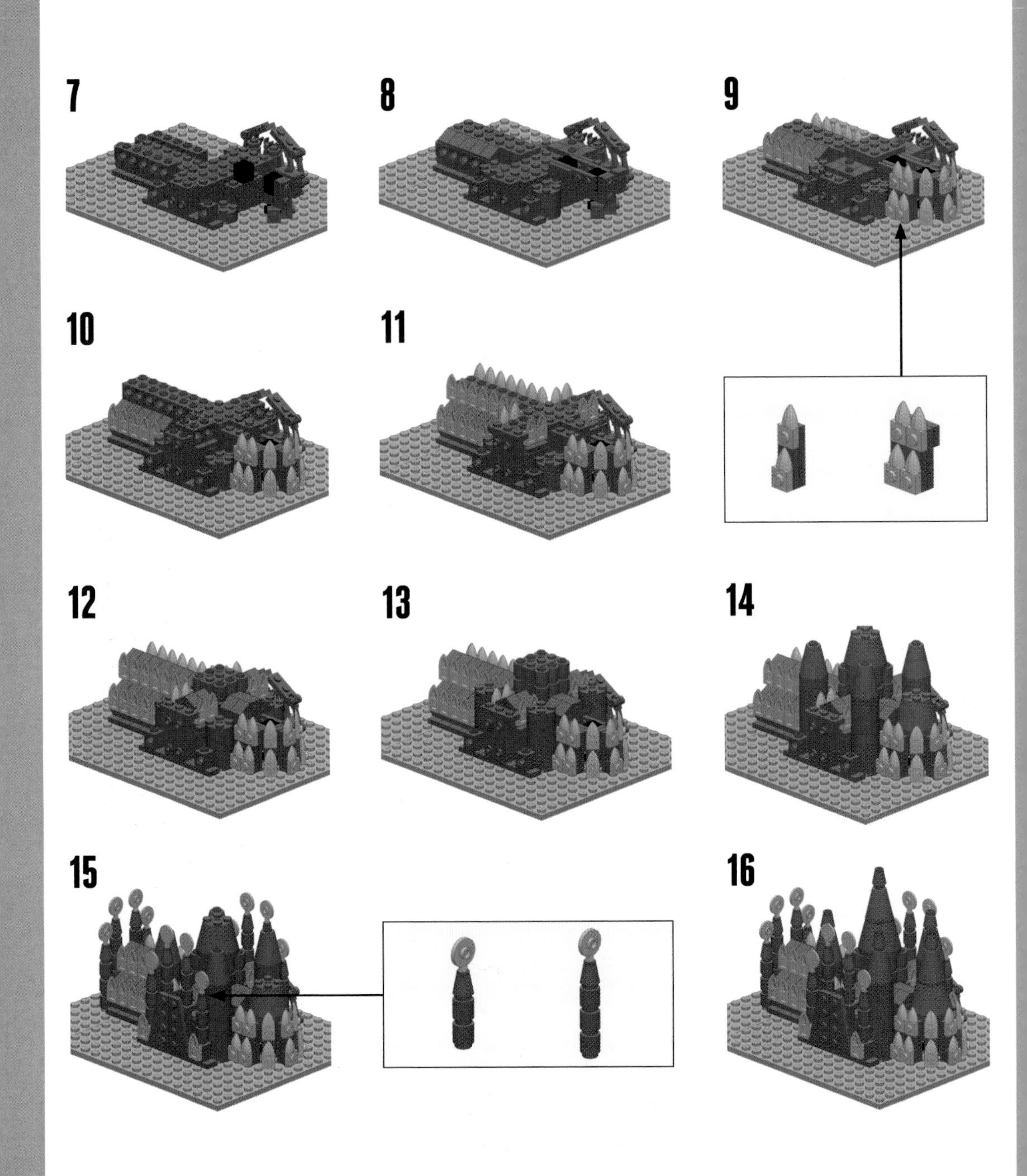
7
8
9
10
11
12
13
14
15
16

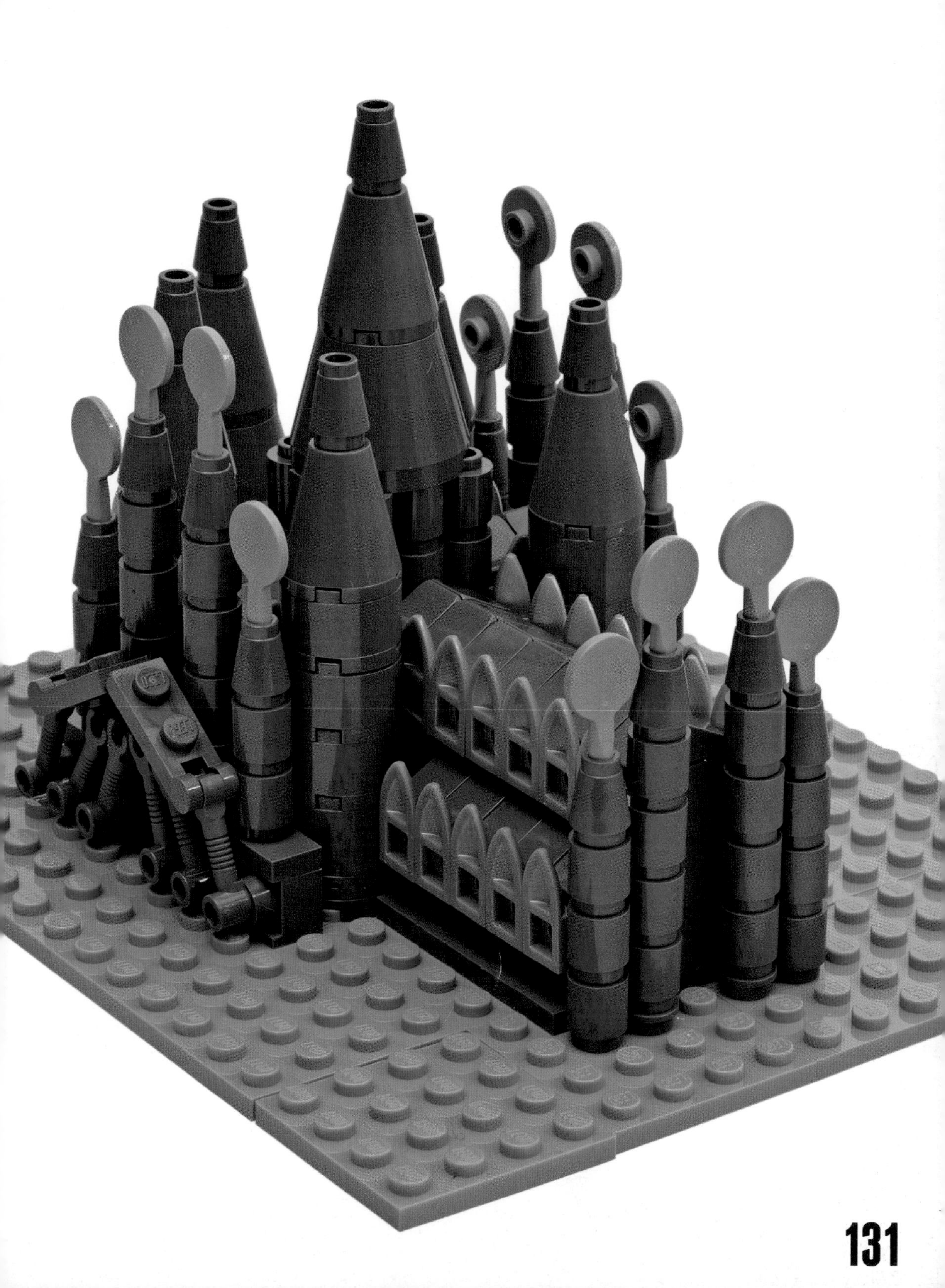

BARCELONA SALAMANDER

Artist: Antoni Gaudí

LEGO® Edition by Warren Elsmore

Size: 72 cm (30 in) high, 36 cm (14½ in) wide

Bricks: 600

The beautiful Salamander was created by Gaudí as part of the Park Güell, a large park in the hills above Barcelona built between 1900 and 1914. Gaudí designed the entire park, making it one of the largest architectural works in Europe. The Salamander is commonly known as 'El Drac', meaning 'the dragon'.

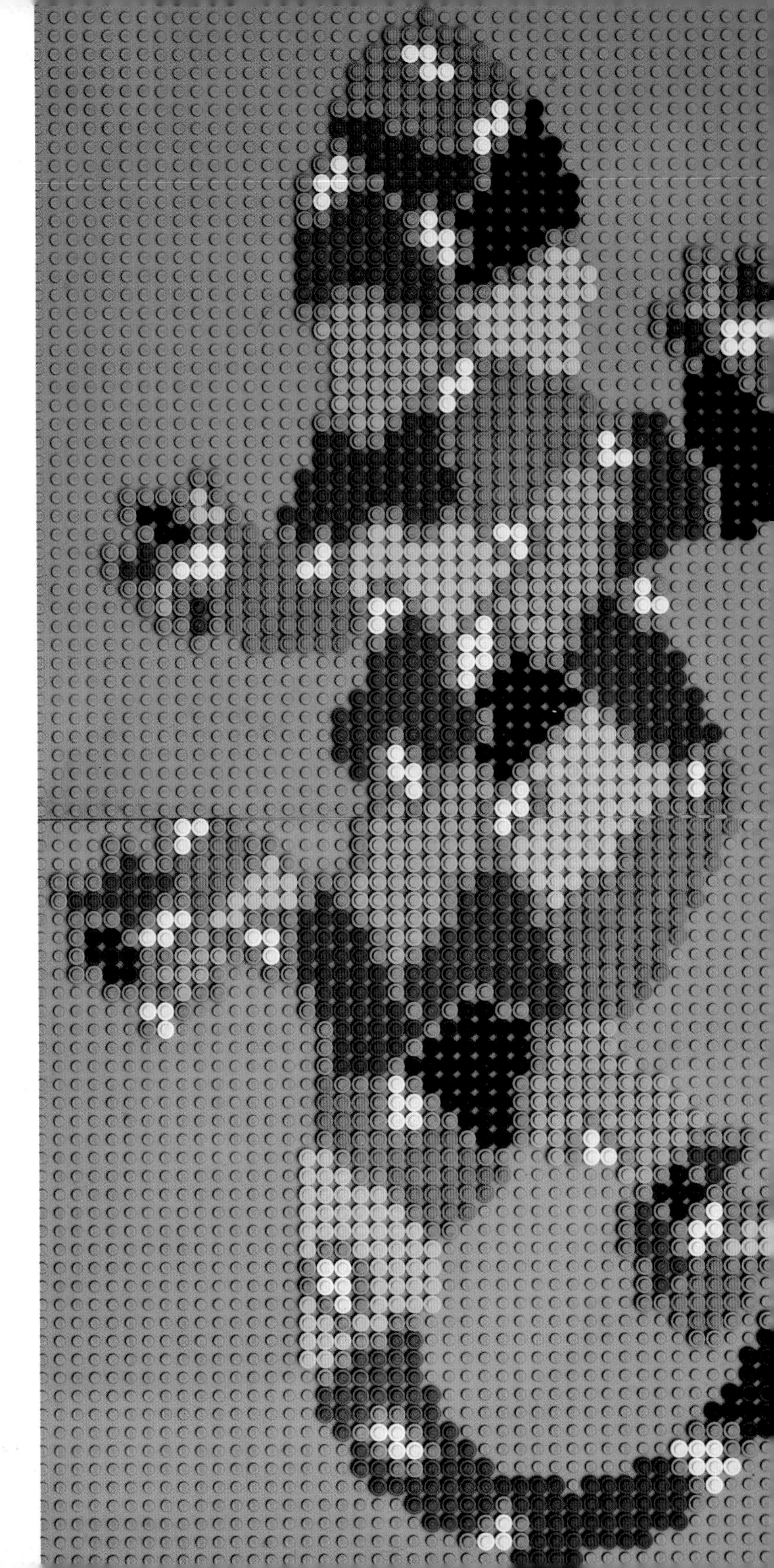

MADRID

EL ESCORIAL

This is the historical seat of the King of Spain, situated in the northwest of Madrid. Built in the sixteenth century, it is an unusual palace in that it was historically the seat of power not only for Spain's royalty, but also for the head of the Roman Catholic Church in Spain. It remains a monastery to this day.

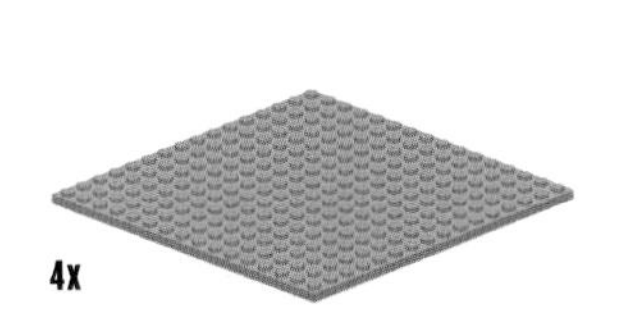

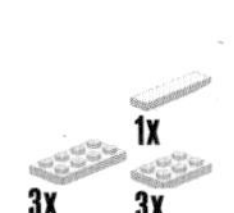

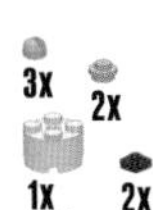

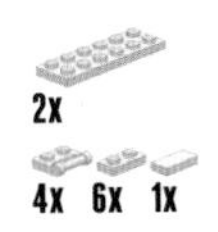

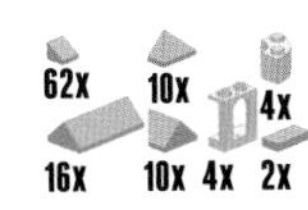

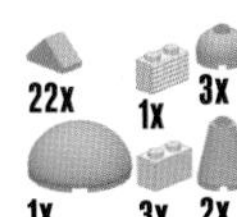

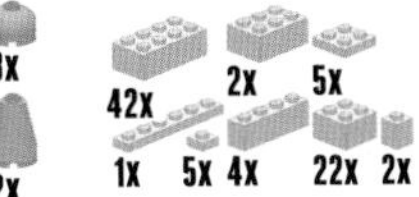

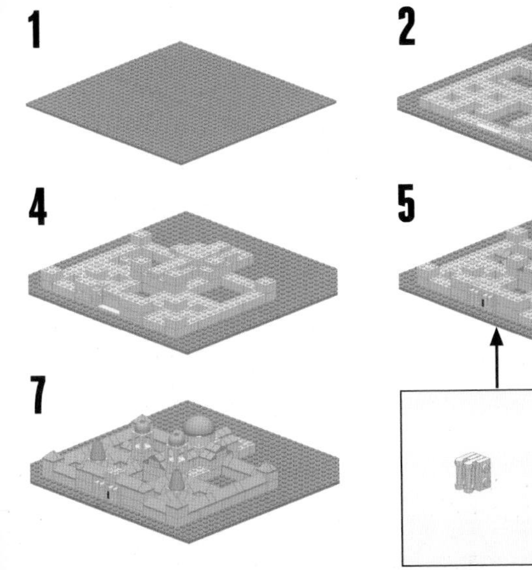

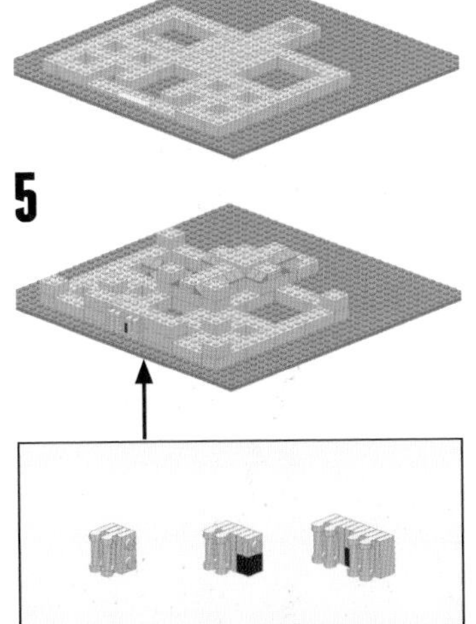

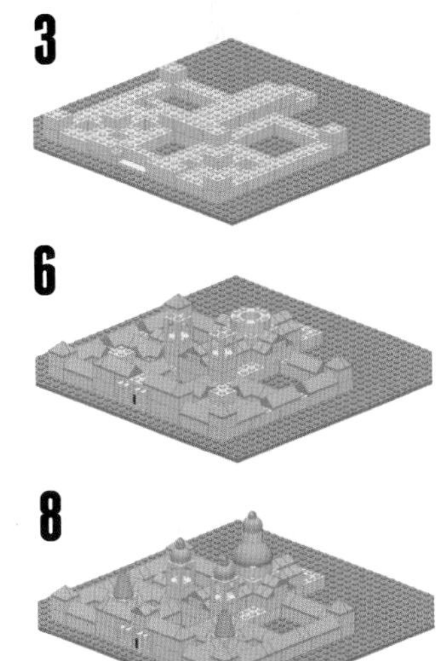

PARIS

Think of Paris and you immediately think of famous landmarks: the Eiffel Tower, the Arc de Triomphe and Montmarte. But to capture the spirit of the city in LEGO® bricks, I decided not to concentrate just on the obvious. The spirit of Paris is just as easily evoked by cafés and boutiques, so it was only natural to include those.

The Eiffel Tower in particular is one monument that does not easily lend itself to modelling in LEGO. The sleek, angled ironwork is particularly difficult to render in what are traditionally square pieces, and in the end the solution found by Spencer Rezkalla for his extraordinary model was to use LEGO Flexi-tube. Flexi-tube is a bendable tubing that LEGO produces for highlights on models, and it was the perfect material with which to create the tower's legs. In a similar way to the Olympic Stadium, this tubing is held in place by the numerous LEGO pieces designed to clip onto a bar, pulling the tube into a shape that is instantly recognisable.

A similar structural landmark of Paris is the Centre Pompidou. In this modern construction, the structural aspects of the building are fully exposed – along with pipework and other infrastructure which are usually hidden away. Thankfully, the regular steel columns have an obvious LEGO counterpart. Designed for exactly the same purpose, a LEGO panel exists with a crossed steel bracing. This was the ideal part to use to render the Centre's exterior, and to set the scale of the building.

The more intimate Paris landmarks, the small boutiques and cafés, gave us the chance to increase the scale and include LEGO minifigs. Of course, we have created buildings for LEGO minifigs before, so this was an opportunity to examine which elements could be used to create the most convincing features. The curved glass store fronts immediately call to mind the city's characteristic high-end fashion boutiques, and the shuttered windows of the apartments above can only be from Paris.

THE EIFFEL TOWER (OPPOSITE)

This model took nearly two months to design and build. The design is an example of using LEGO flexible tube elements to define the outline of a complex sweeping shape. Constructing the model presented some difficulty in that many of the parts were threaded over flexible tubes. Its overall shape and appearance were achieved by a process of trial and error. Simply changing a single piece required the arduous task of sliding all of the neighbouring pieces off the tube, swapping out the element in question, and then reassembling the entire string in the original order.

Although it appears quite fragile, it is actually the strongest of all my models, and can be flipped upside down without any pieces falling off.

THE EIFFEL TOWER

Stephen Sauvestre (1889)

LEGO® Edition by Spencer Rezkalla

Size: 50 cm (19½ in) high, 25 cm (10 in) deep and wide

Bricks: 4,812

Scale: approximately 1:650

Photography by Alex Mandrilla

ARC DE TRIOMPHE

The statues on the front of the Arc de Triomphe are in relief. They're made from pieces designed to be used the other way up, but I've turned them upside down for this model. When they're the right way up, they're a lion's head and a hubcap! When used like this, though, they make good carvings.

This was a good example of a model with bricks facing in all directions: some pieces were used upside down, and others back to front.

The main challenge was making them fit together, stay together, and still look right.

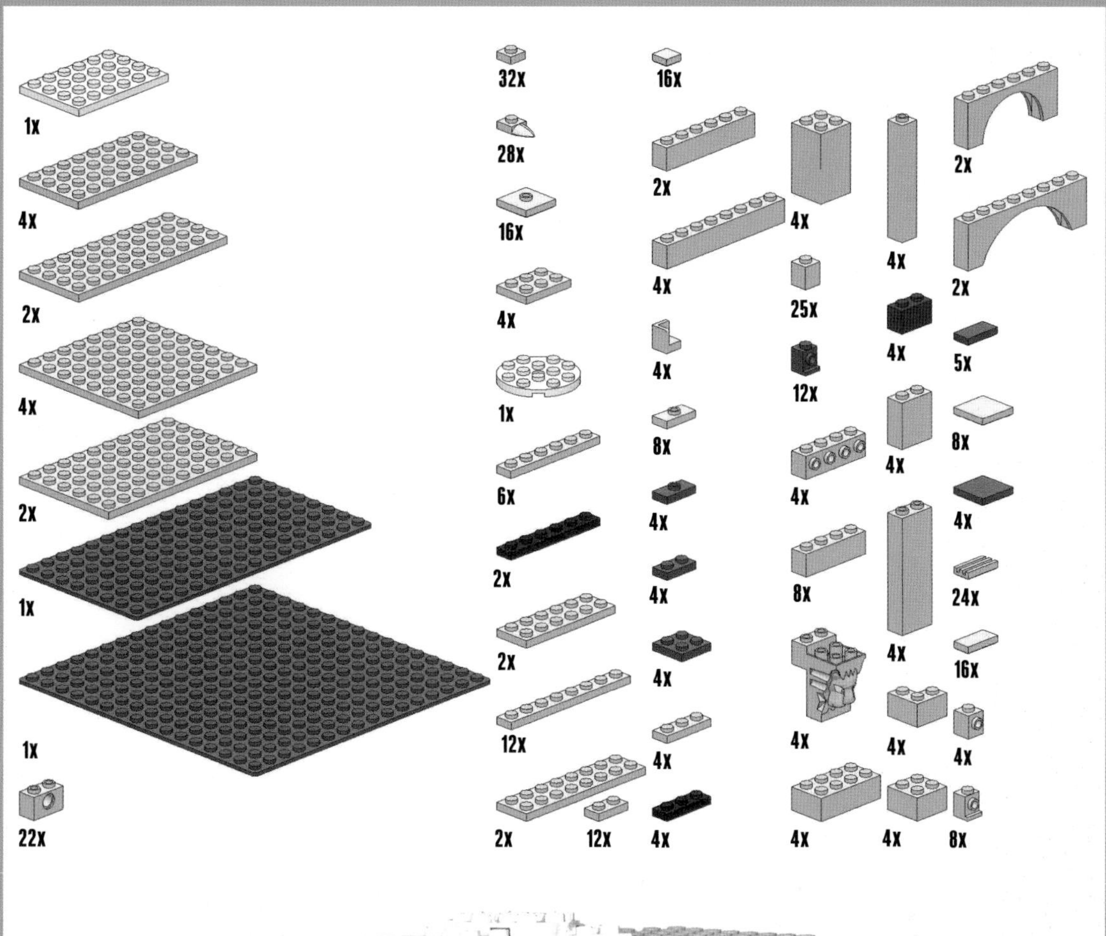
1x
4x
2x
4x
2x
1x
1x
22x
32x
28x
16x
4x
1x
6x
2x
2x
12x
2x
12x
16x
2x
4x
4x
8x
4x
4x
4x
4x
4x
4x
25x
12x
4x
8x
4x
4x
4x
4x
4x
4x
4x
4x
2x
2x
5x
8x
4x
24x
16x
4x
8x

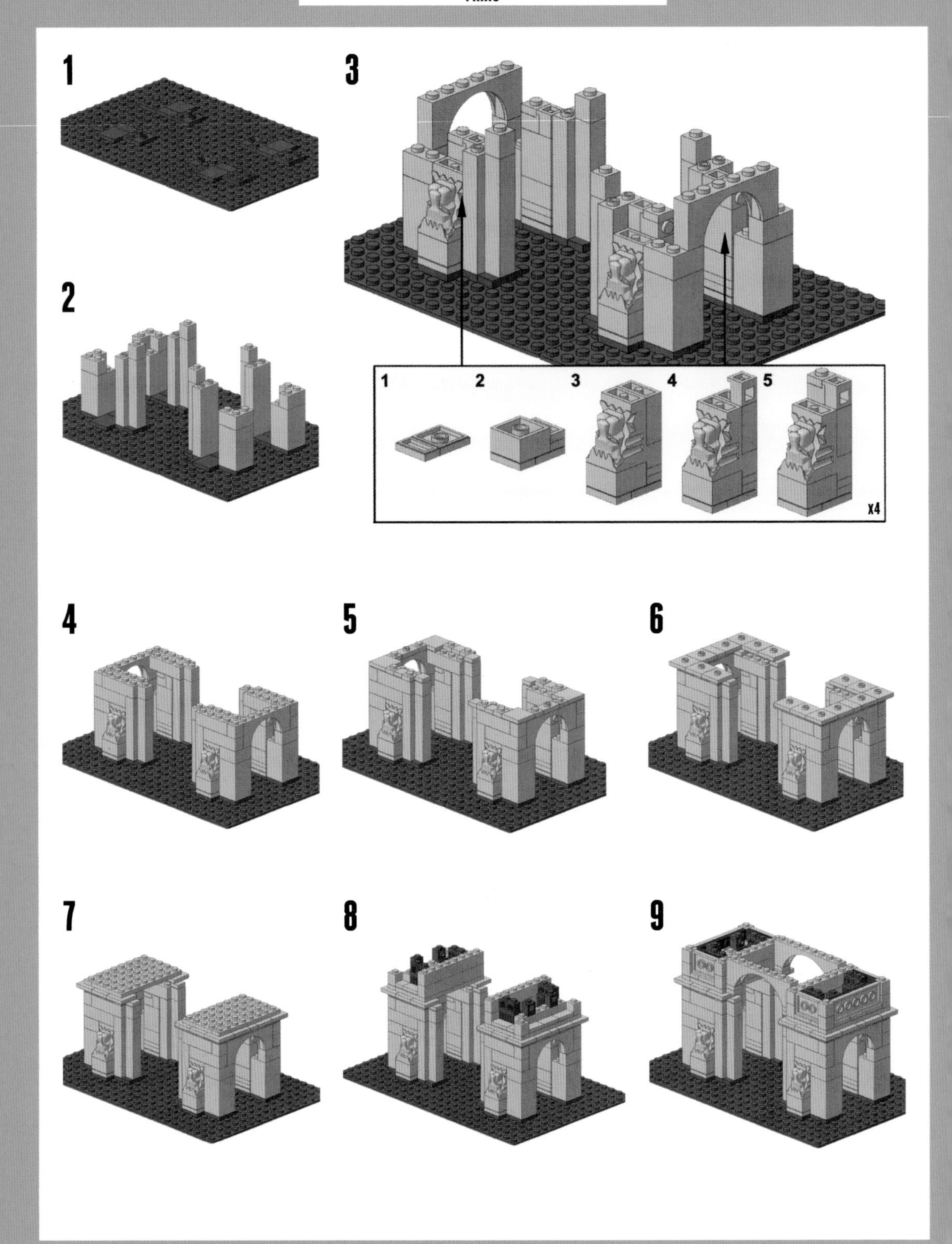
1
2
3
1
2
3
4
5
x4
4
5
6
7
8
9

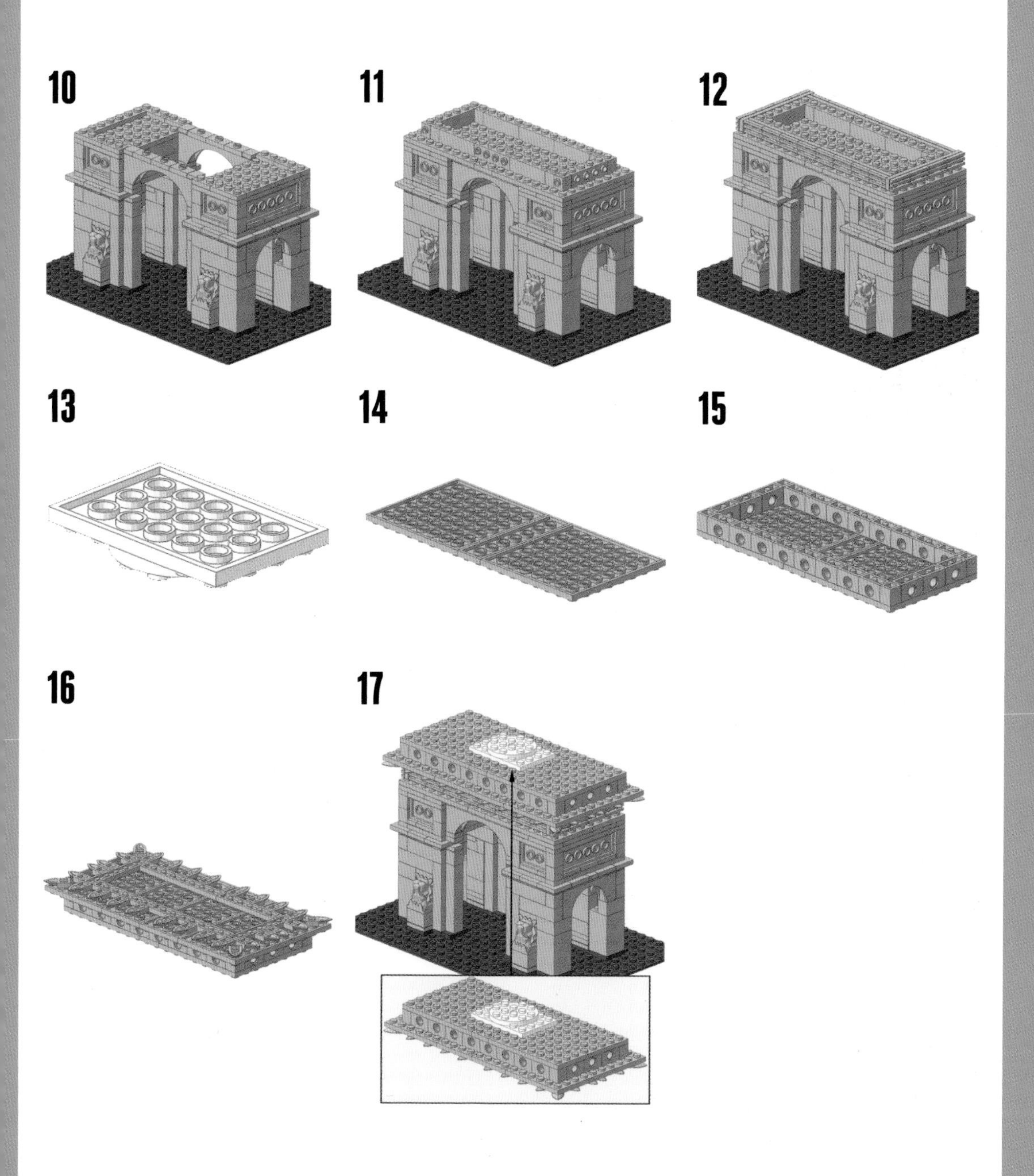
10
11
12
13
14
15
16
17

METRO STOP

Hector Guimard (1900)

LEGO® Edition by Warren Elsmore

Size: 13 cm (5⅛ in) tall and long, 14 cm (5½ in) wide

Bricks: 250

Scale: Minifig scale

The original arches above the entrances to many stations on the Paris Metro rail network are distinctive and iconic examples of wrought-iron work in the style of the Art Nouveau movement. The piece used to represent this metalwork in the model is itself a malleable LEGO part designed to be a creeper from a tree – it can bend into any shape – and so forms the distinctive look needed here.

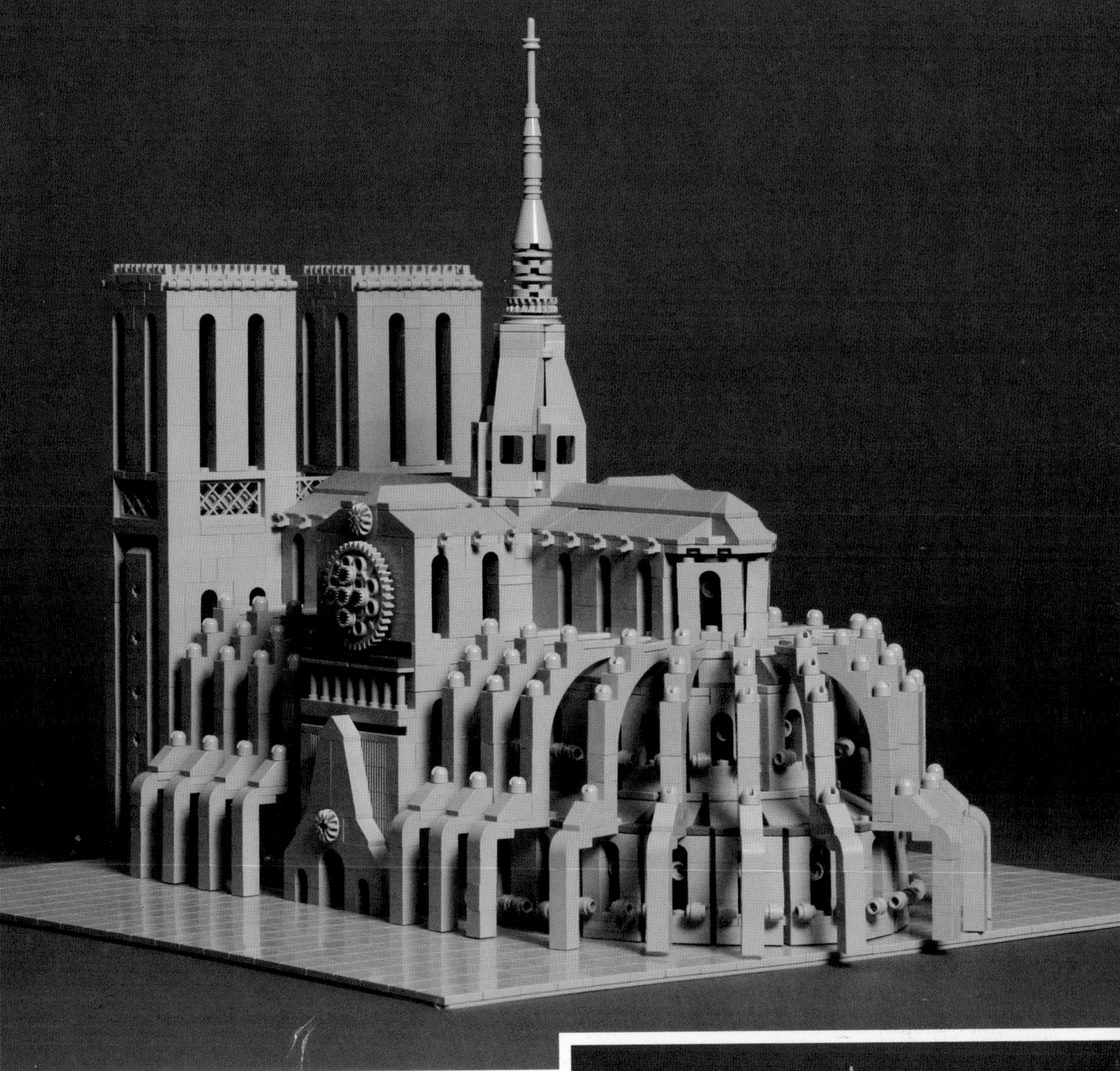

NOTRE DAME

Architect: Various (constructed 1163–1345)

LEGO® Edition by Arthur Gugick

Size: 30.5 cm (12 in) high, 38 cm (15 in) long and wide

Bricks: 5,000

Scale: Approximately 1:335

This is a tiny model of one of the largest churches in the world. The original building was begun in 1163, and is probably the finest example of gothic architecture in Europe. This micro-landmark has as much detail in the smallest space possible. This model is currently on display at the Cleveland Hopkins airport in Ohio.

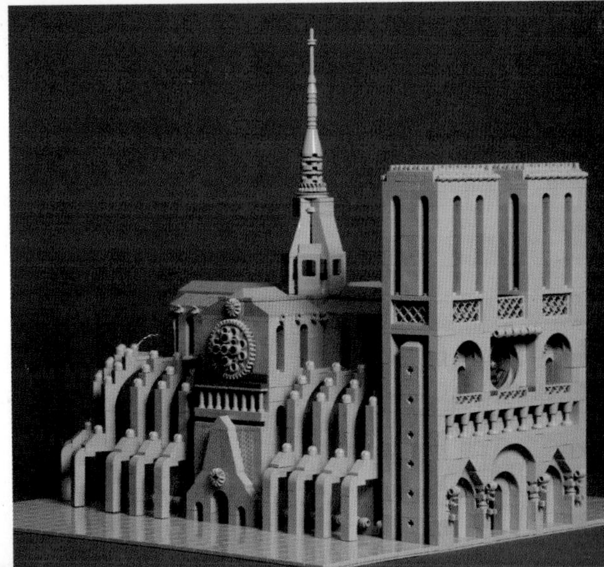

MONA LISA

Depicting the mysterious noblewoman as a mosaic had its own challenges. We haven't gone into high enough resolution to depict the world-famous smile, but it was hard enough trying to re-create a painting that is so dark and orange from LEGO®'s palette! It is still an instantly recognisable image, even at low resolution. The instructions below demonstrate how to make the frame, but for the artwork itself I recommend copying the mosaic as it's shown across the page as best you can, or else converting your own image into a LEGO mosaic (see p.25 for tips on mosaic techniques and software). Of course you don't have to limit yourself to da Vinci – Piet Mondrian or Mark Rothko are also strong choices.

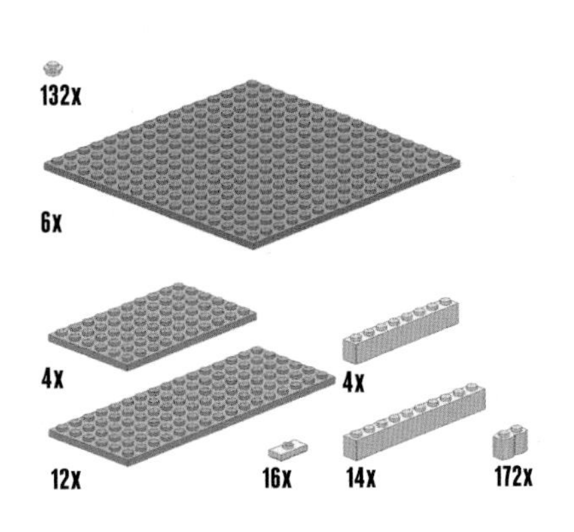

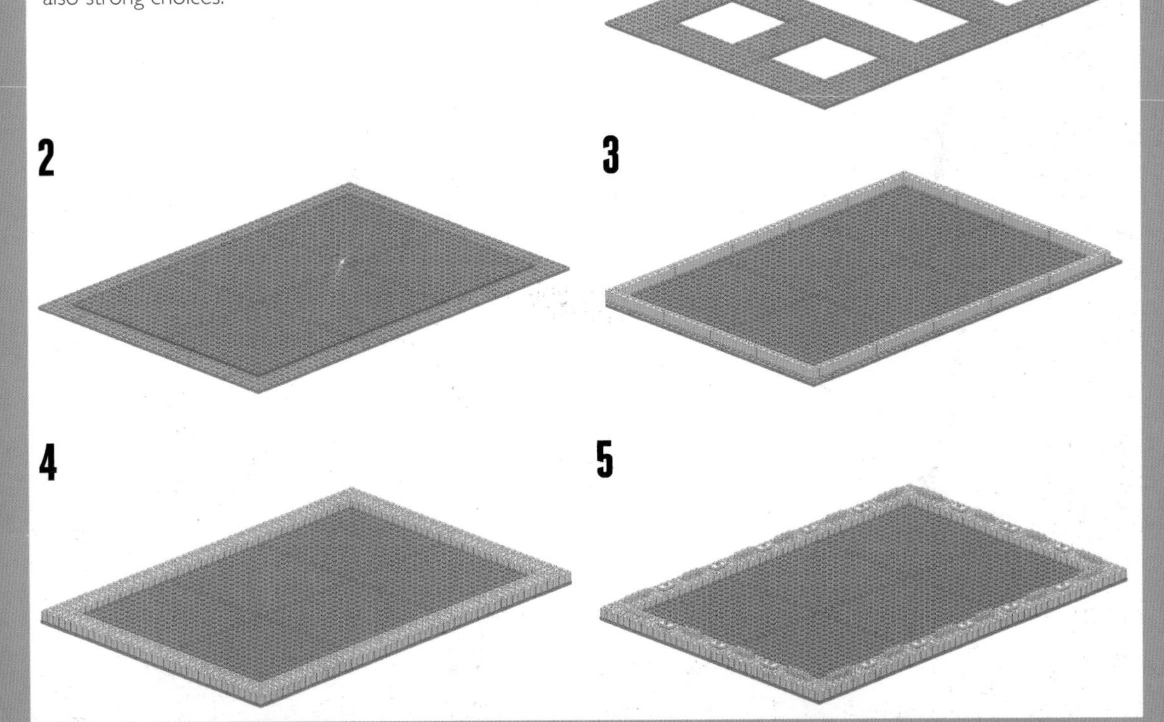

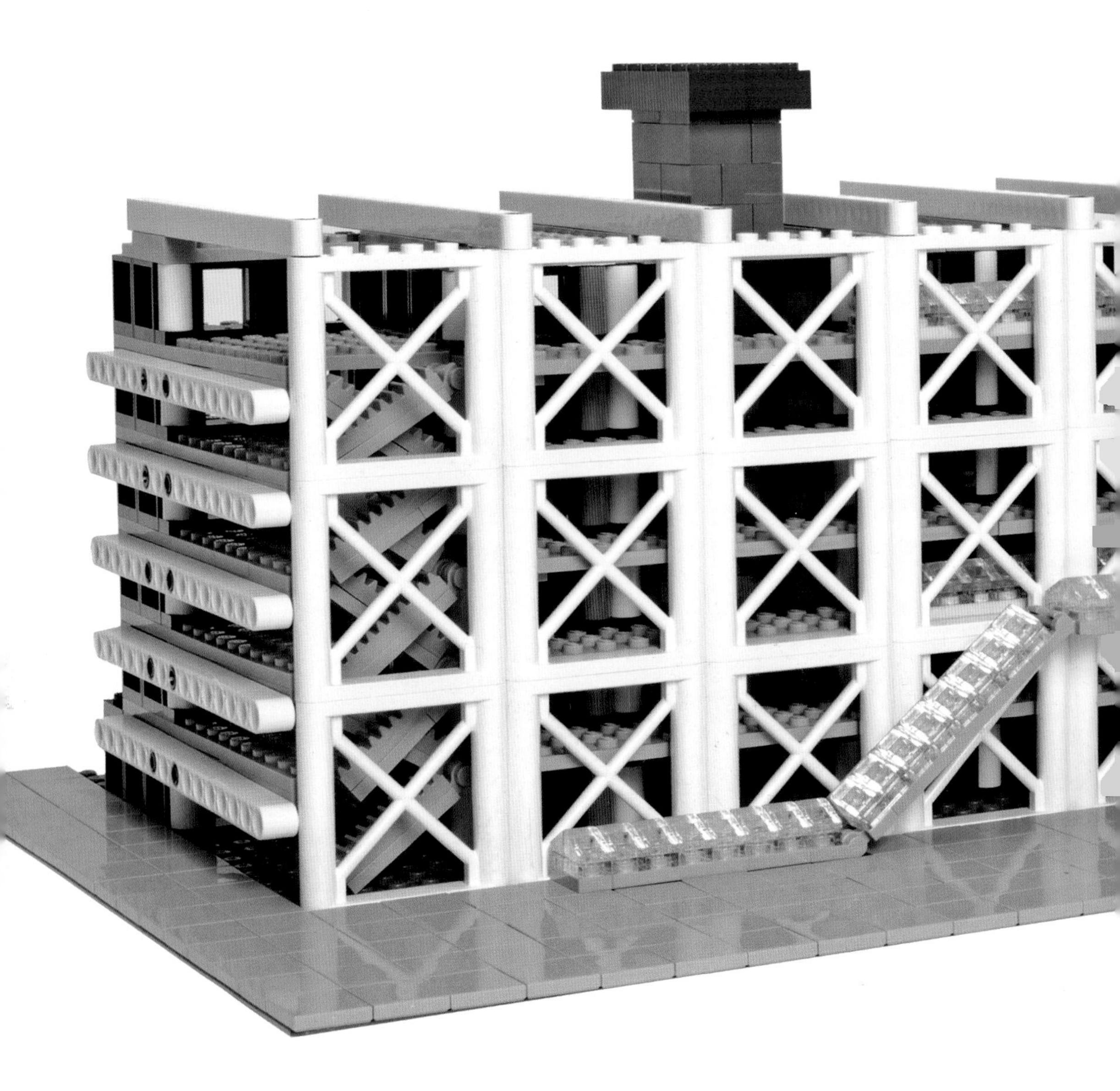

CENTRE POMPIDOU

Architects: Renzo Piano & Richard Rogers (1977)

LEGO® Edition by Warren Elsmore

Size: 15 cm (6 in) high, 54 cm (21 in) wide

Bricks: 21,700

Scale: 1:260

This is one of the most renowned and popular art museums in the world. Like the Lloyd's building in London, it's famous for having its interior visible on the outside. The white lattice piece that decorates the exterior is the piece this model started from, and then it just kept going and the model was scaled up from there.

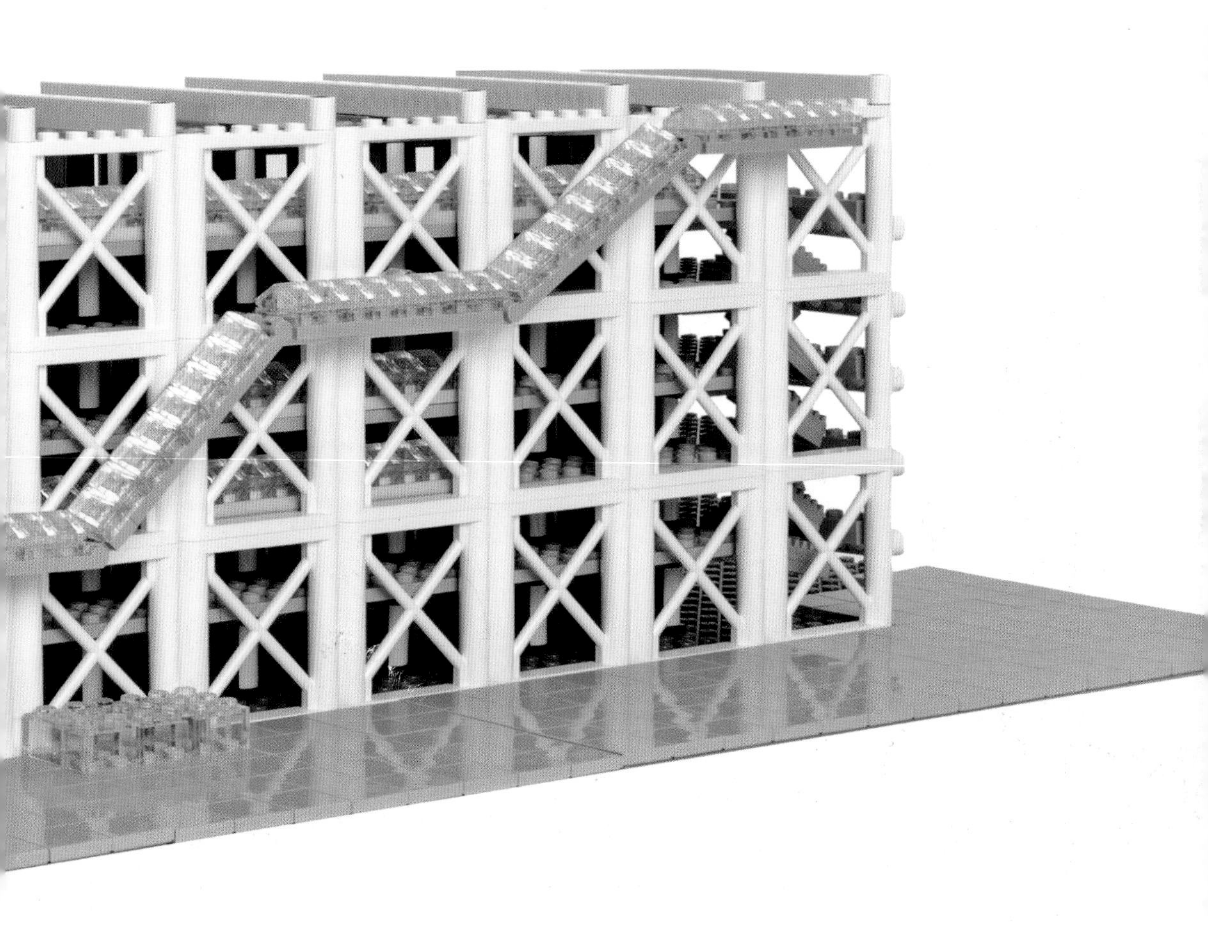

PARKOUR SCENE

LEGO® Edition by Warren Elsmore
Scale: Minifig scale
Bricks: 300

The fashionable sport of parkour (or 'freerunning'), represented here, originated in Paris. It's much easier to depict in LEGO than to try it in real life...

PALAIS DE VERSAILLES

The palace and gardens of Versailles are laid out in such a way that, when seen from above, they have a symmetrical beauty. Considering how vast the real property is, the relative scale of this small model is absolutely tiny – possibly the smallest in the whole book.

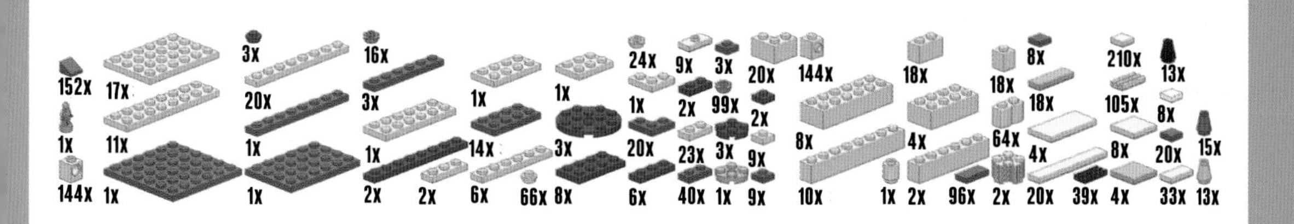
152x
1x
144x
17x
11x
1x
1x
3x
20x
1x
1x
16x
3x
1x
2x
2x
1x
14x
6x
66x
1x
3x
8x
24x
1x
20x
6x
9x
2x
23x
40x
3x
99x
3x
1x
2x
9x
9x
20x
144x
8x
10x
1x
18x
4x
2x
96x
18x
64x
2x
8x
18x
4x
20x
39x
210x
105x
8x
4x
13x
8x
20x
33x
15x
13x

1

2

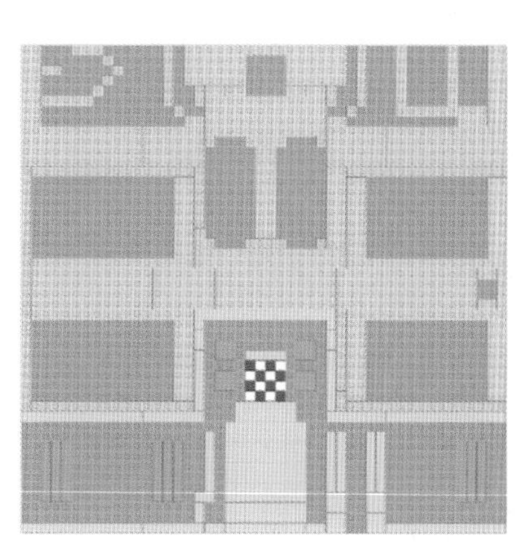

3

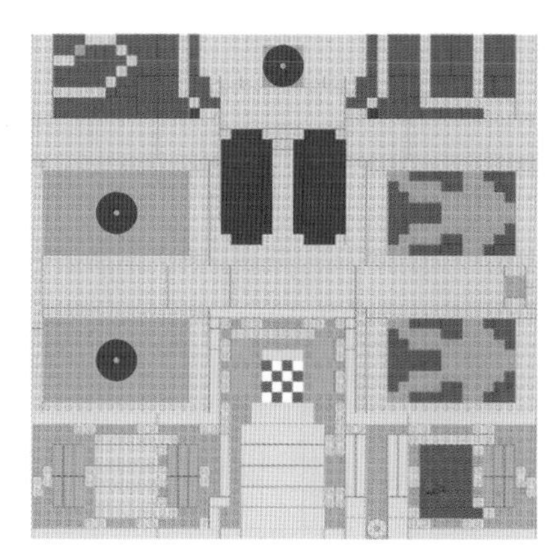

4

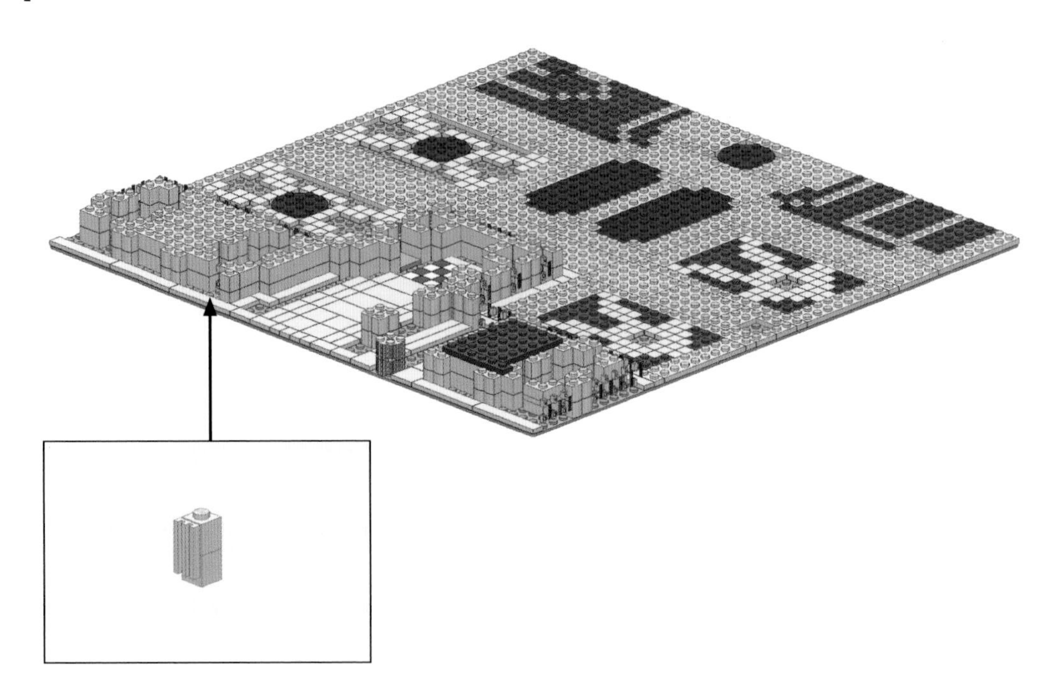

5

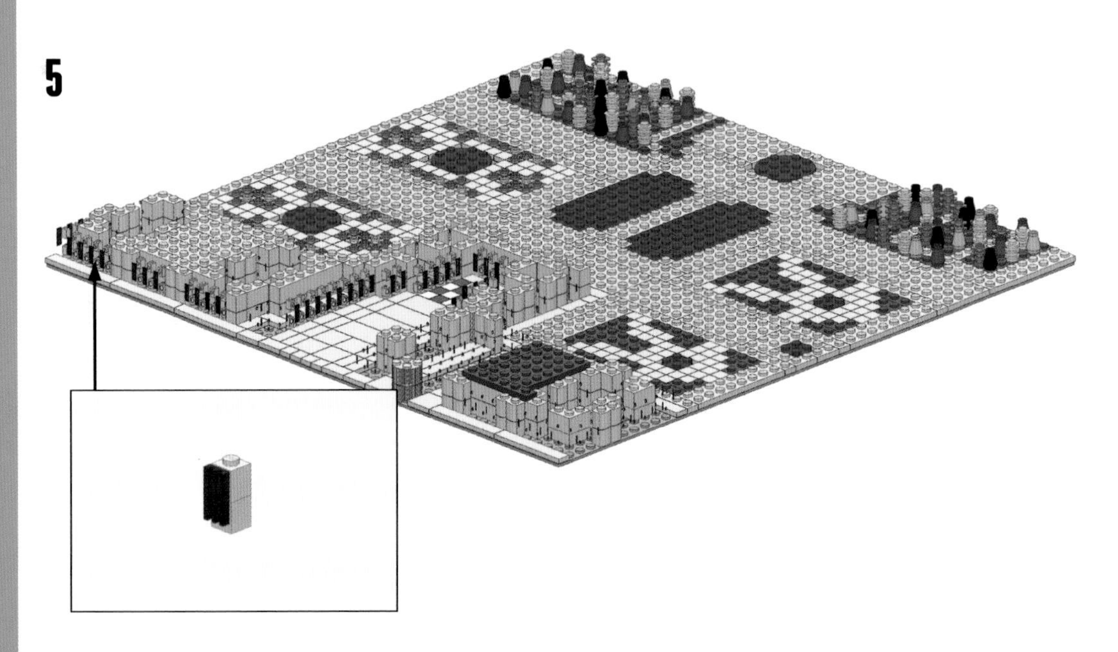

6

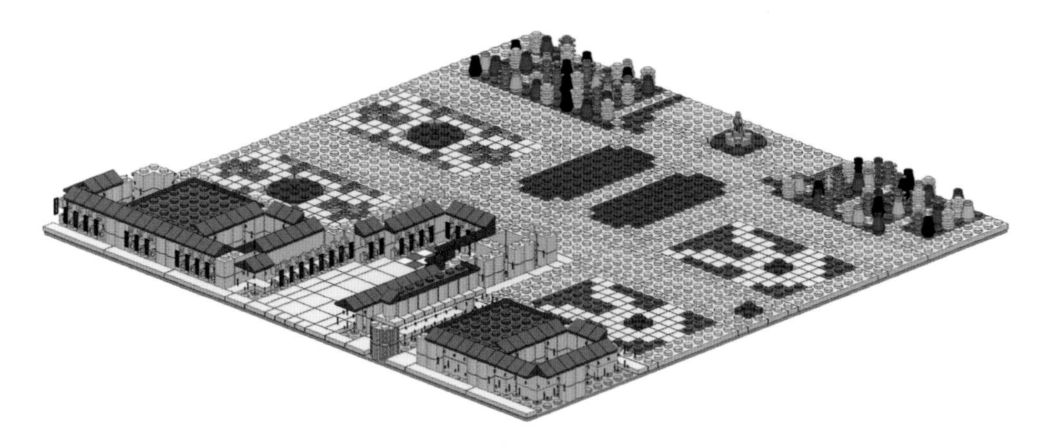

7

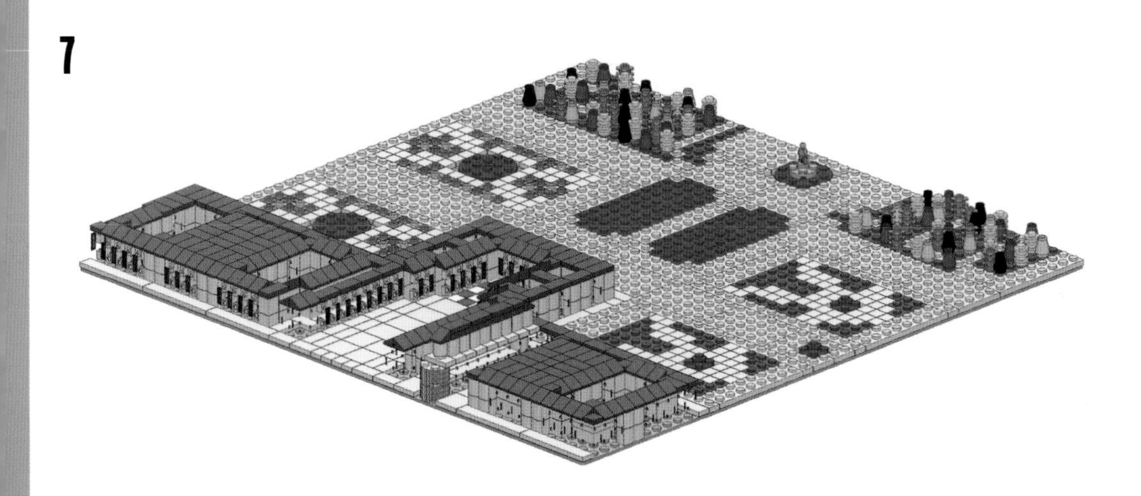

PARISIAN CAFE

This typical Parisian café has lots of tables on the pavement, and a large overhanging awning to evoke the feel of the real city. The French flag flies from the windows, which have the characteristic French slatted-shutter look. The bars in the interior are designed to evoke the feel of an old neighbourhood hub, including the very large coffee machine in the back which is both highly realistic and easy to make.

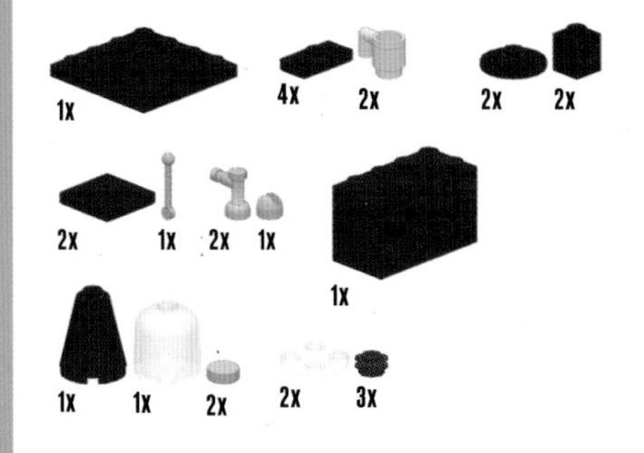

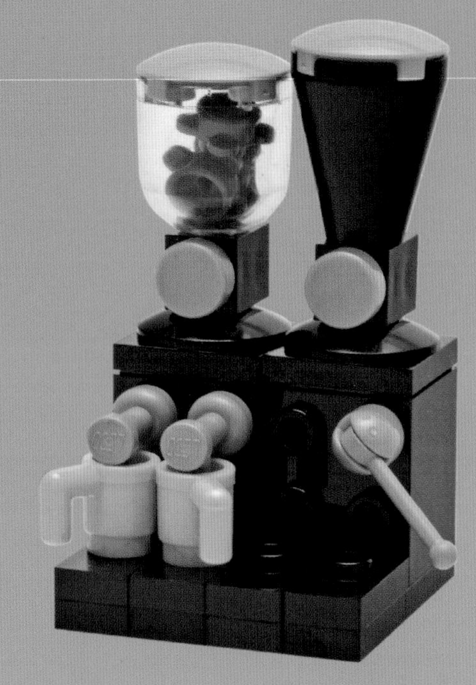

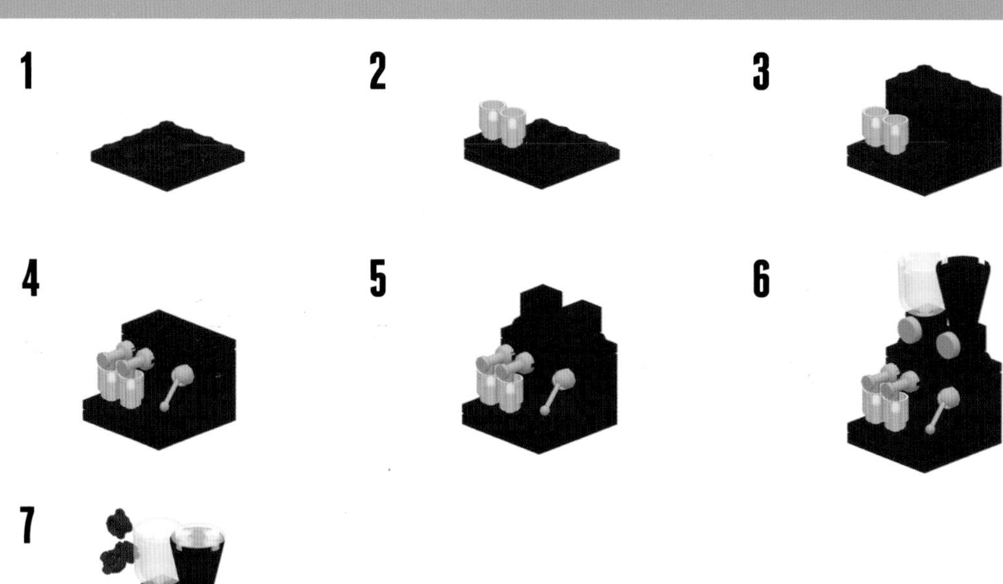

BOUTIQUE

LEGO® Construction by Teresa 'Kitty' Elsmore

Scale: Minifig scale

To depict a Paris street scene, the windows of the shop fronts have to be interesting, so they've got curved glass frontages, a feature adapted from a recent LEGO set.

MOULIN ROUGE

Adolphe Willette and Édouard-Jean Niermans (1889)

LEGO Edition by Alastair Disley

Size: 42 cm (16½ in) high to the top of the windmill's blade, 25 cm (10 in) wide and deep

Bricks: 1,500

Scale: 1:50 (with some selective compression of width)

Aside from being featured in the famous Baz Luhrmann film, Le Moulin Rouge cabaret has a long history as a landmark of the lawless and racy side of the French capital. Unusually, the LEGO windmill is nine-sided, just as the real building is in Montmartre – this was the most difficult part to re-create, and we don't even know why they built it like this and made life so hard for us LEGO builders!

AMSTERDAM

WINDMILL

There was a time when the Netherlands had over 10,000 windmills, milling corn or pumping excess water from the lowlands. Eight windmills remain standing in Amsterdam, of which most are from the 17th and 18th centuries – this model is a small and representative example of their style.

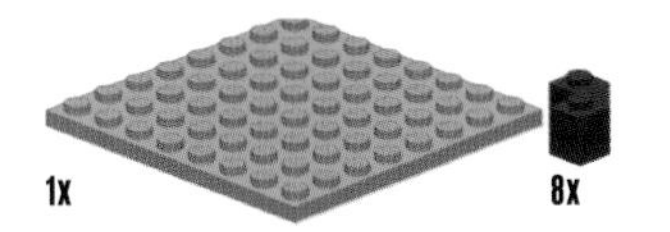

1x

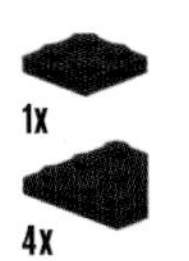

8x

1x

4x

1x 1x

1x 1x 1x

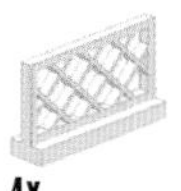

4x

1

2

3

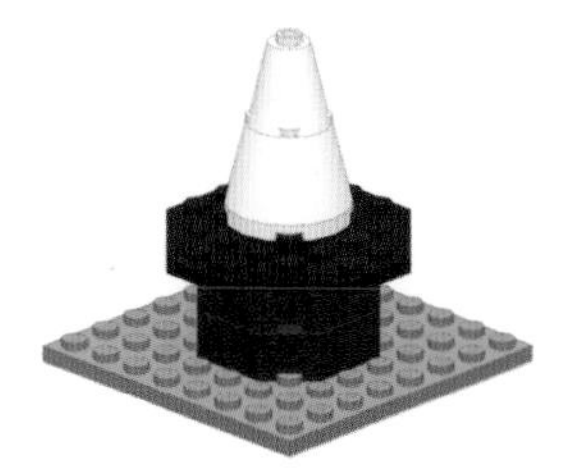

4

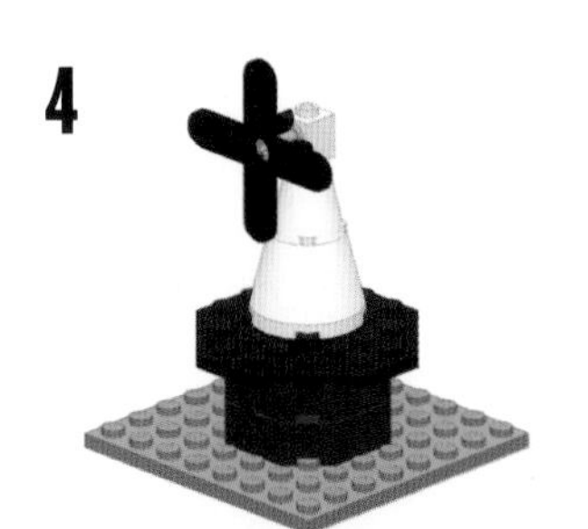

5

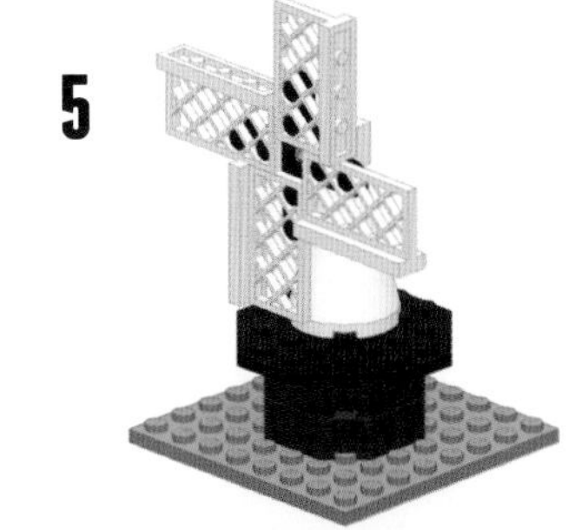

AMSTERDAM STREET SCENE

LEGO® Construction by Alastair Disley

Size: 36 cm (14¼ in) high, 77 cm (30½ in) deep, 115 cm (42½ in) wide

Bricks: 5,000

Scale: 1:40

Many of these buildings are built using thousands of little 1x2 plates to simulate the texture of brickwork. Although this scene isn't based on one specific place in Amsterdam, every building is modelled on a single real building, from the colour to the characteristic style of Dutch gables.

VENICE

CAMPANILE

This is the distinctive bell tower of St. Mark's Basilica in the Piazza San Marco. The building itself has been rebuilt many times over the centuries. The first tower was built in the ninth century, and the current building is an exact copy of the one that completely collapsed in 1902, remarkably killing no one except the caretaker's cat.

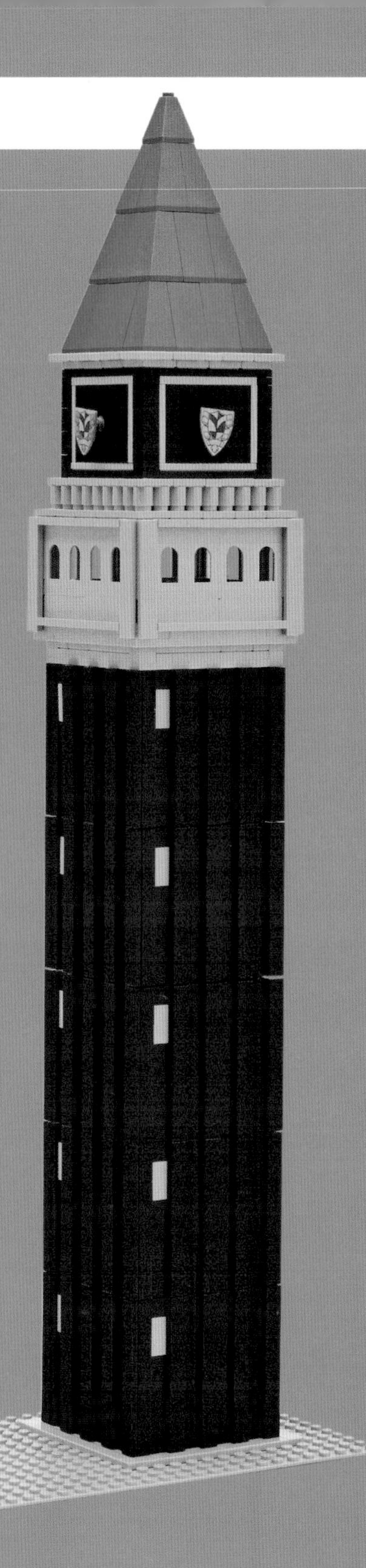

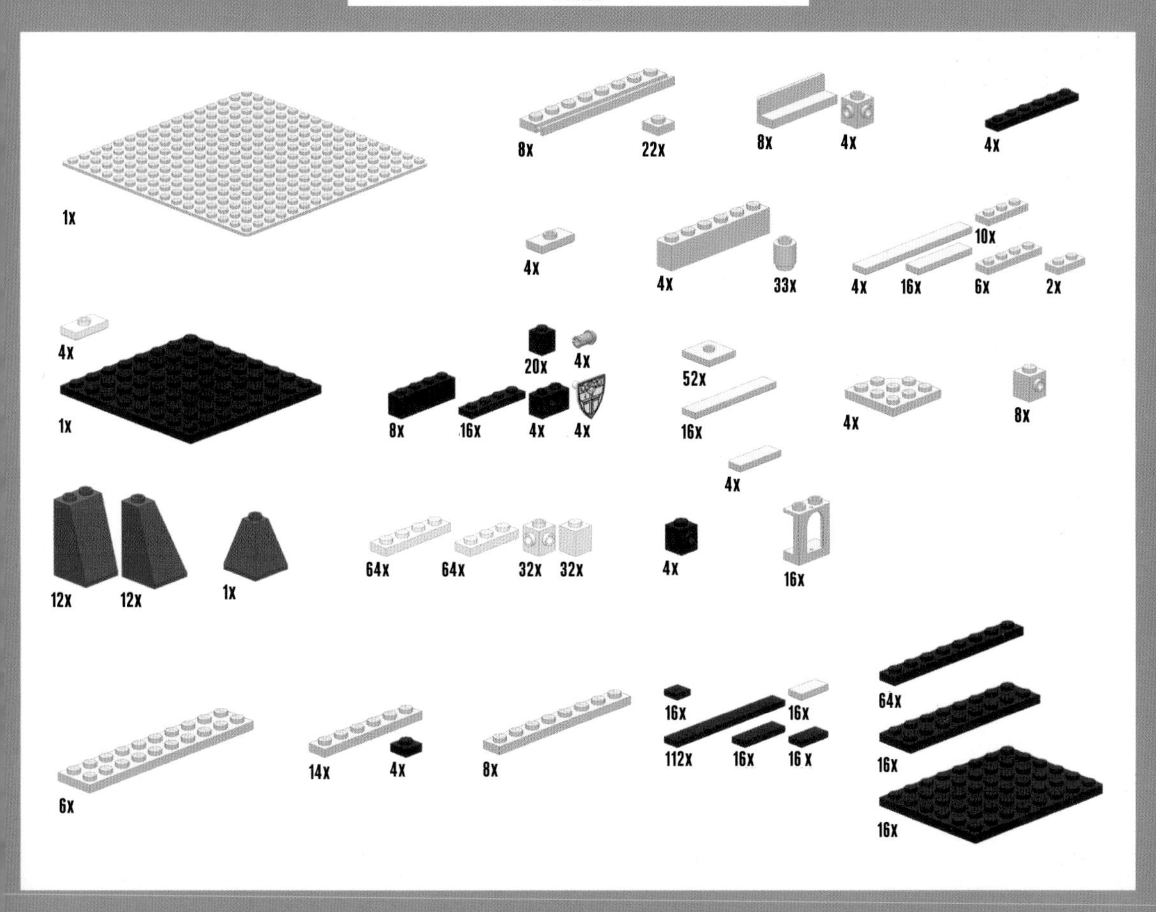
1x
8x
22x
8x
4x
4x
4x
4x
33x
10x
4x
16x
6x
2x
4x
1x
20x
4x
8x
16x
4x
4x
52x
16x
4x
8x
4x
12x
12x
1x
64x
64x
32x
32x
4x
16x
6x
14x
4x
8x
16x
16x
112x
16x
16 x
64x
16x
16x

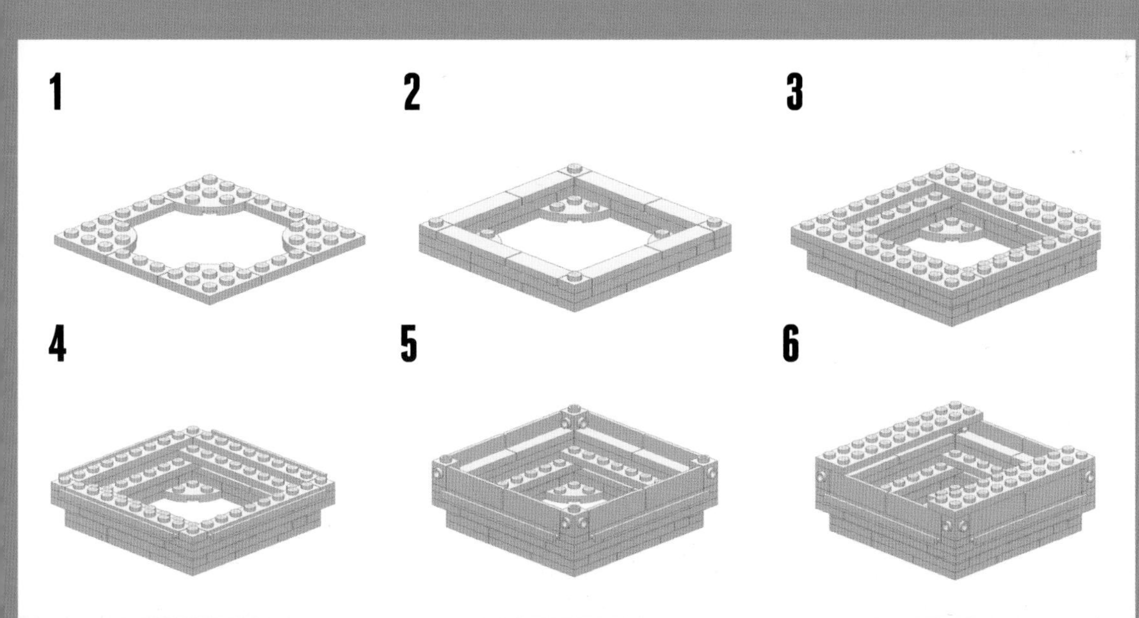
1
2
3
4
5
6

7

8

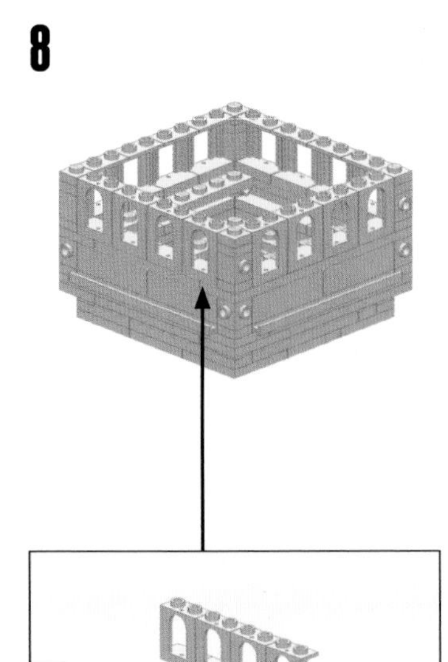

9

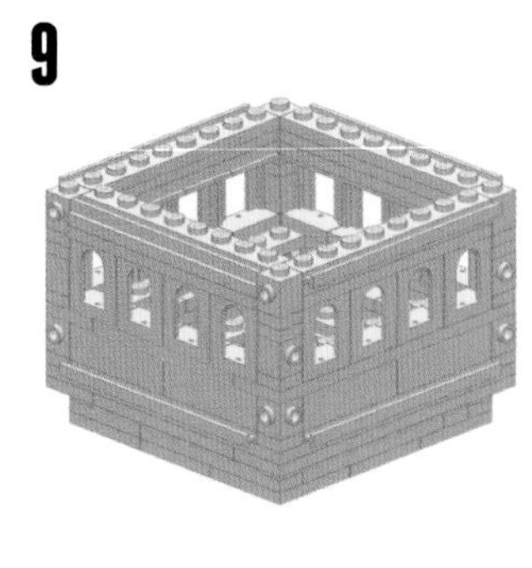

10

11

12

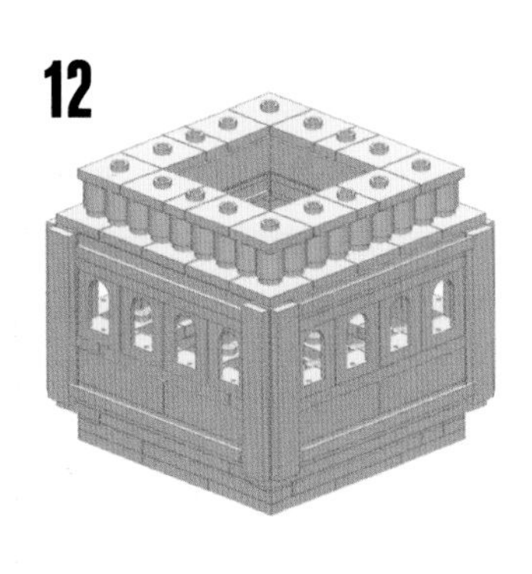

13

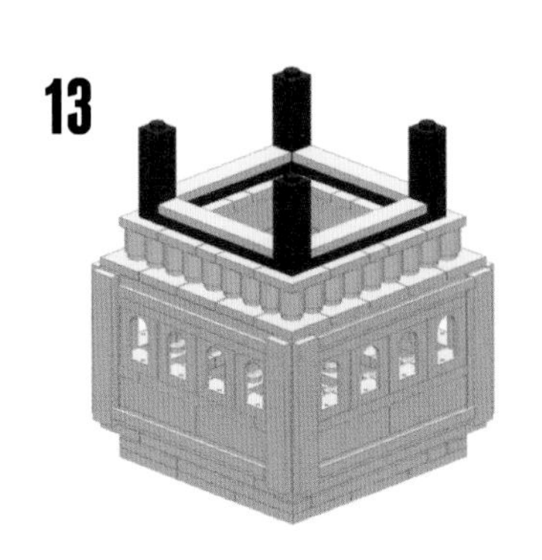

14

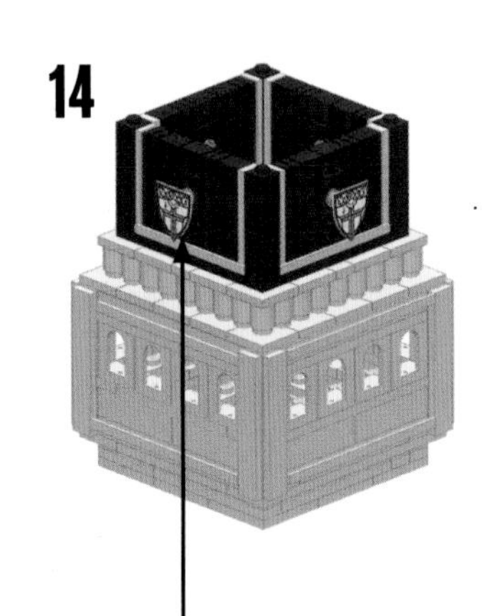

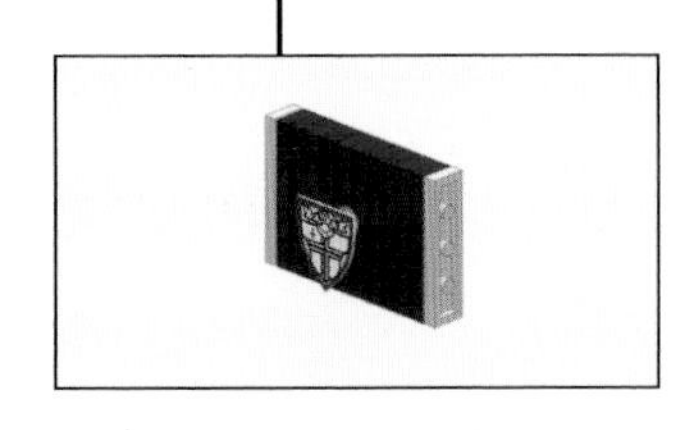

15

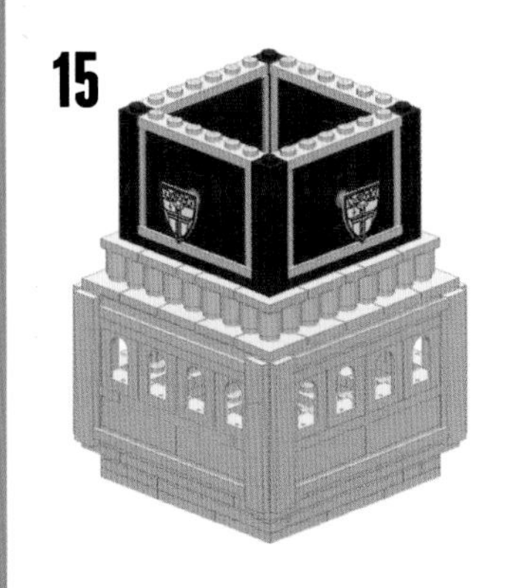

16

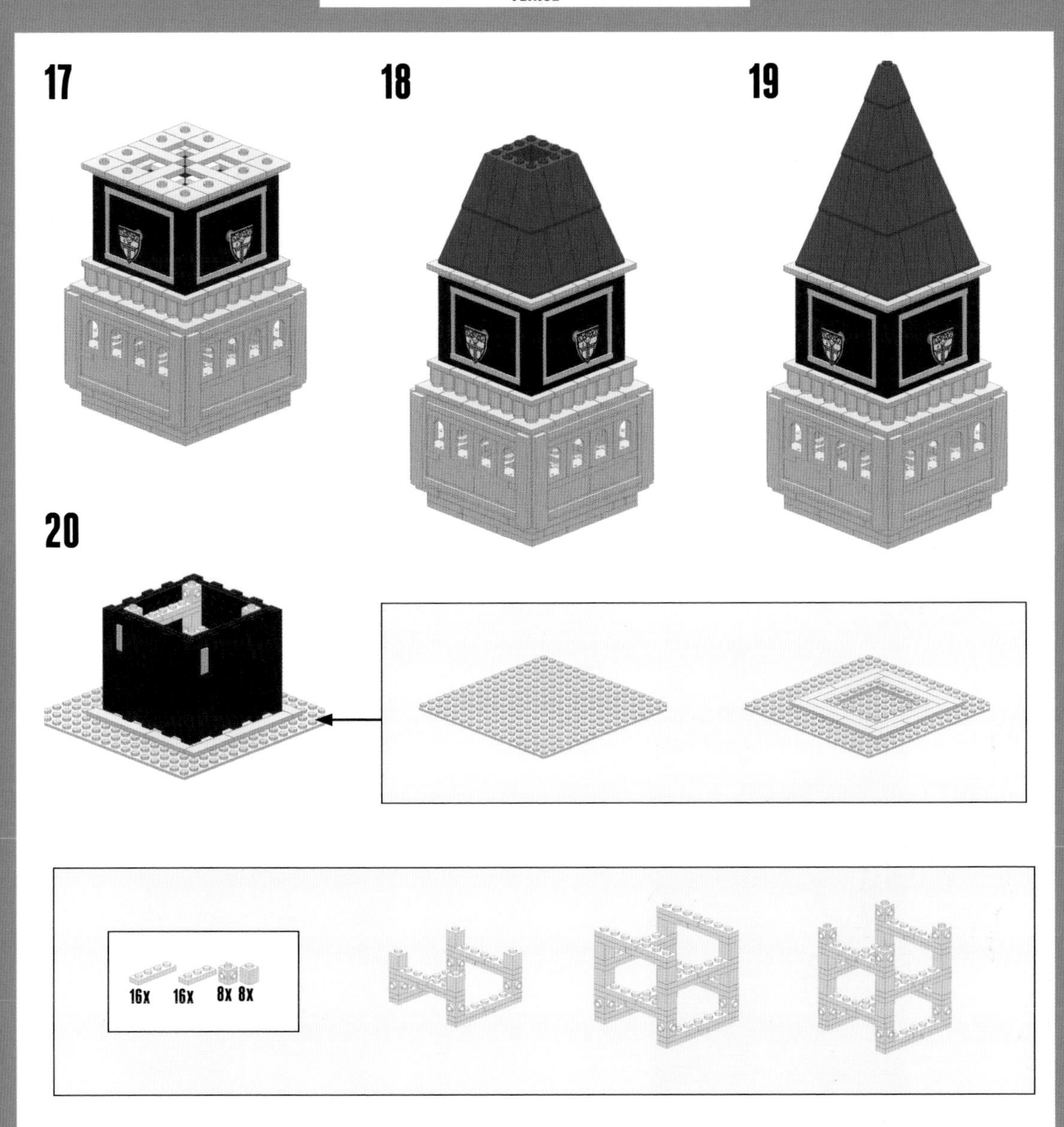
17
18
19
20
16x
16x
8x
8x

4x
1x
1x
1x
7x
1x
1x
1x
x4
x4

21

22

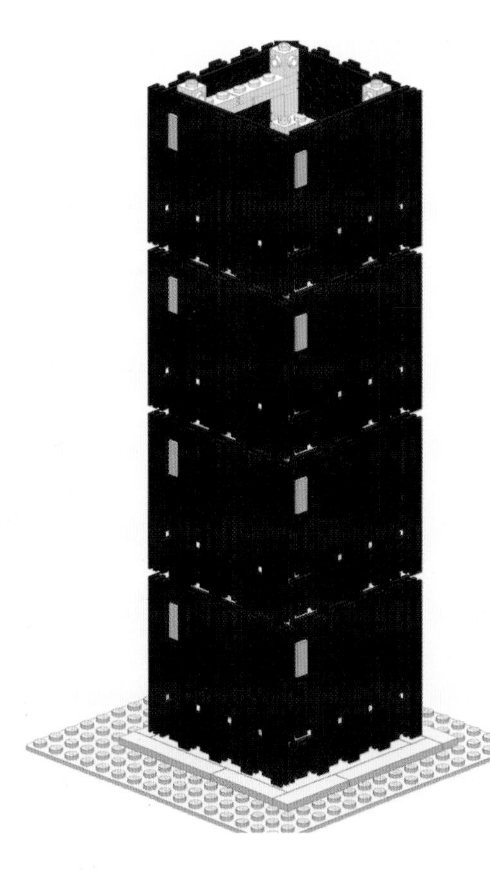

23

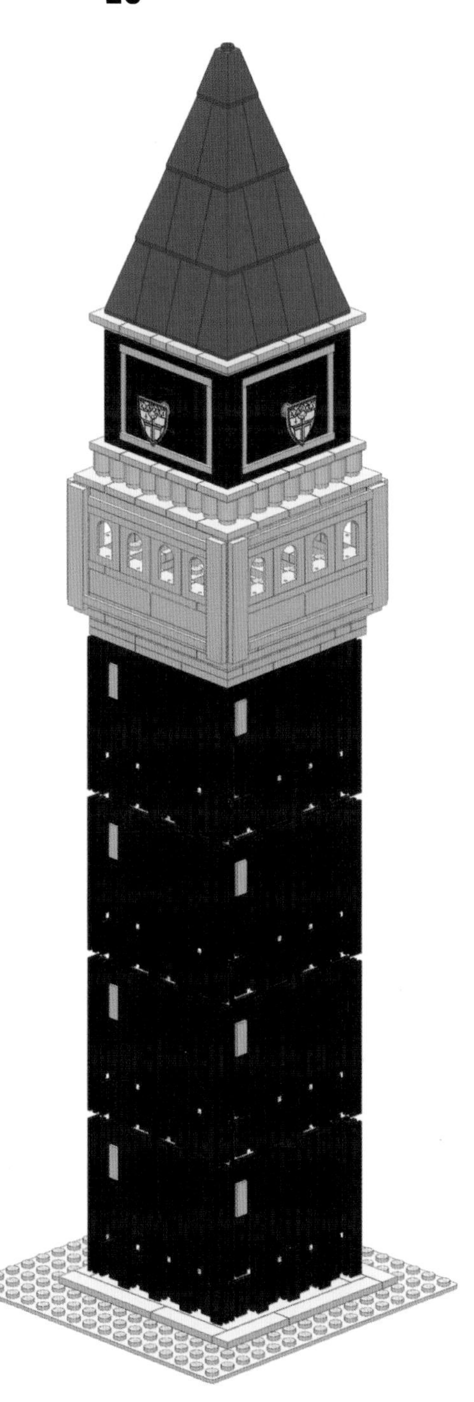

GONDOLA

LEGO® Construction by Warren Elsmore

Size: 2 cm (¾ in) high and wide, 13 cm (5⅛ in) long

Bricks: 61

Scale: Minifig scale

This gondolier had to be shown transporting some young lovers along the canals of Venice. A simple model to design and construct, the gondola is made instantly recognisable by the distinctive white piece (called a 'ferro') at the prow.

TREVI FOUNTAIN

In this scene we have minifigs throwing coins in the fountain for good luck. Having visited the fountain myself, this is one instance where I can say that I have performed the very same action as the minifigs!

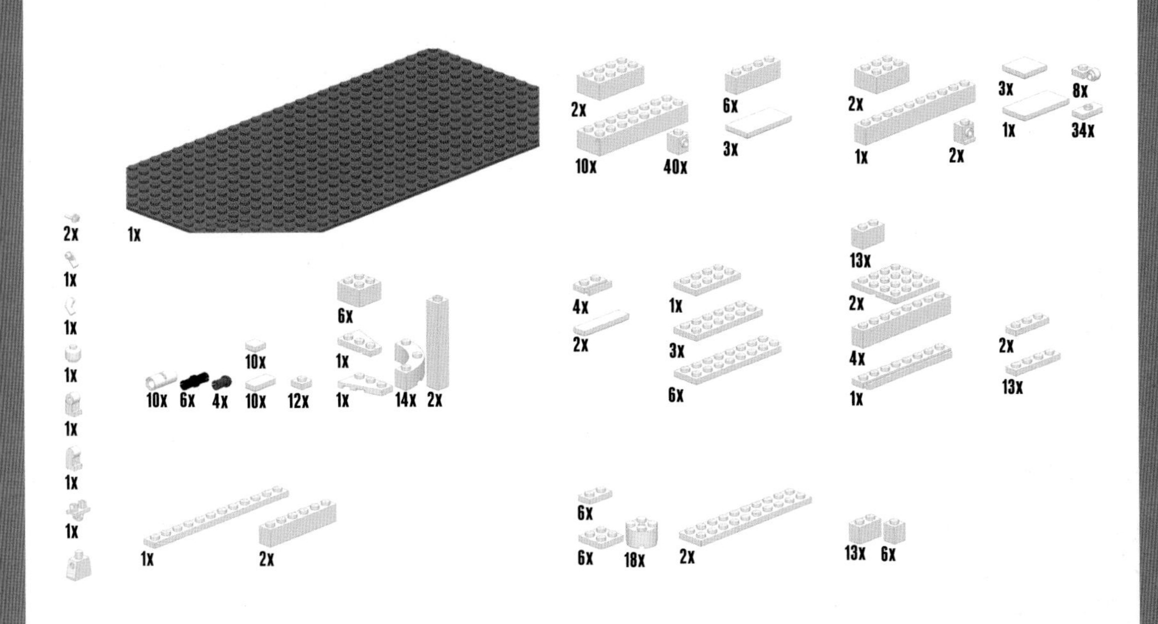

1x
2x
1x
1x
1x
1x
1x
1x
10x
6x
4x
10x
10x
12x
6x
1x
1x
14x
2x
1x
2x
2x
10x
40x
6x
3x
2x
1x
2x
3x
1x
8x
34x
13x
2x
4x
1x
4x
2x
1x
3x
6x
2x
13x
6x
6x
18x
2x
13x
6x

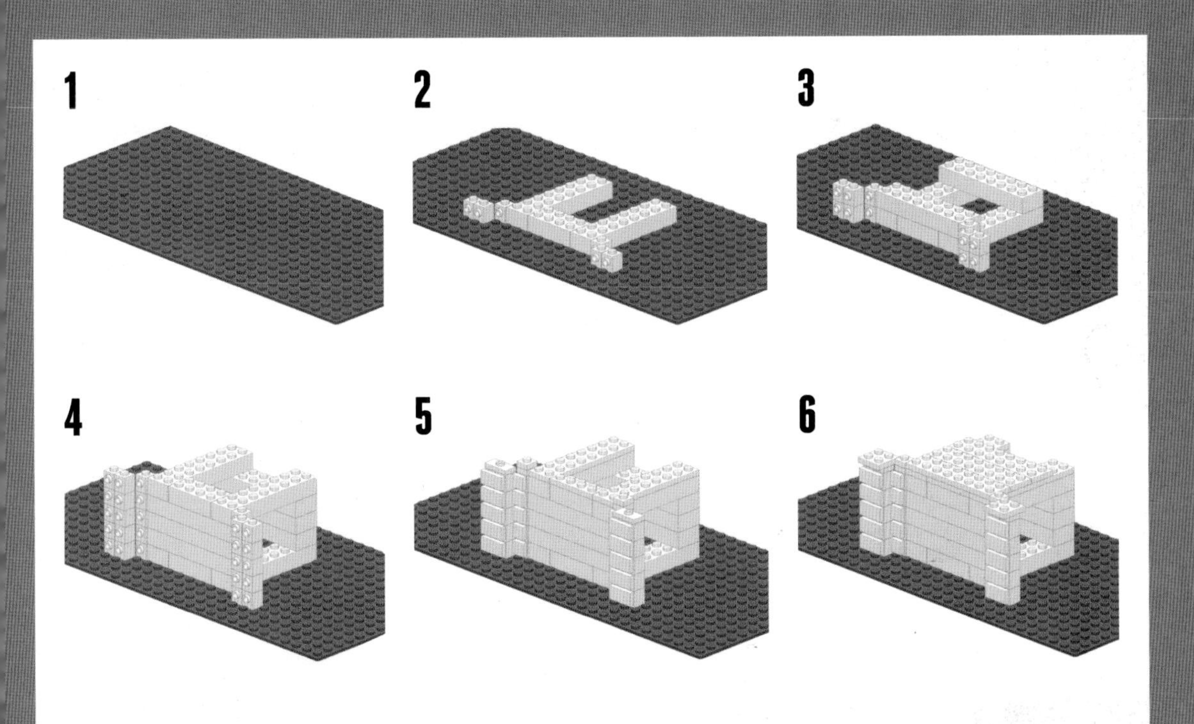

1
2
3
4
5
6

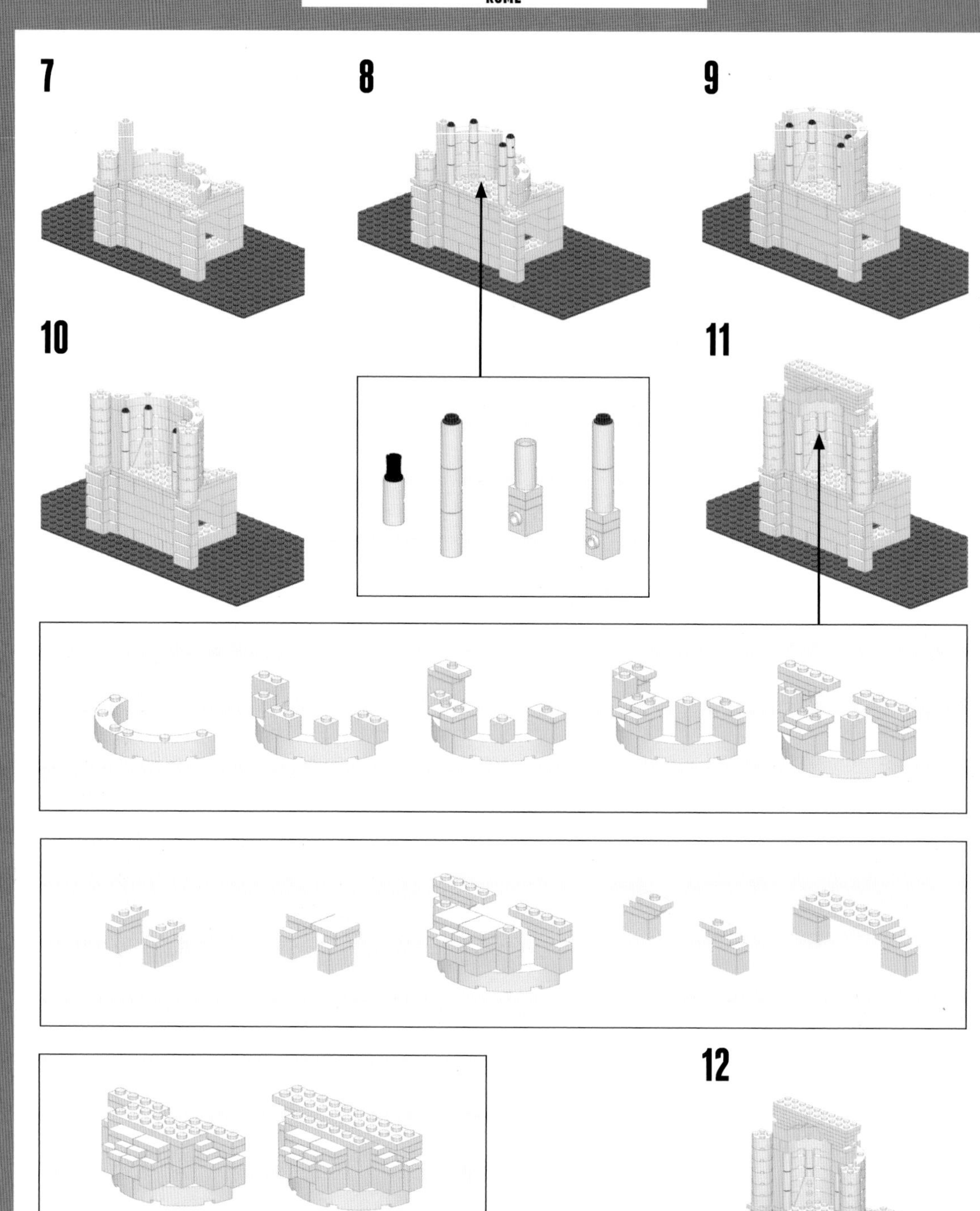
7
8
9
10
11
12

13

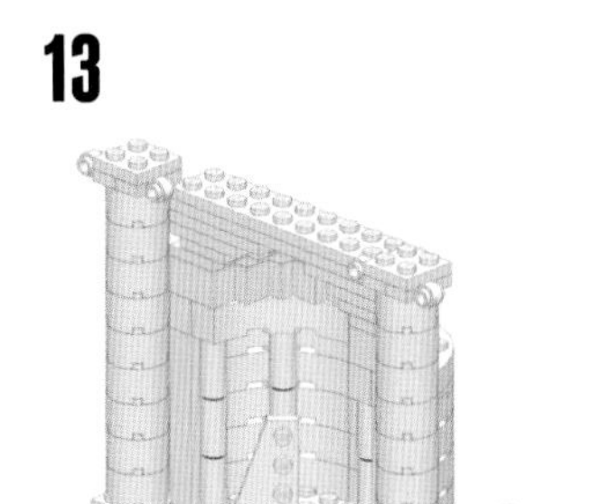

14

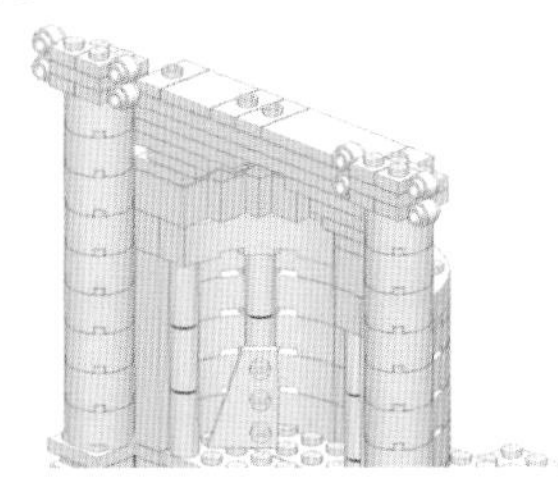

15

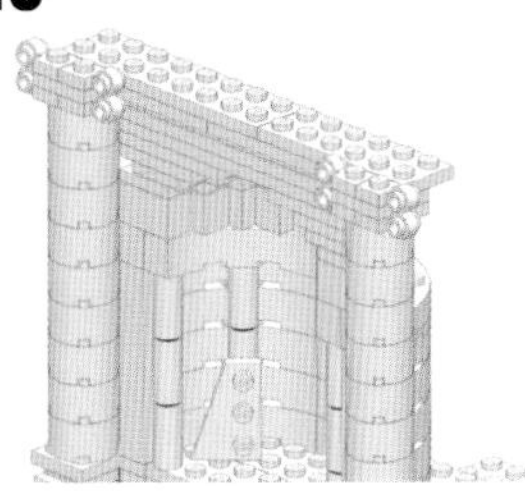

16

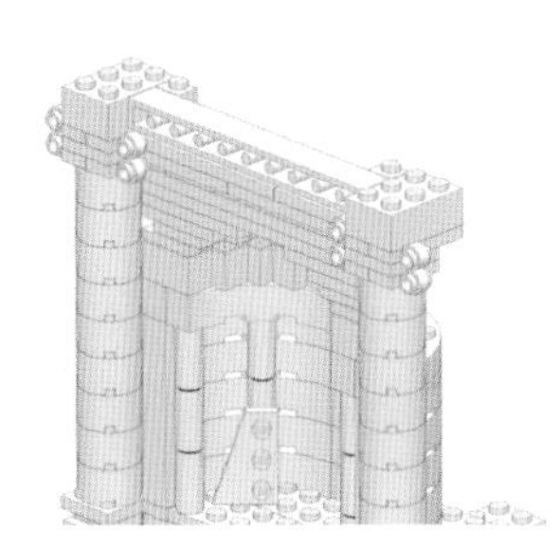

17

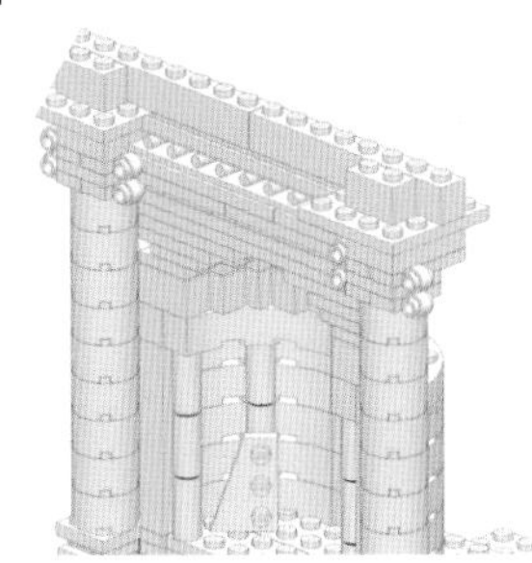

18

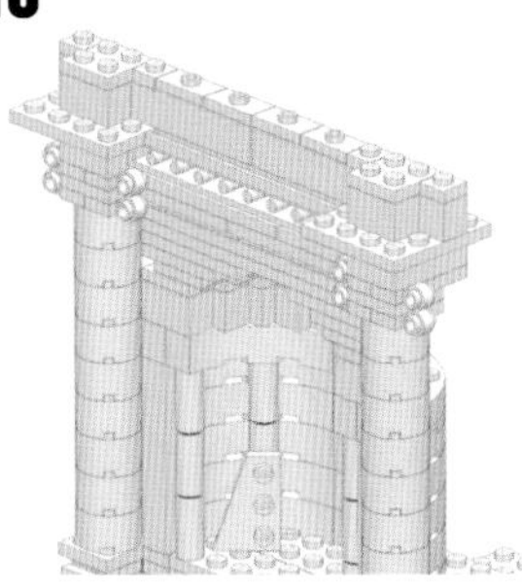

19

20

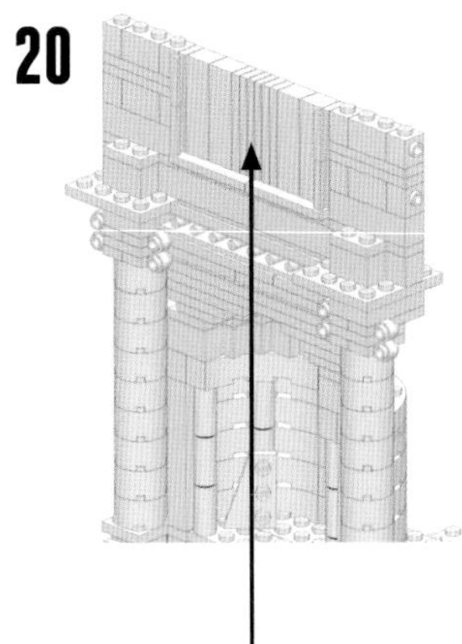

21

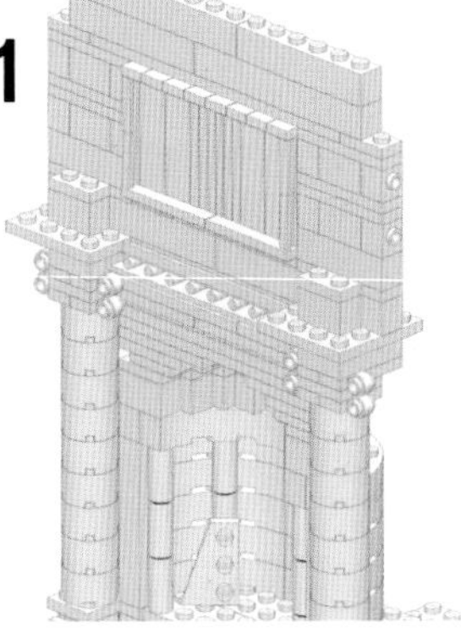

22

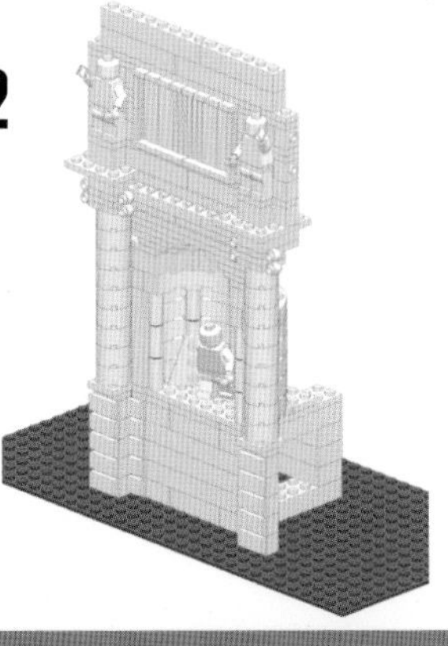

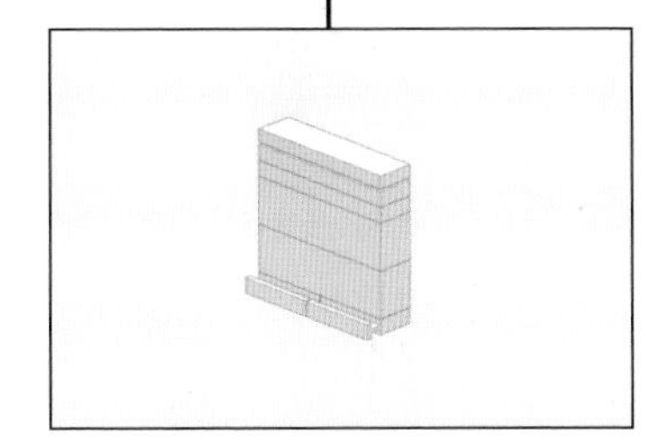

Photography by Gareth Butterworth

TEMPLE OF CLAUDIUS

LEGO® Construction by James Pegrum

Size: 40 cm (15¾ in) high and wide,
80 cm (31½ in) long

Bricks: 20,000

Scale: approximately 1:44

Although this is a classic temple of the kind to be found across the Roman Empire, it is in fact based on a temple built in Colchester, England, to honour the Emperor Claudius, who oversaw the Roman invasion of Britain. Building the columns for this model was a challenge, as there are 32 of them, each with four plates, so in total thousands of pieces are needed to build them. The design was also an upgrade from James's previous project, which was a reconstruction of the Pantheon in Rome. The roof is very lightweight but surprisingly strong – a curious and mischievous kitten walked across it without any damage to model or cat!

COLOSSEUM

This is probably the most complex model that includes instructions in the book. From a LEGO® point of view, it's all based around one particular piece that has a small arch in it, used hundreds and hundreds of times over. It was interesting to create a model for a building that is ruined – in order to be precise, it had to remain unfinished!

Nothing in the model is square, which in the world of LEGO makes it difficult to achieve. If you do build it, then you're well on your way to being a proper enthusiast – this can be a centrepiece in your own Brick City.

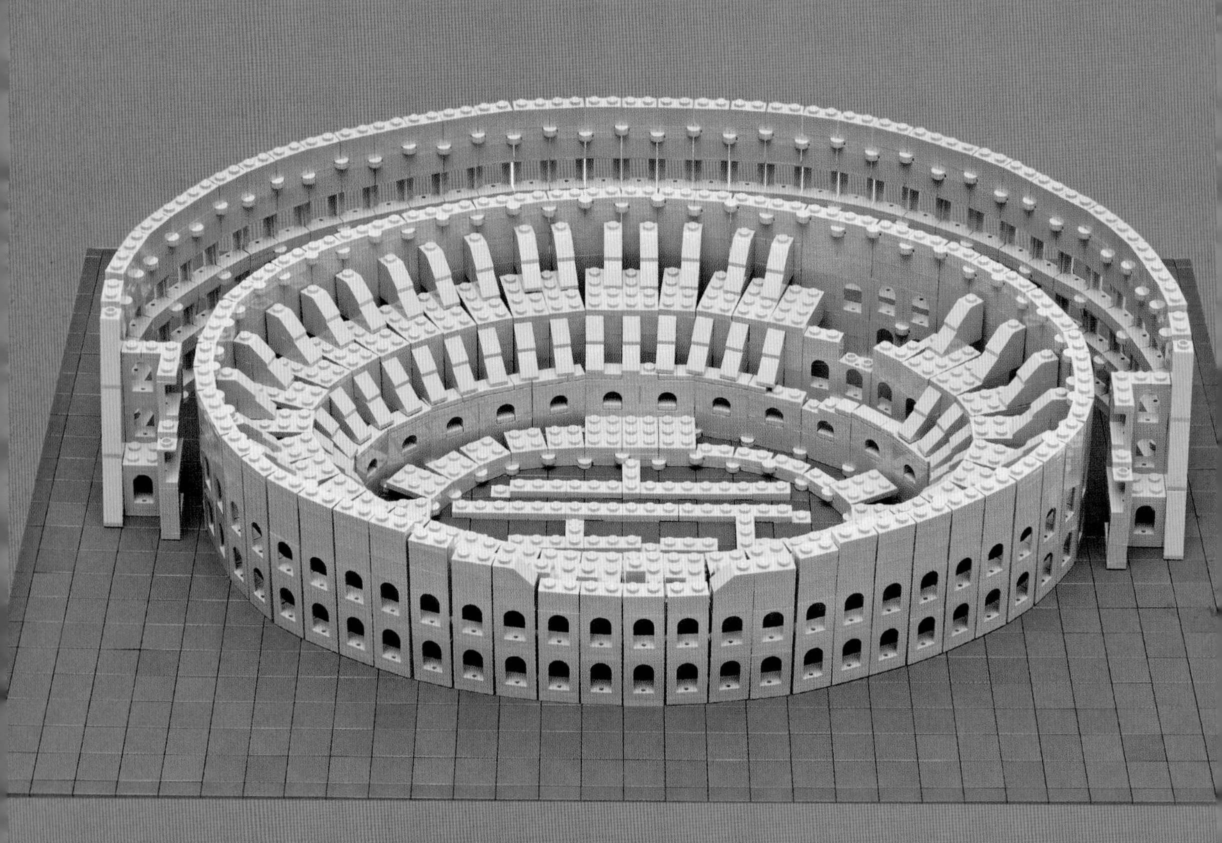

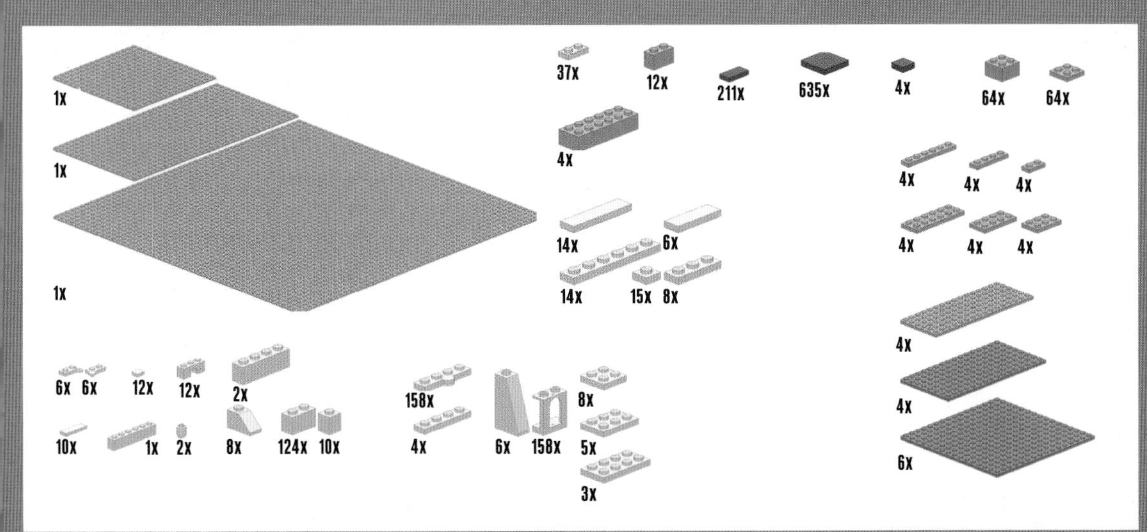
1x
1x
1x
37x
12x
211x
635x
4x
64x
64x
4x
4x
4x
4x
14x
6x
4x
4x
4x
14x
15x
8x
4x
6x 6x
12x
12x
2x
158x
8x
4x
10x
1x
2x
8x
124x
10x
4x
6x
158x
5x
6x
3x

BASE

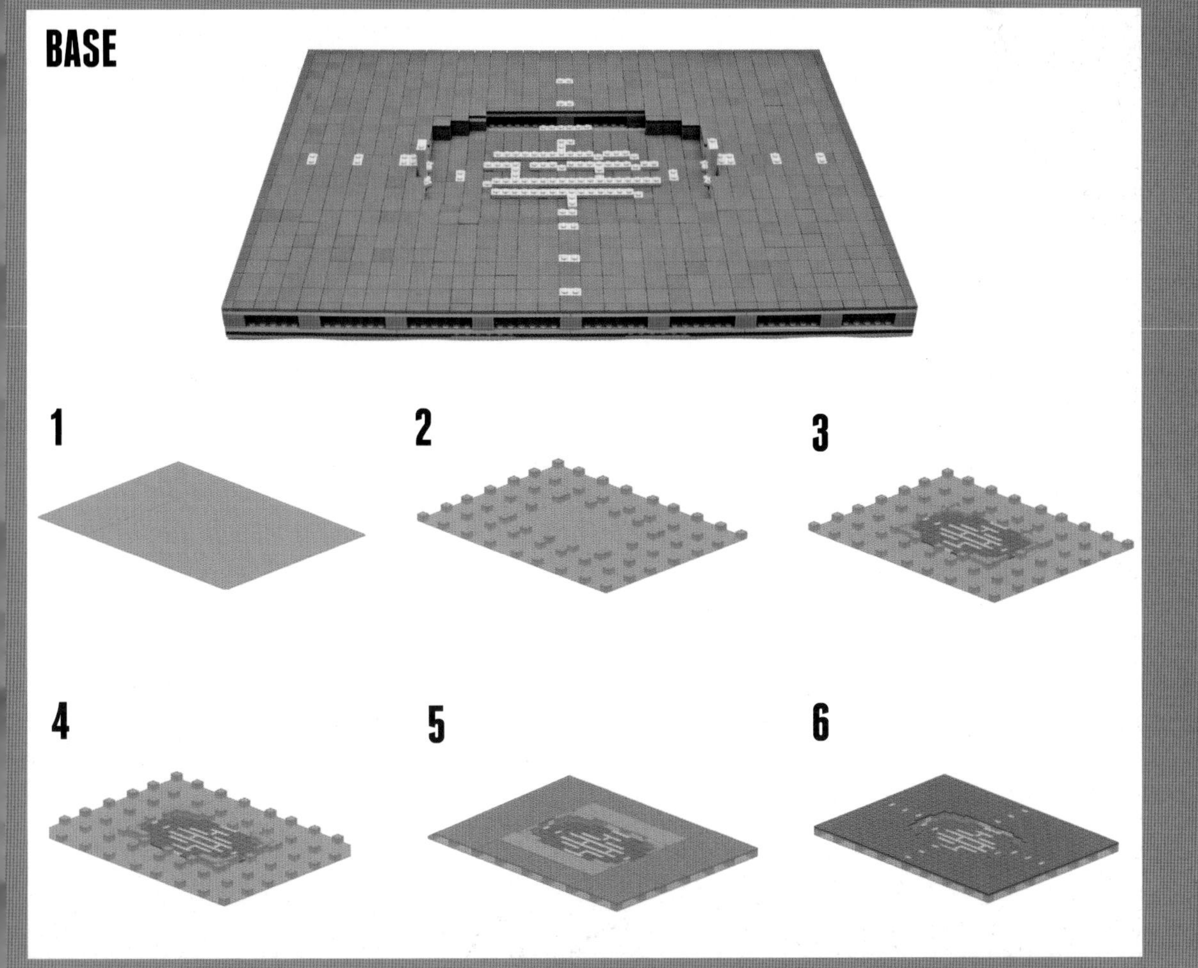
1
2
3
4
5
6

RING 1

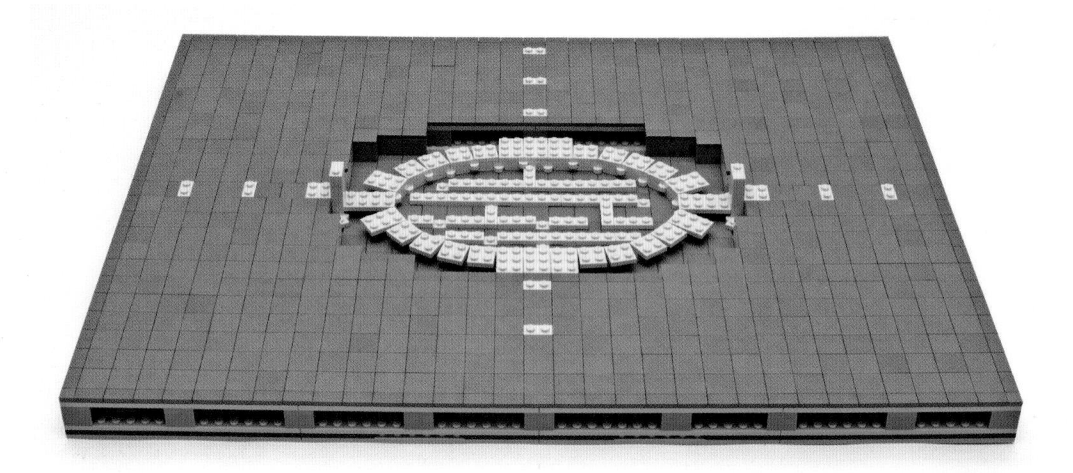

7

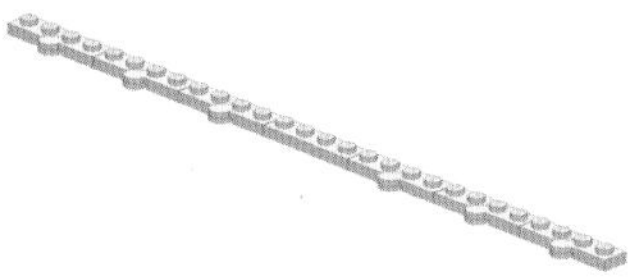

8

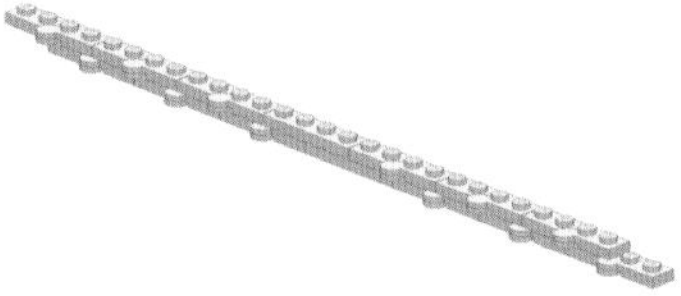

9

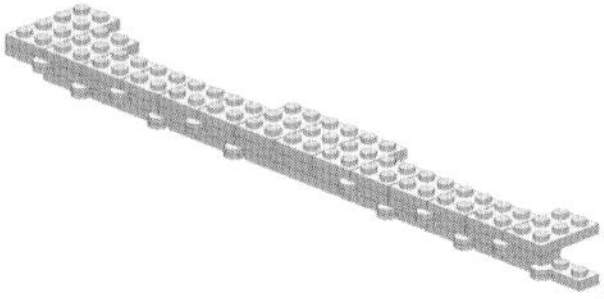

x2

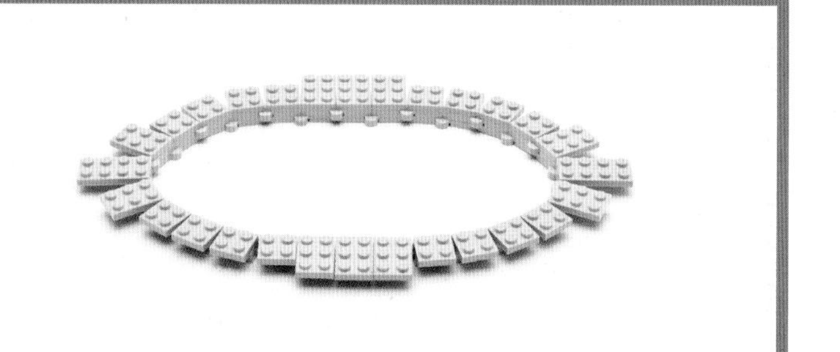

RING 2

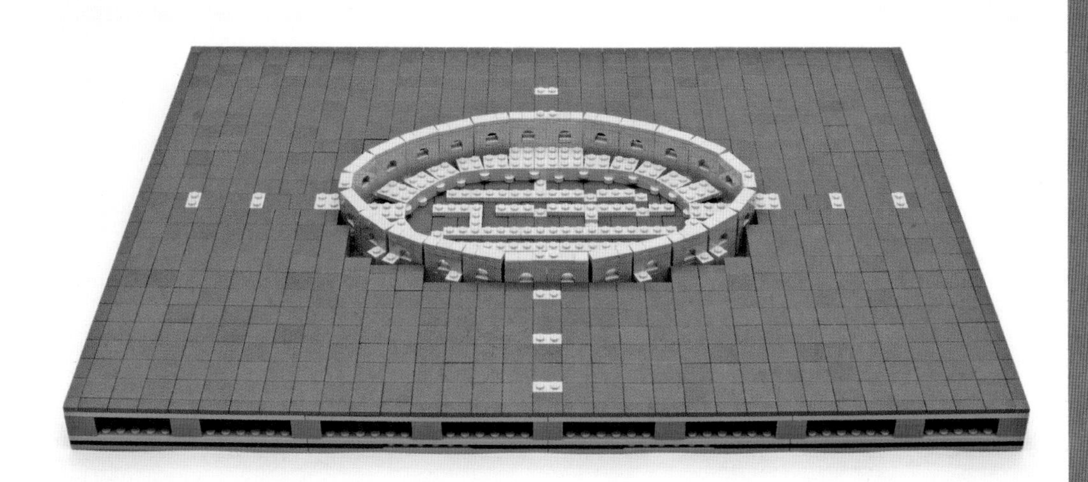

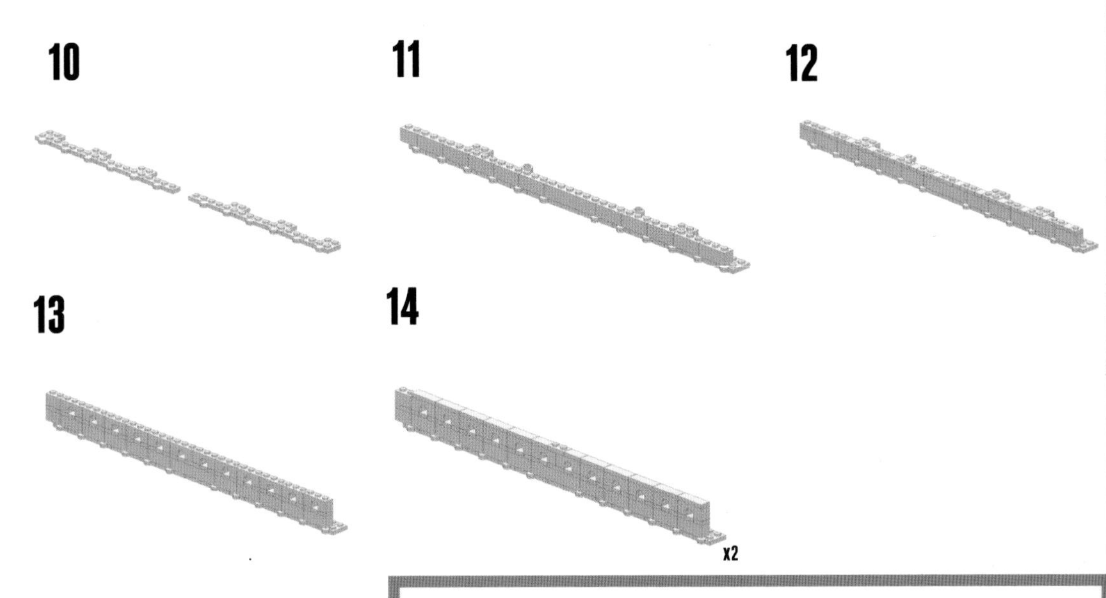

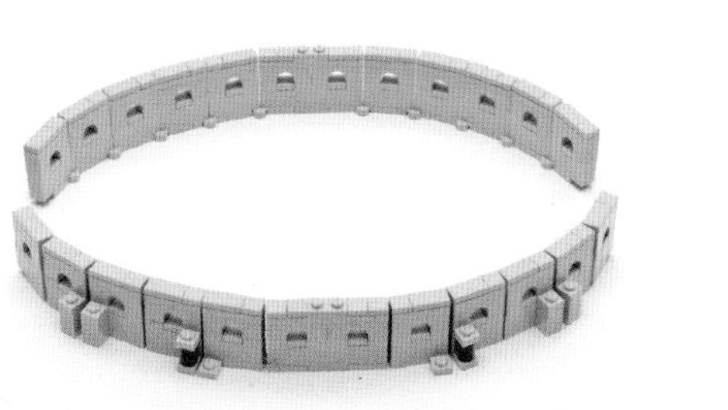

RING 3

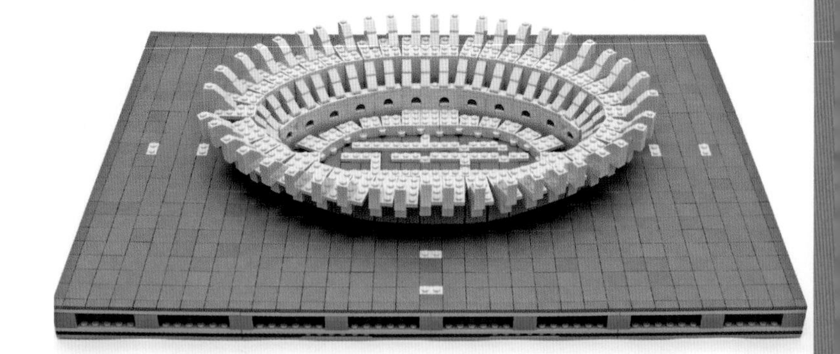

15

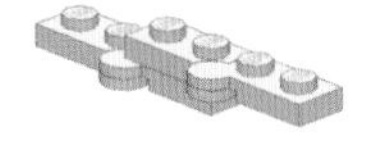

16

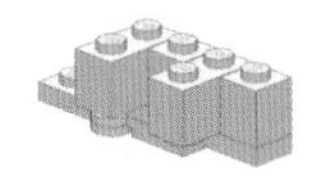

17

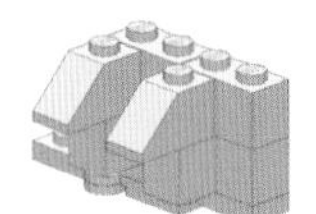

18

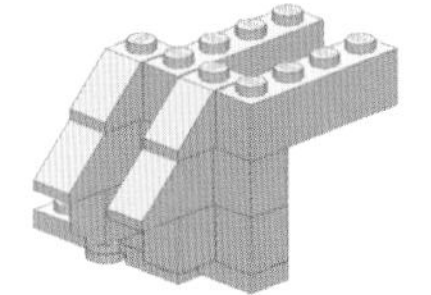

19

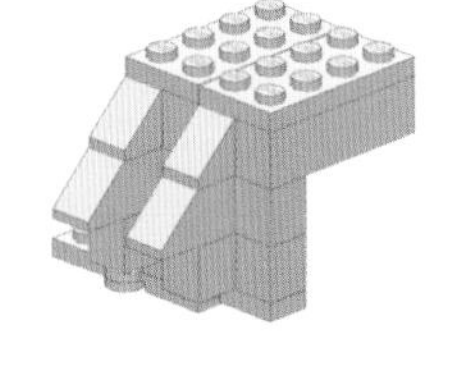

20

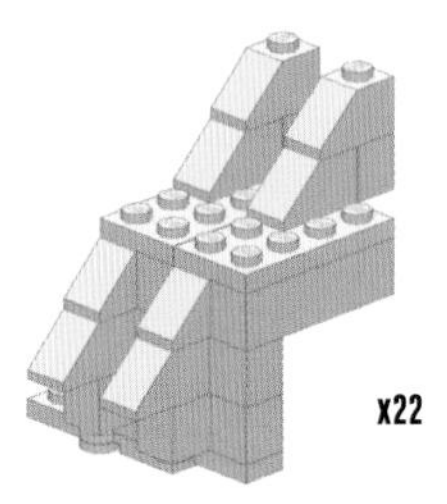

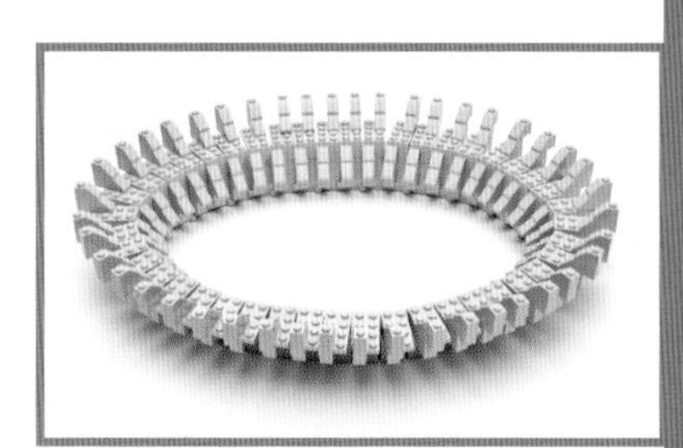

21

22

23

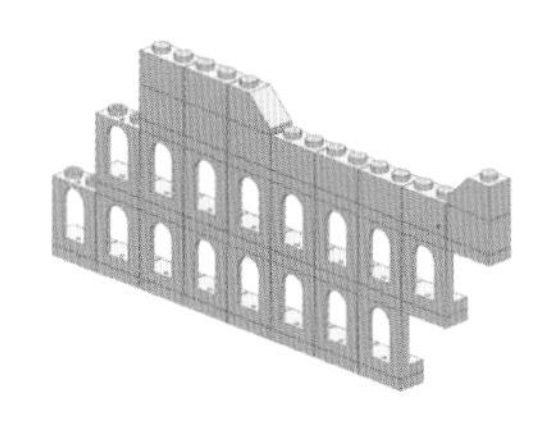

24

x22

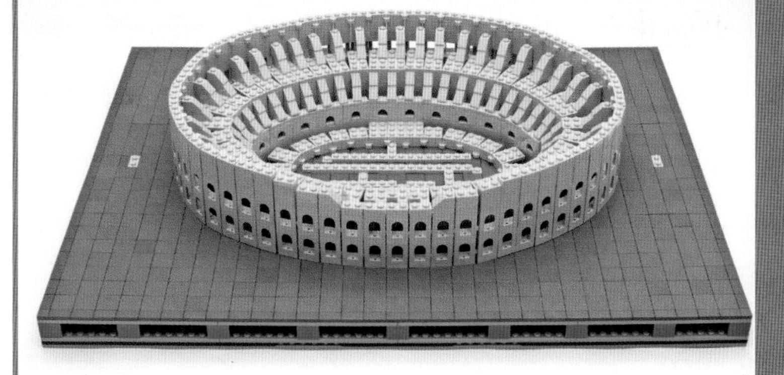

RING 5

25

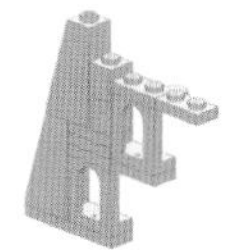

26

27

28

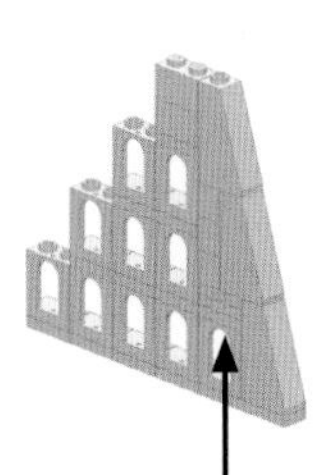

29

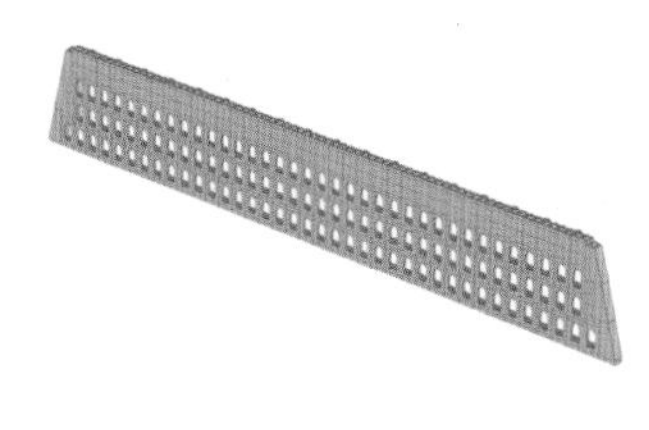

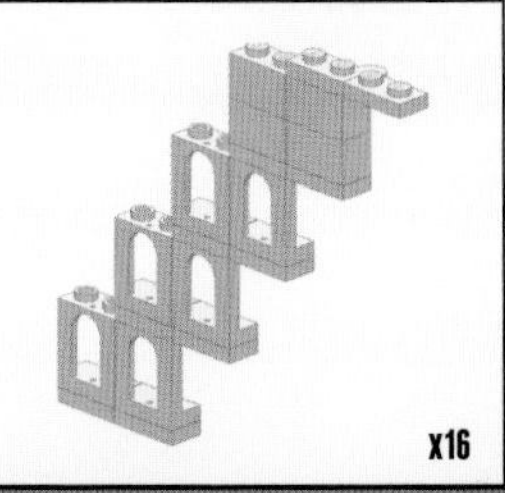

x16

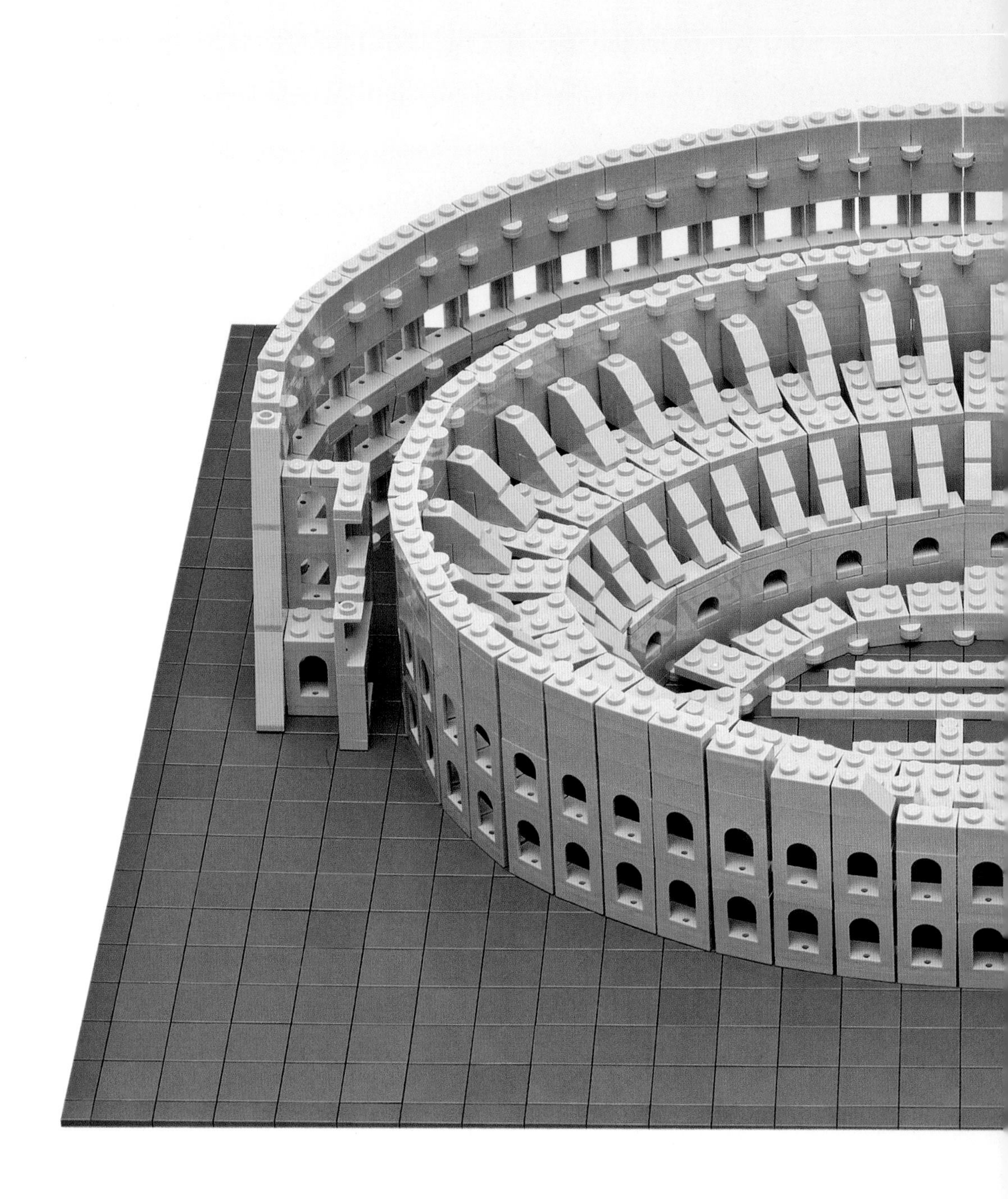

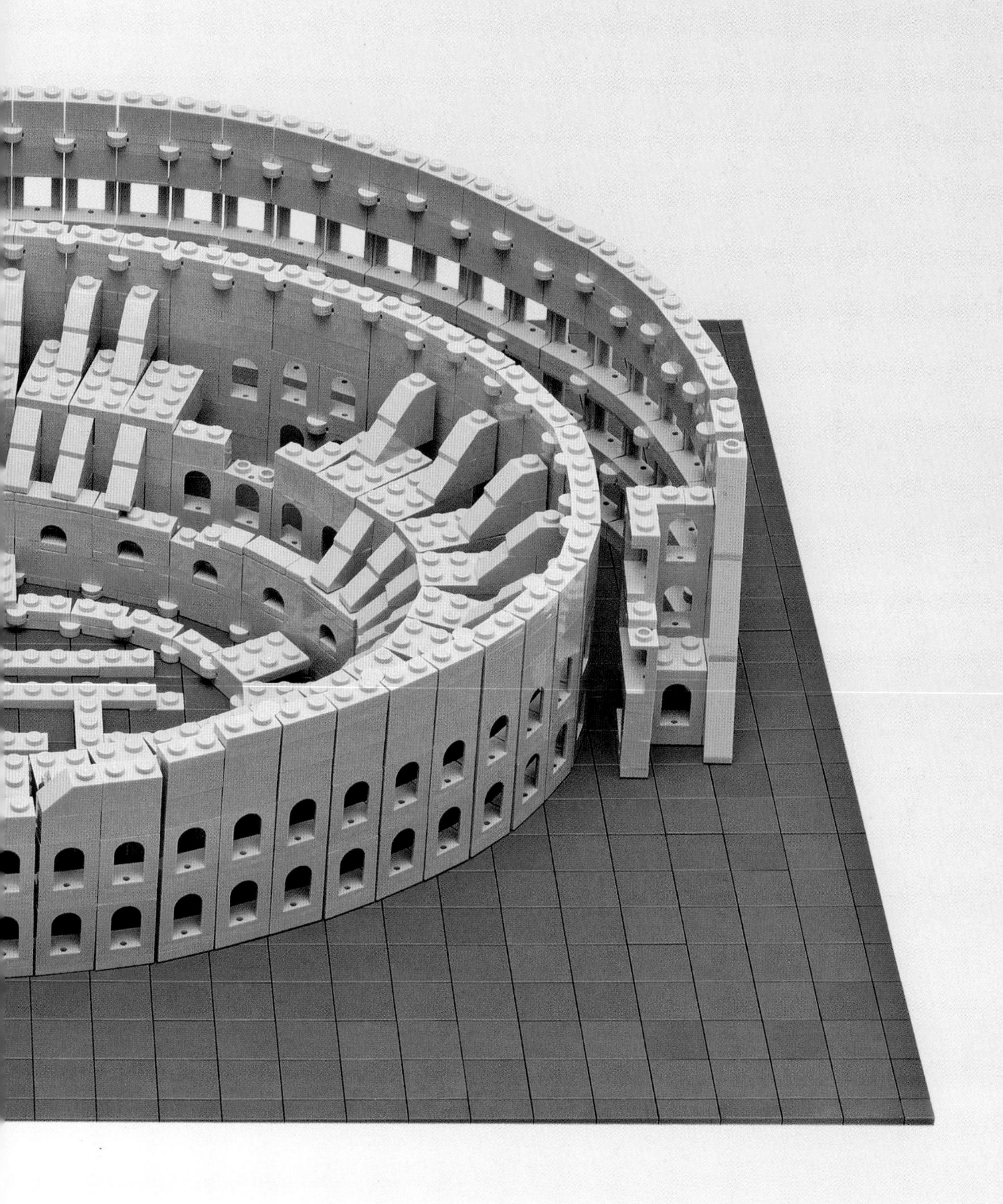

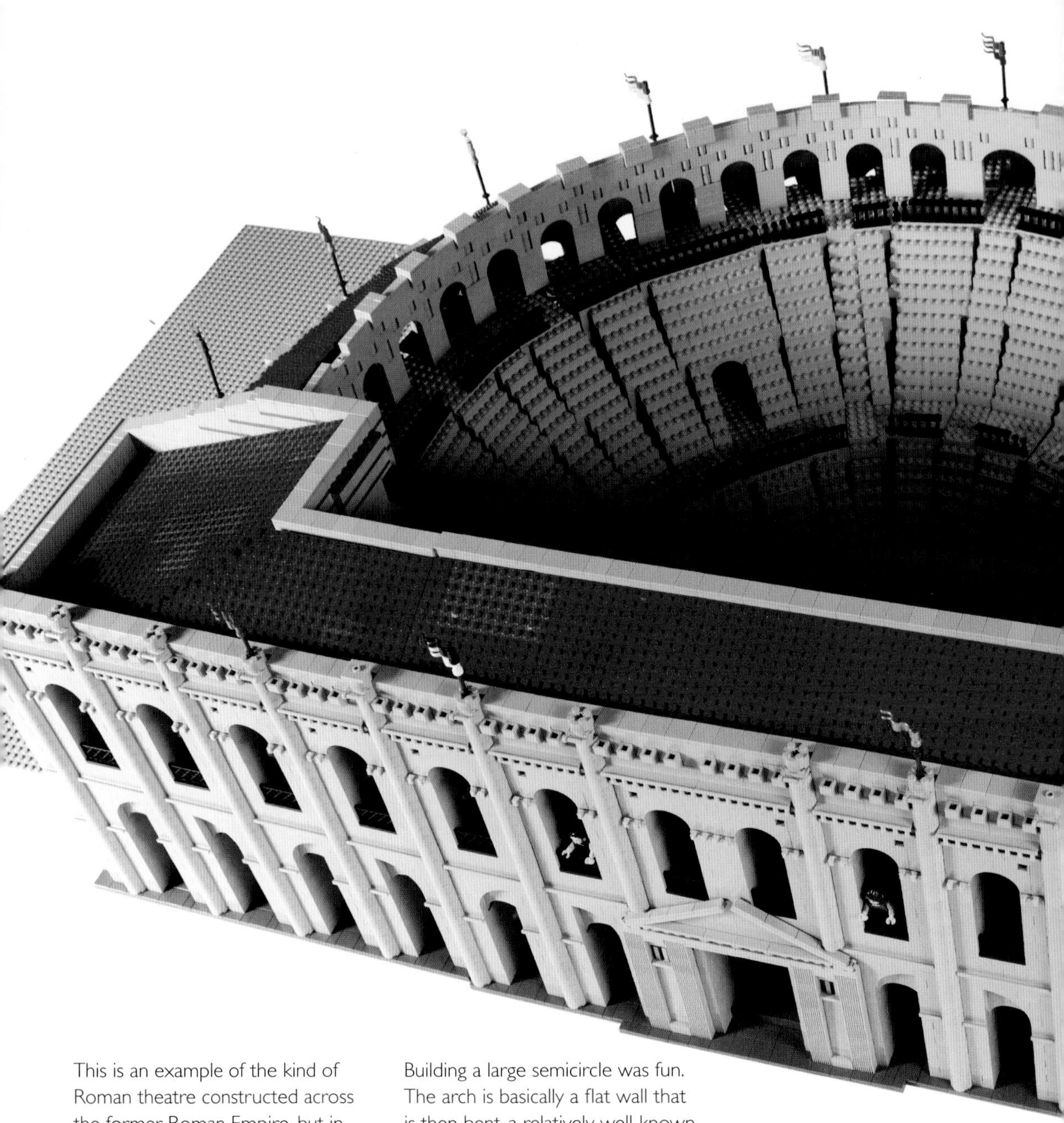

This is an example of the kind of Roman theatre constructed across the former Roman Empire, but in fact it is specifically modelled on one discovered in Colchester, England. The Roman theatre was a less violent place than the amphitheatre (which hosted gladiatorial combat and murderous chariot races), and was instead a venue for plays, music and public speeches.

Building a large semicircle was fun. The arch is basically a flat wall that is then bent, a relatively well-known technique, but an interesting one to execute given that James tried to get as much architectural modelling into it as possible. The shape also presented a challenge with the seating, but James managed it using wedge plates. The roof is simple and not very strong, but visually satisfying.

ROMAN THEATRE

LEGO® Edition by James Pegrum
Size: 30 cm (11¾ in) high, 80 cm (31½ in) long, 60 cm (23½ in) wide

Bricks: 30,000

Scale: approximately 1:44

Photography by Gareth Butterworth

Constructed across every part of the Empire, Roman theatres were semi-circular, unlike round amphitheatres, to improve the acoustics for the audience.

COPENHAGEN

LITTLE MERMAID STATUE

Sculptor: Edvard Eriksen (1913)
LEGO® Edition by Sean Kenney
Scale: Minifig scale
Bricks: 16

This statue is from one of Hans Christian Andersen's most famous stories. To create the mermaid-like stance of leaning forwards on her fishtail, the minifig's legs are bent back in an unnatural way, which if you look closely enough, seems quite uncomfortable.

RUNDETAARN

This curious-looking tower was built by Denmark's King Christian IV in the seventeenth century as an astronomical observatory. The piece we used to represent the windows is commonly called the LEGO® tooth (used as dentures for large-scale monsters, for instance) which, used on its side, creates the desired gothic pointed window shape.

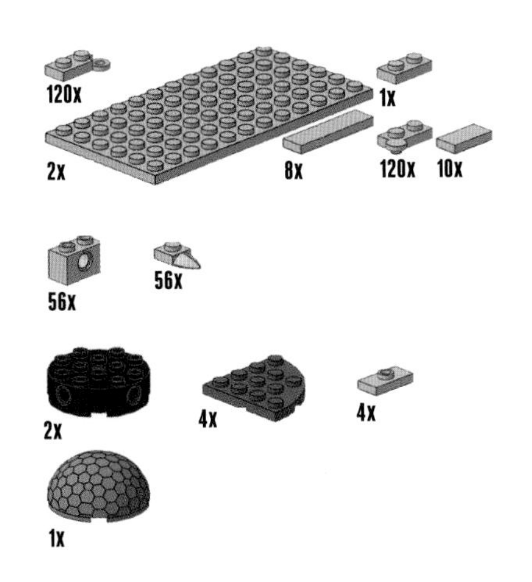

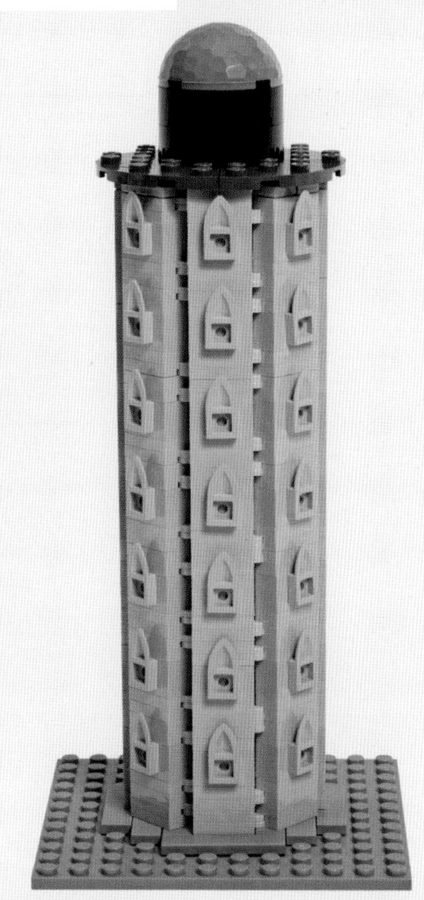

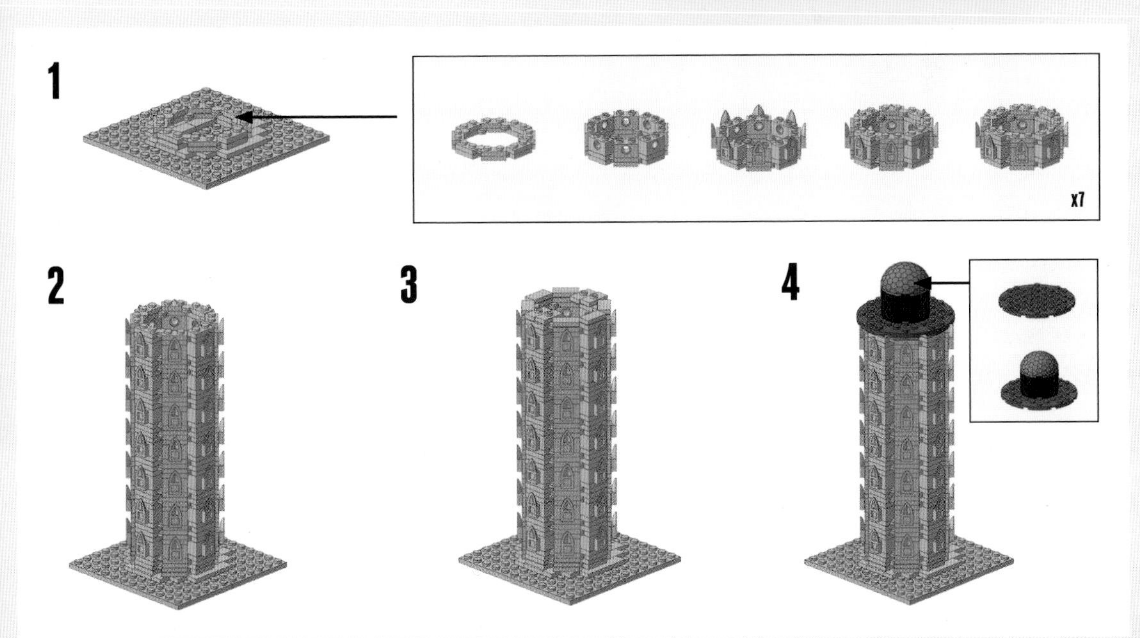

CHRISTIANSBORG PALACE

The windows in this model (the Danish State Assembly building) are created by headlamp bricks placed backwards, which give the right look. The building does seem rather forbidding and almost prison-like when modelled in LEGO®, but the real thing is the only building in the world that houses all three of any country's divisions of government power: the executive, legislative and judicial branches are all based there.

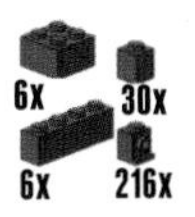
6X
30X
6X
216X

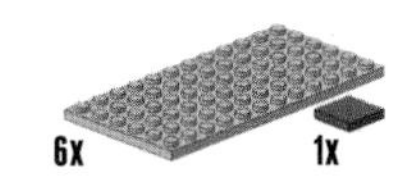
6X
1X

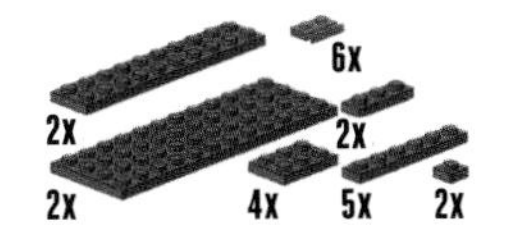
6X
2X
2X
2X
4X
5X
2X

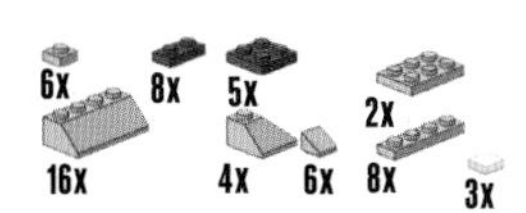
6X
8X
5X
2X
16X
4X
6X
8X
3X

1X 1X 5X 1X
1X
3X

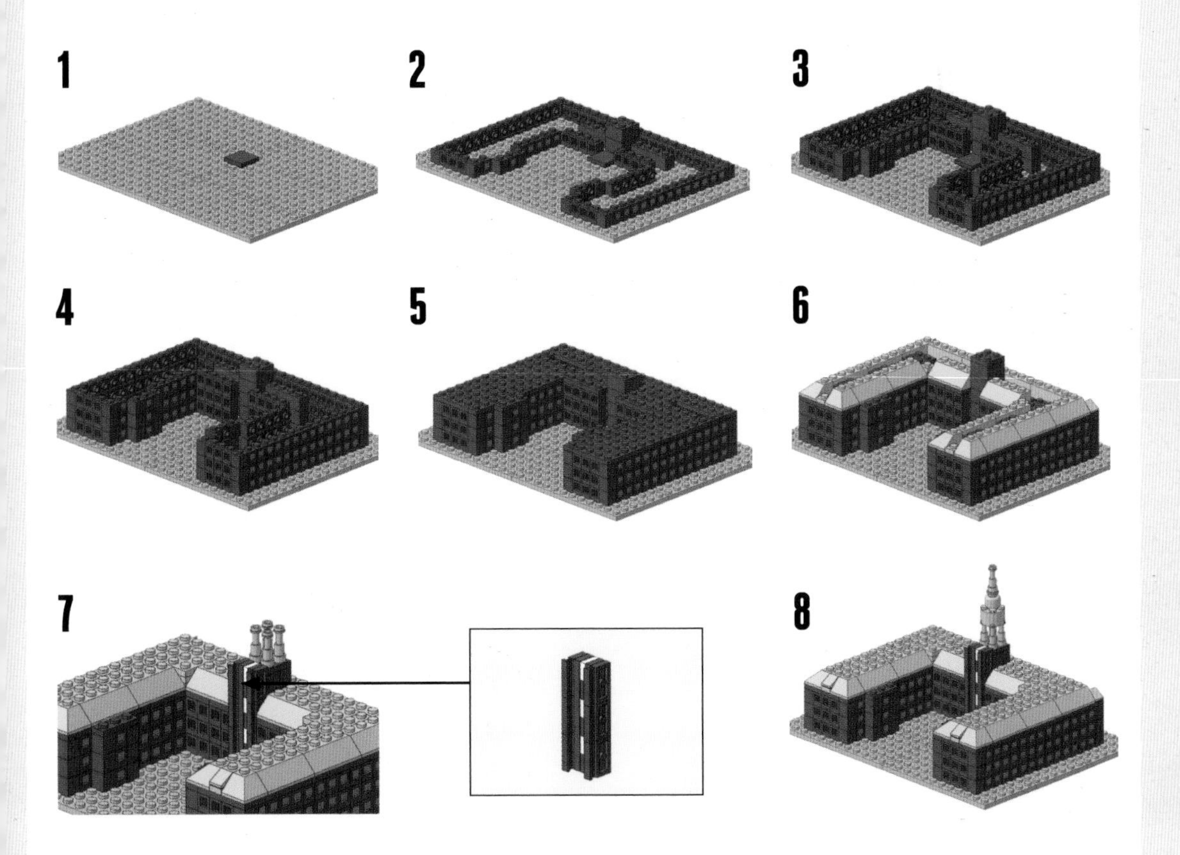
1
2
3
4
5
6
7
8

STOCKHOLM

STADSHUSET

This pretty and unusually square red building is made to microscale. It is Stockhom's City Hall, and each year the banquet to celebrate the Nobel Prize winners is held here.

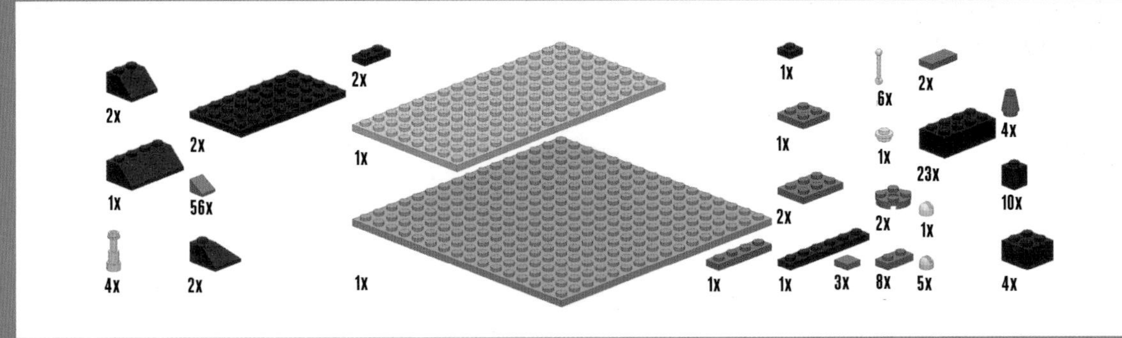
2x
2x
1x
56x
4x
2x
2x
1x
1x
1x
6x
2x
1x
1x
4x
23x
10x
2x
2x
1x
1x
1x
3x
8x
5x
4x

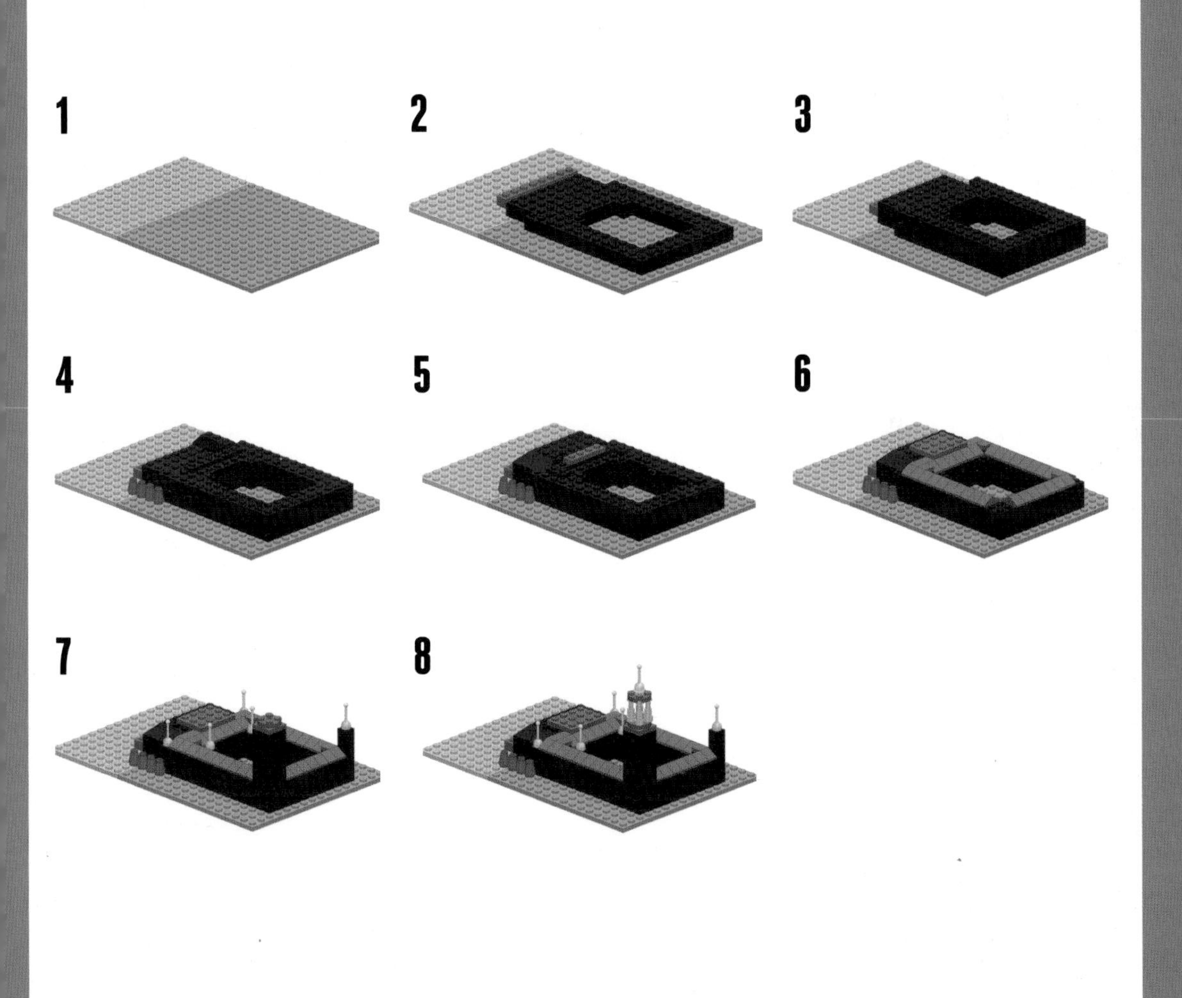
1
2
3
4
5
6
7
8

TENGBOMS KONCERTHUSET

Home to the Royal Stockholm Philharmonic, this concert hall is where the Nobel Prize is awarded each year. The building is relatively easy to represent in LEGO® since it has a very square form. However, to scale the building down to a manageable size, it has been built below minifig scale — each door and window is built from bricks. Included opposite are instructions for just a section of the front wall, which includes all the salient features. You can see from the finished picture that to complete the model you will need to build a number of these sections next to each other, some with balconies and some without, and box them in with solid ends. This model is a great example of how adding a few highlights to a plain brick wall can add real character to the building.

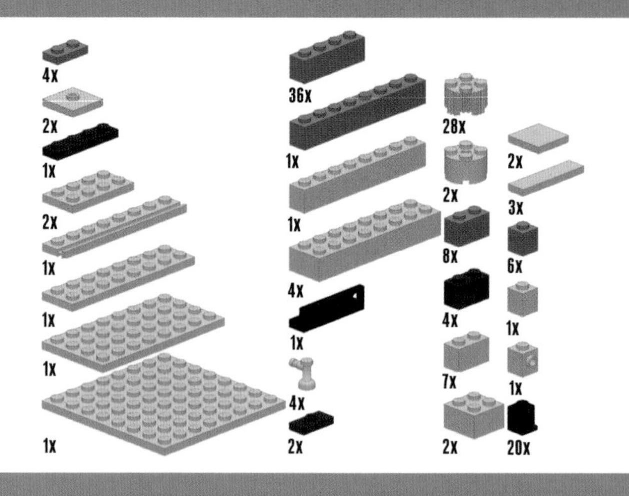

1

2

3

4

5

6

7

8

9

10

11

12

13

BERLIN

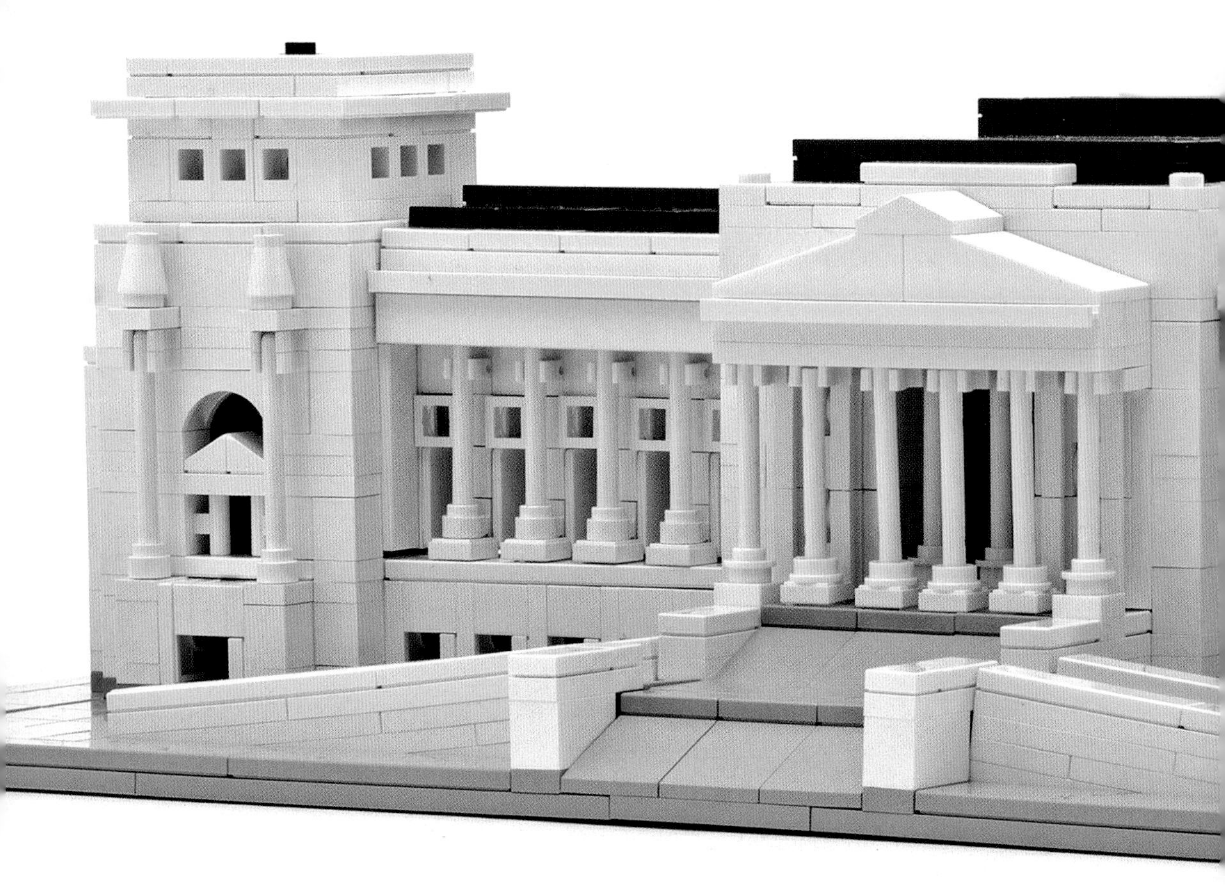

REICHSTAG

Architect: Paul Wallot (1894)
LEGO® Edition by Alastair Disley
Size: 11 cm (4½ in) high, 22 cm (8½ in) long and wide
Bricks: 2,000
Scale: 1:370

This building was one of the most difficult to build for this book, largely because it is so small. To get all the features looking right, lots of LEGO pieces are used in ways that they weren't originally designed for – as well as on their sides, back to front and even upside down. Alastair used trial and error, comparing the results to photographs of the real building, and rebuilt the main entrance three times before he was satisfied with it.

AMPELMANN

This rather jolly-looking man striding forwards is the iconic East German variation of the green or white walking man who appears on pedestrian traffic lights. Unusually, this whole model is built on a 45-degree angle, and then tilted to balance on the points of his heels and toes to create the right image.

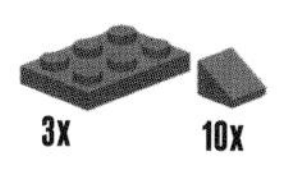

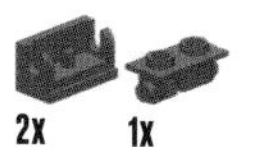

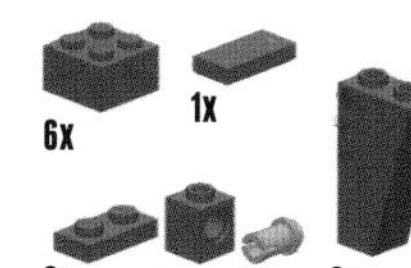

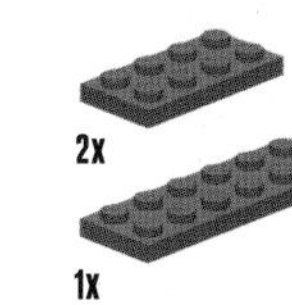

2x

1x

1

2

3

4

5

6

7

8

9

10

TV TOWER

A replica of a remarkable building which was built in the 1960s as a television studio and which, in the centre of the sphere, hosts a revolving restaurant. It remains the tallest building in Germany, although the model itself is only 30.5 cm (1 foot) tall. The sphere in the middle uses the same technique as on the New York hot dog model (p.60), called 'Bram sphere'. It consists of six pieces solidly connected throughout with studs pointing outward in every direction.

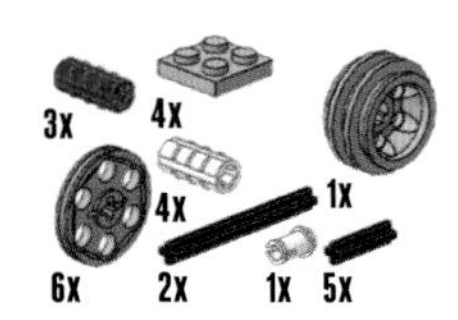

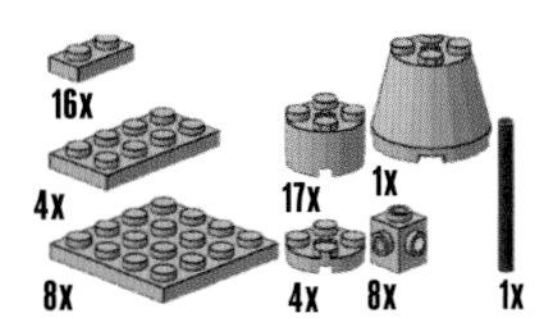

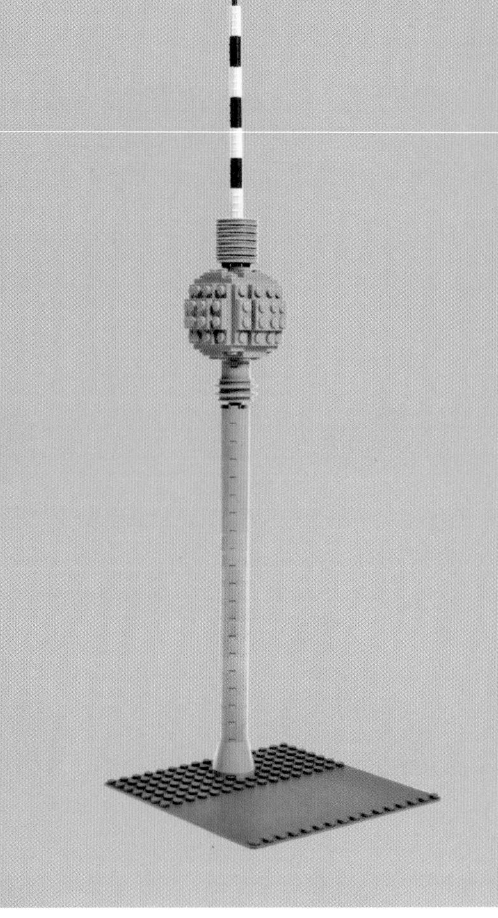

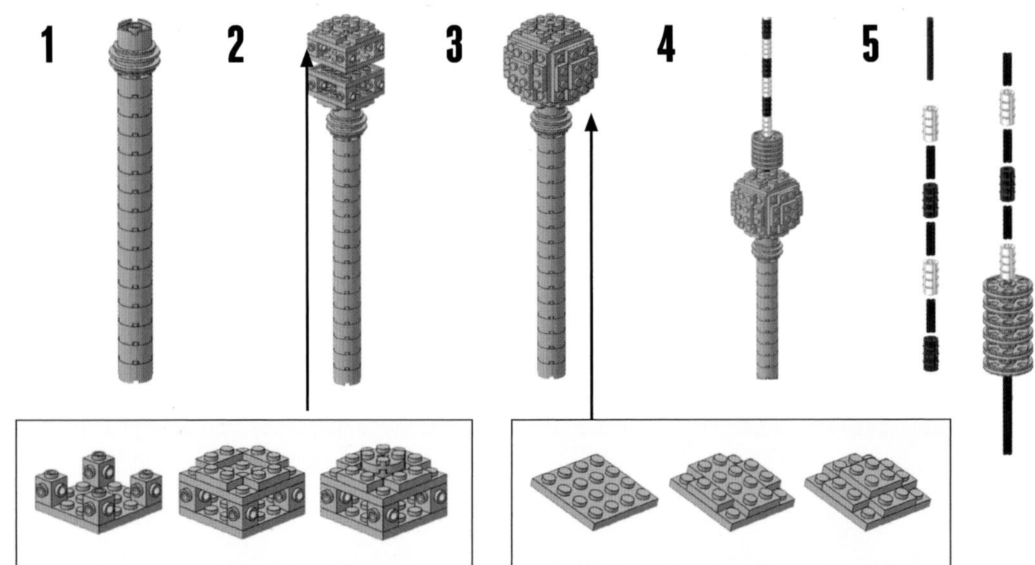

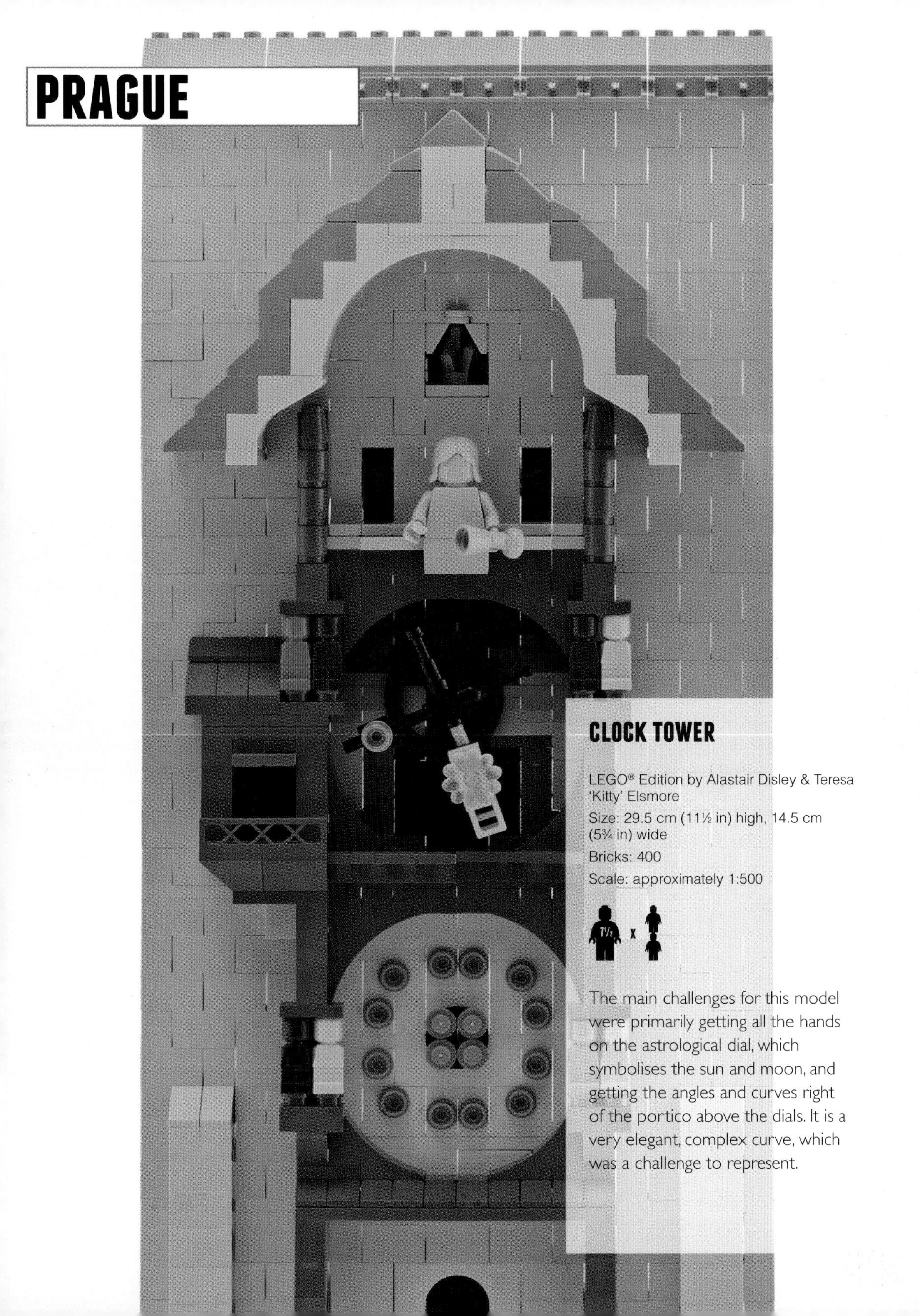

CLOCK TOWER

LEGO® Edition by Alastair Disley & Teresa 'Kitty' Elsmore

Size: 29.5 cm (11½ in) high, 14.5 cm (5¾ in) wide

Bricks: 400

Scale: approximately 1:500

7½ x

The main challenges for this model were primarily getting all the hands on the astrological dial, which symbolises the sun and moon, and getting the angles and curves right of the portico above the dials. It is a very elegant, complex curve, which was a challenge to represent.

CHARLES BRIDGE

This bridge, which connects Prague Castle with the Old Town, has 16 arches in real life, so you can repeat the steps in these instructions to extend it onwards. The statues are simply LEGO® minifigures, all in grey. Using the same colour for all body parts, swords, and hats creates a simple stonework effect.

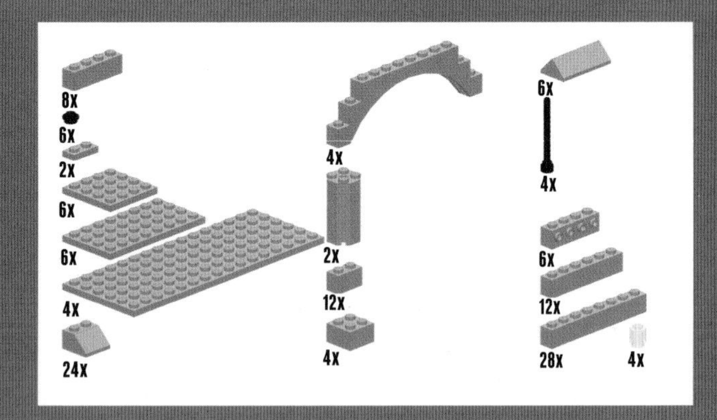

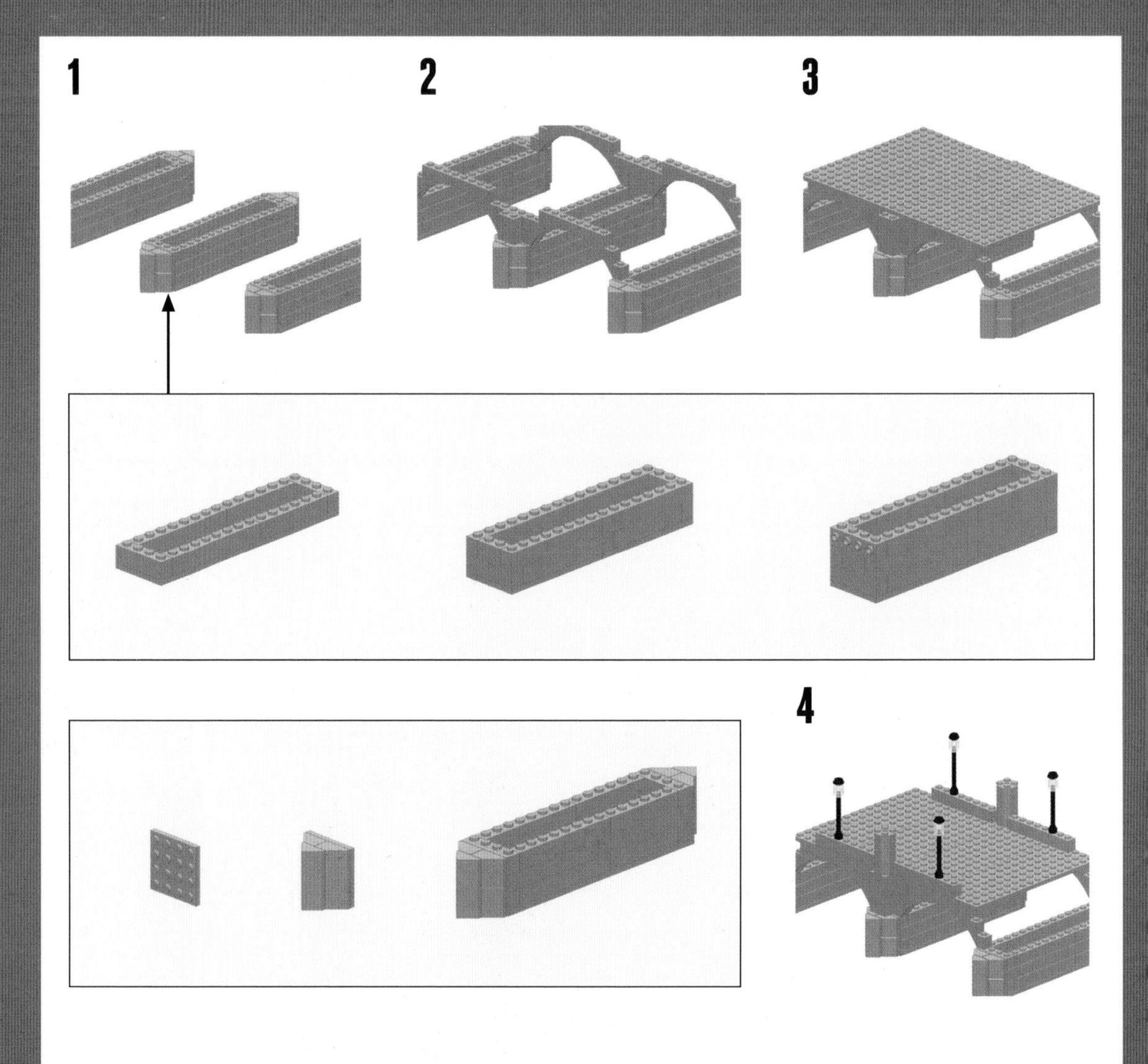

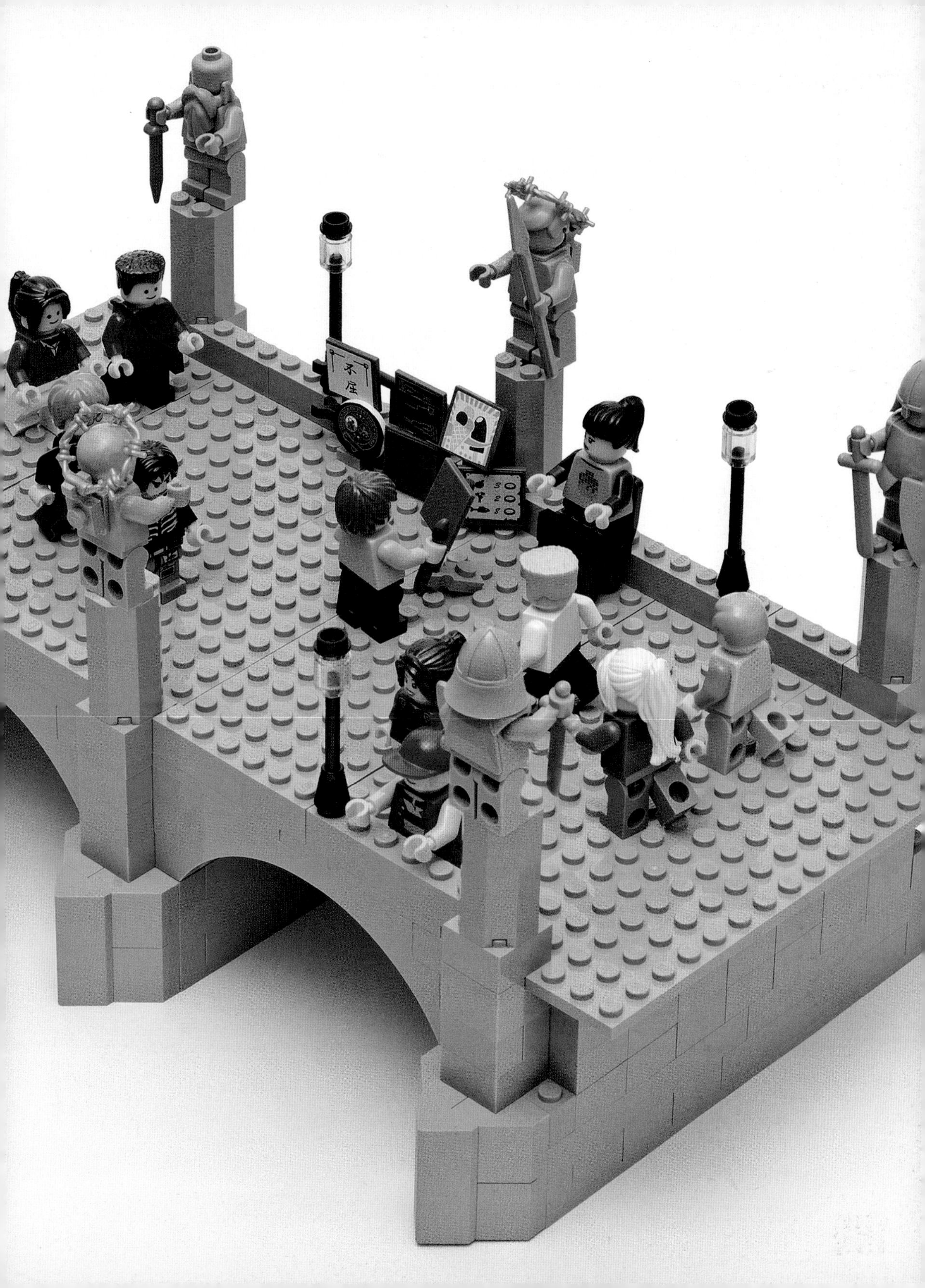
300
200
800

OLYMPIC STADIUM TOWER

Another national monument of a building left behind by the Olympics, as we've seen elsewhere in the book from Montreal and London. The tower is part of the stadium, which dates back to the 1952 Summer Olympics.

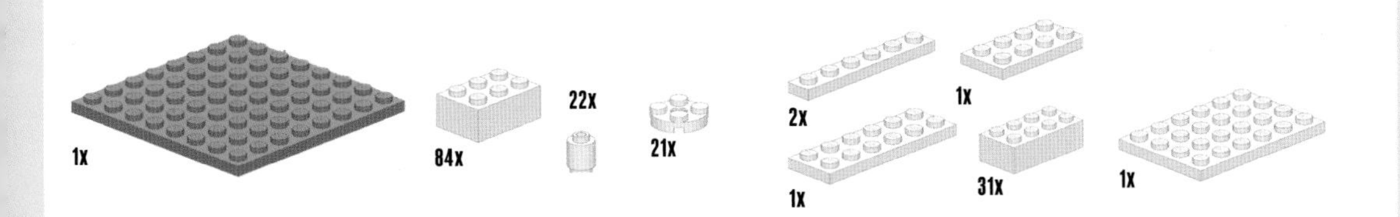
1x
84x
22x
21x
2x
1x
1x
31x
1x
1x

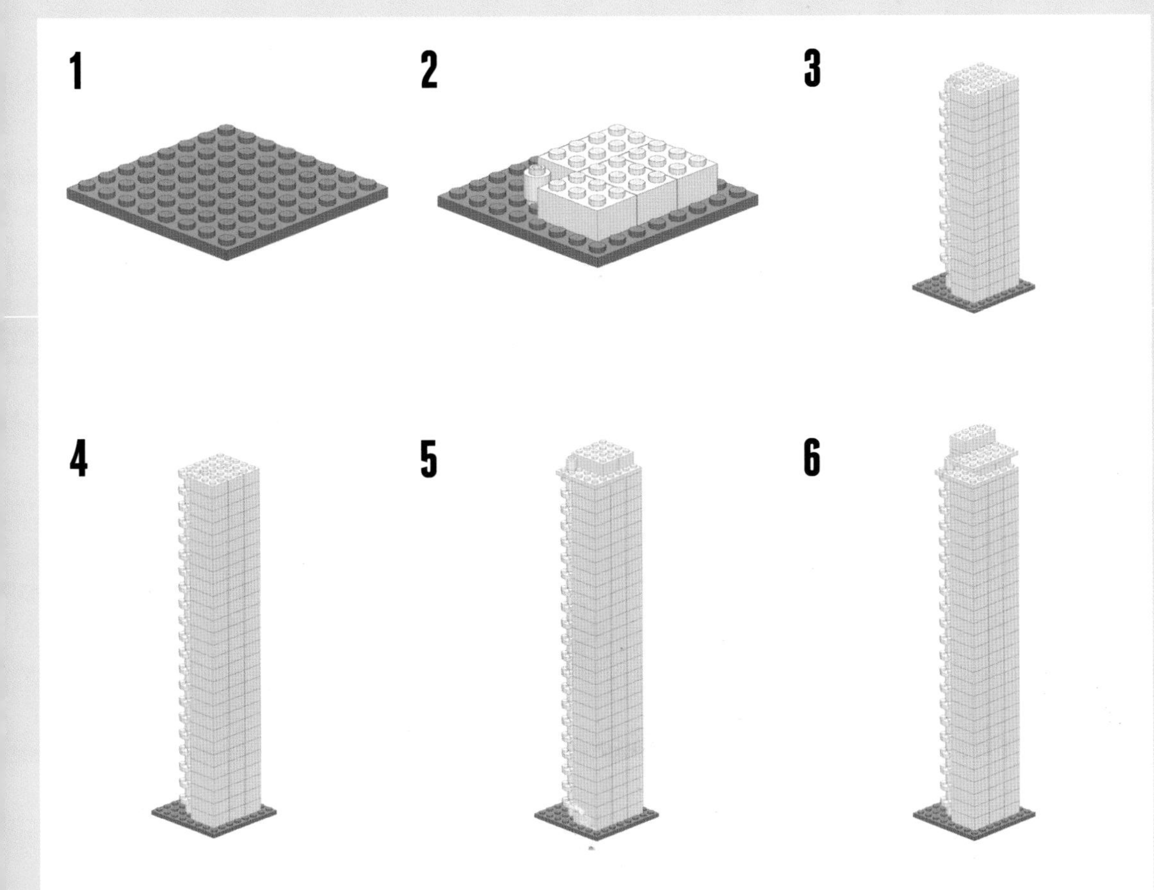
1
2
3
4
5
6

BUDAPEST

SZECHENYI BATHS

This is a famous bath house in Budapest – one of the city's most well-known landmarks. It is fed by two thermal springs and is the largest medicinal bath in Europe.

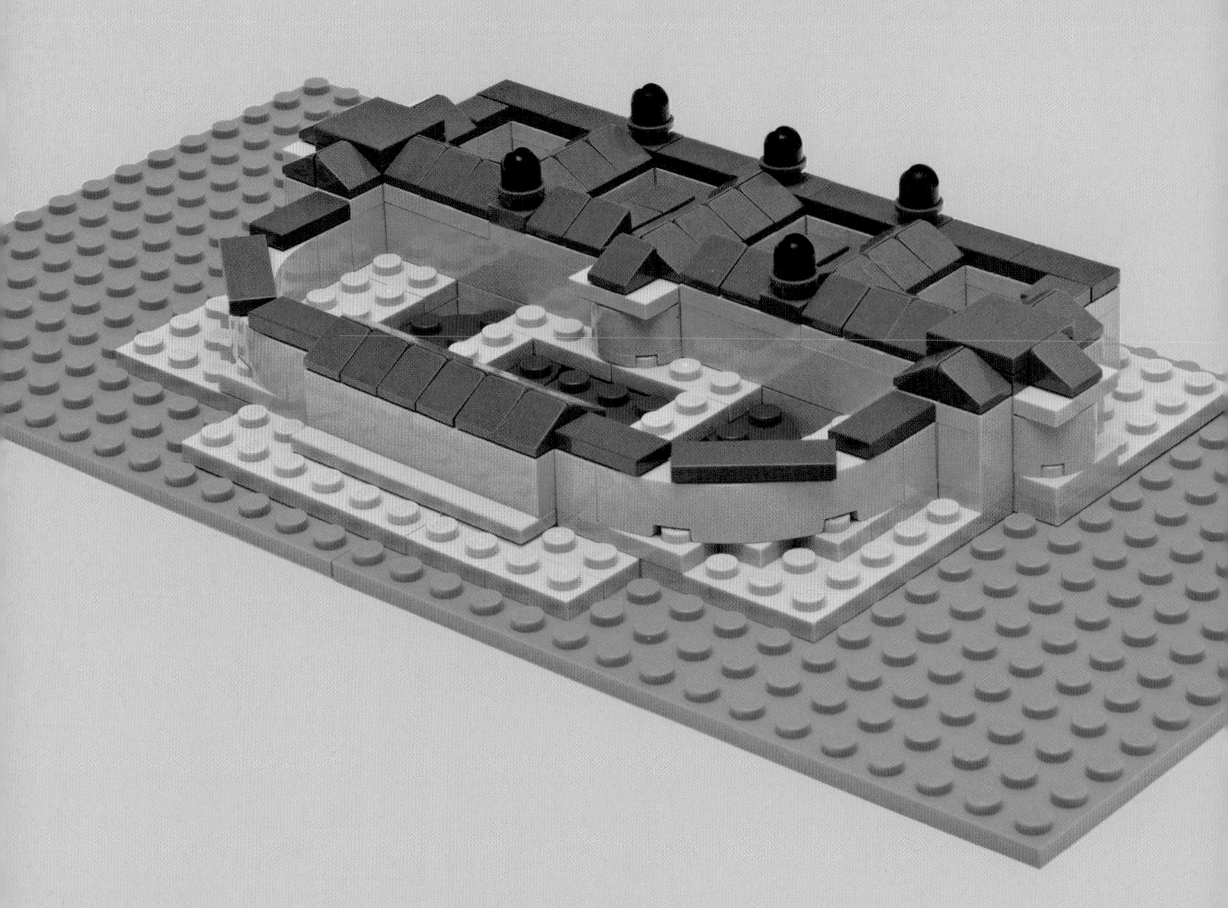

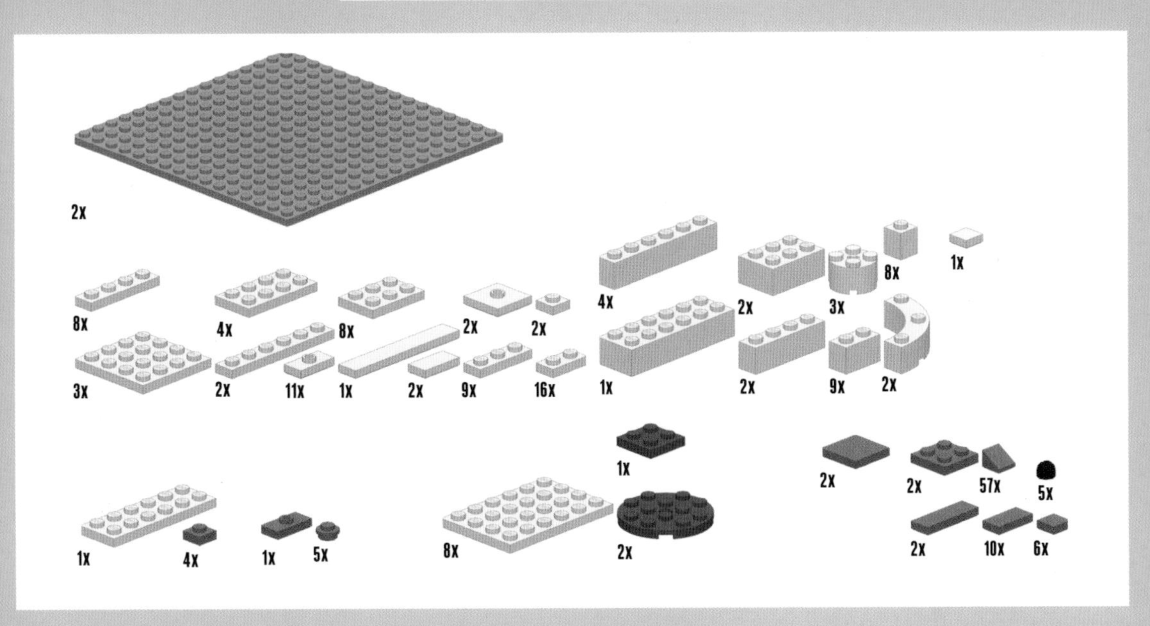
2x
8x
4x
8x
2x
2x
4x
2x
3x
8x
1x
3x
2x
11x
1x
2x
9x
16x
1x
2x
9x
2x
1x
2x
2x
57x
5x
1x
4x
1x
5x
8x
2x
2x
10x
6x

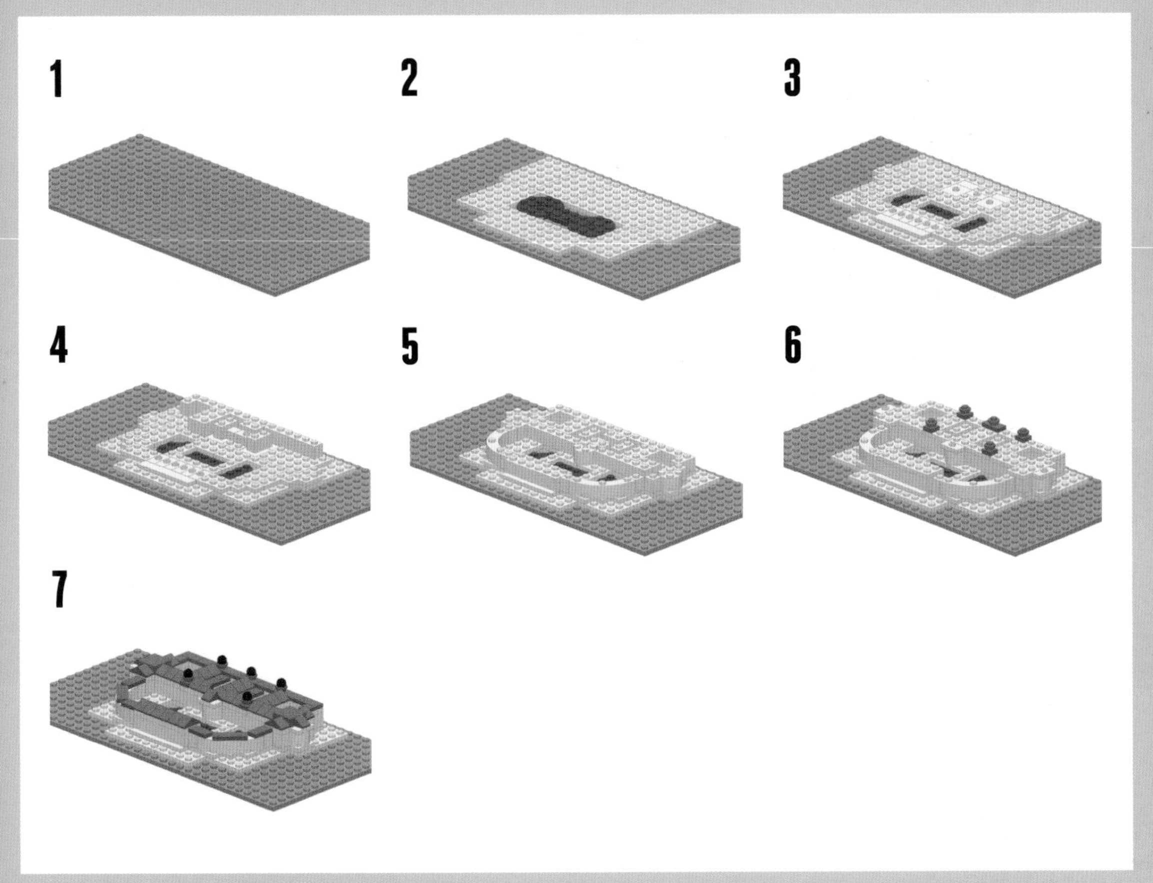
1
2
3
4
5
6
7

KRAKOW

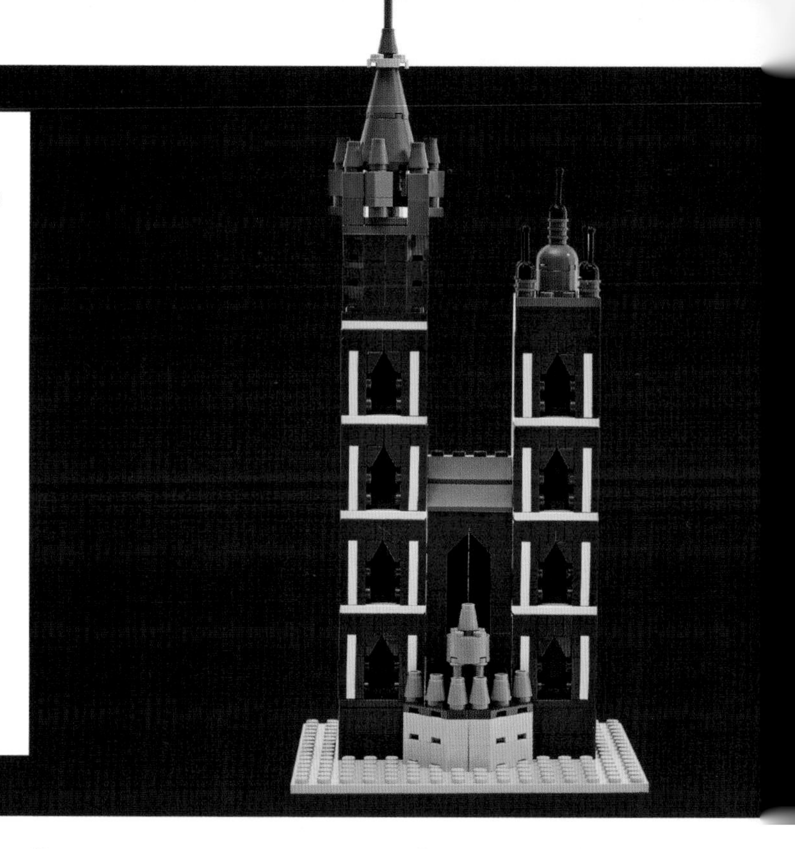

KRAKOW CATHEDRAL

The tower on the left in this picture is an eight-sided tower, which is quite difficult to replicate in LEGO. It consists of eight separate towers rising together around one central, taller tower. It was hard work, but the result is very pleasing!

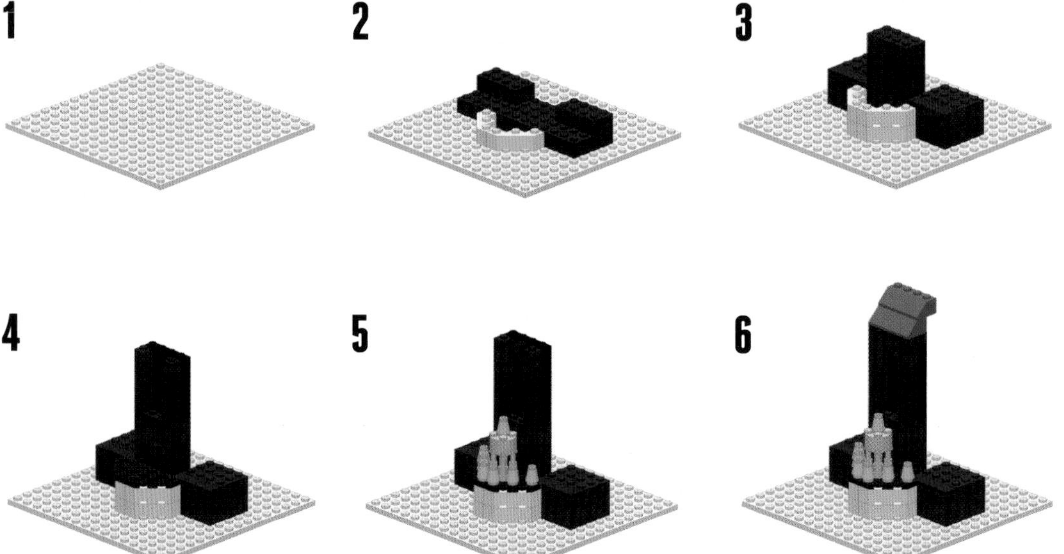

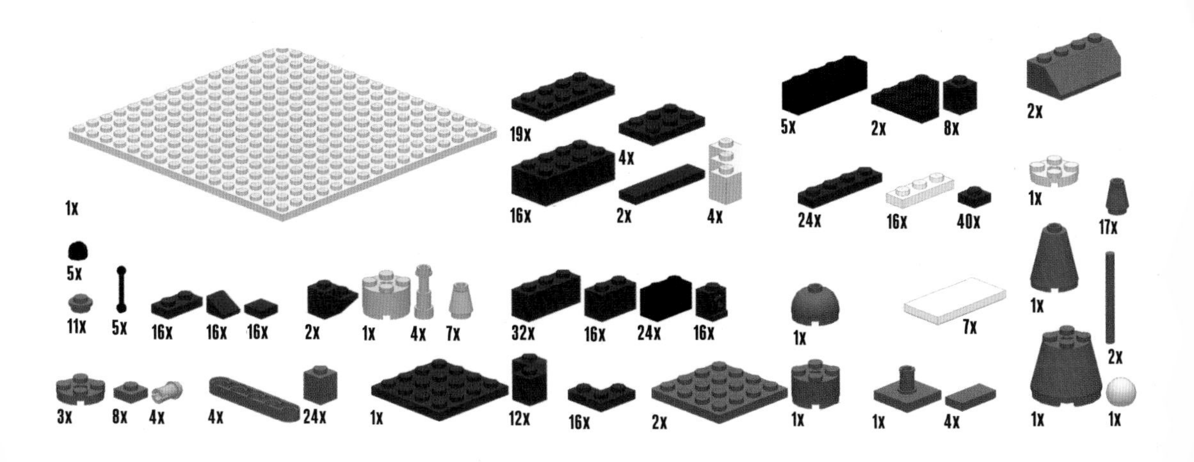
1x
19x
4x
16x
2x
4x
5x
2x
8x
2x
24x
16x
40x
1x
17x
5x
11x
5x
16x
16x
16x
2x
1x
4x
7x
32x
16x
24x
16x
1x
7x
1x
2x
3x
8x
4x
4x
24x
1x
12x
16x
2x
1x
1x
4x
1x
1x

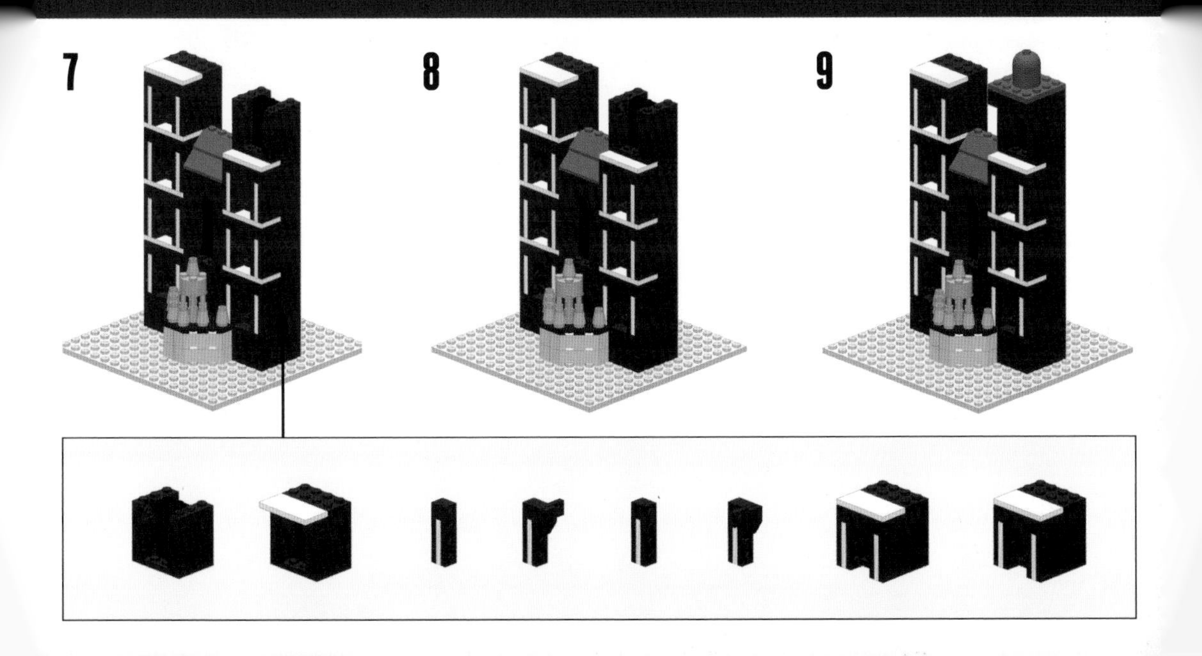
7
8
9

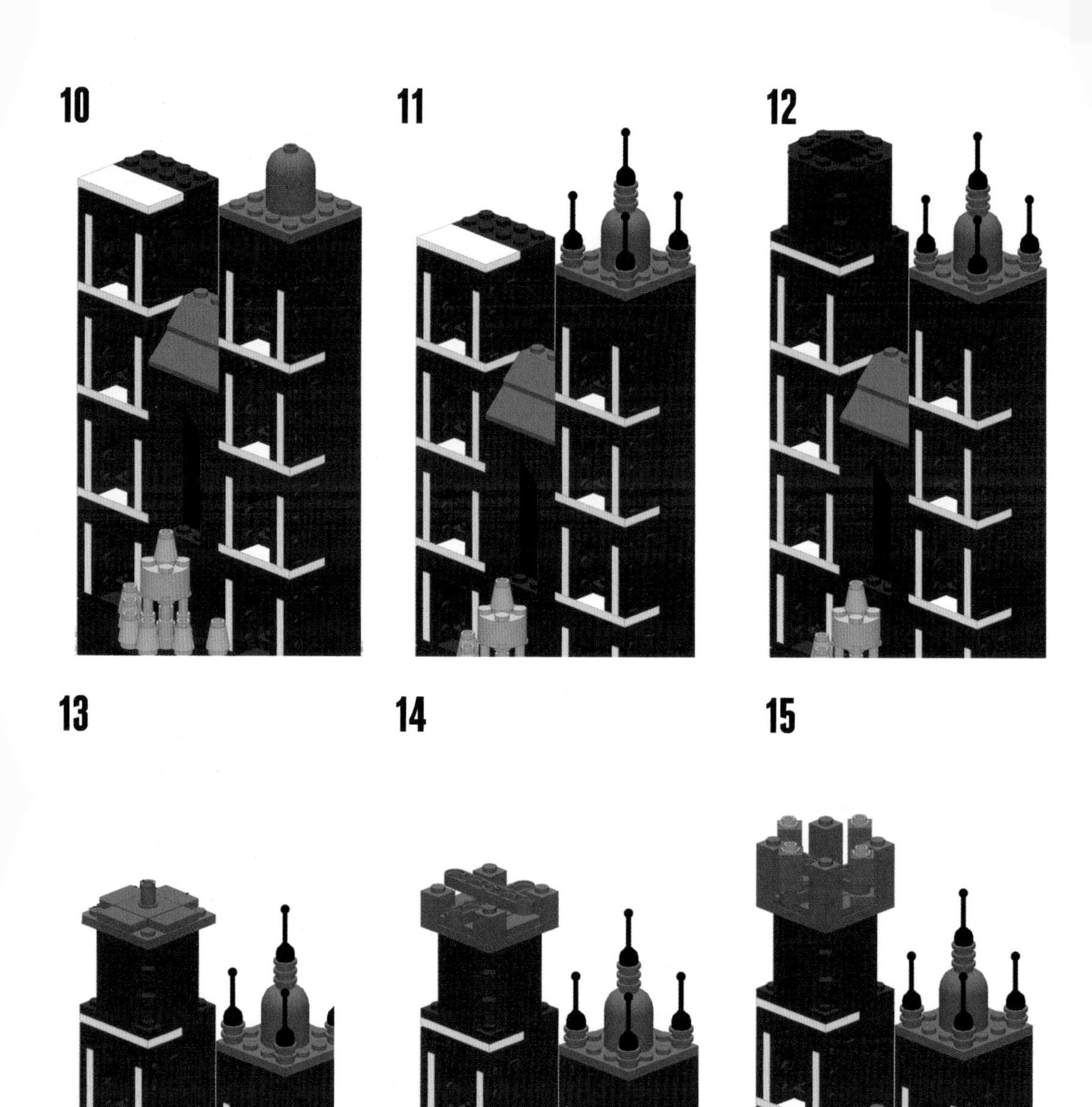
10
11
12
13
14
15

16

17

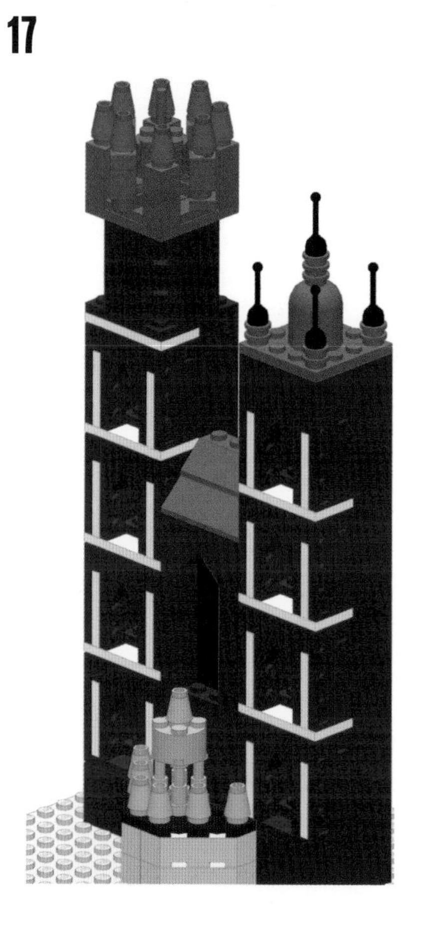

18

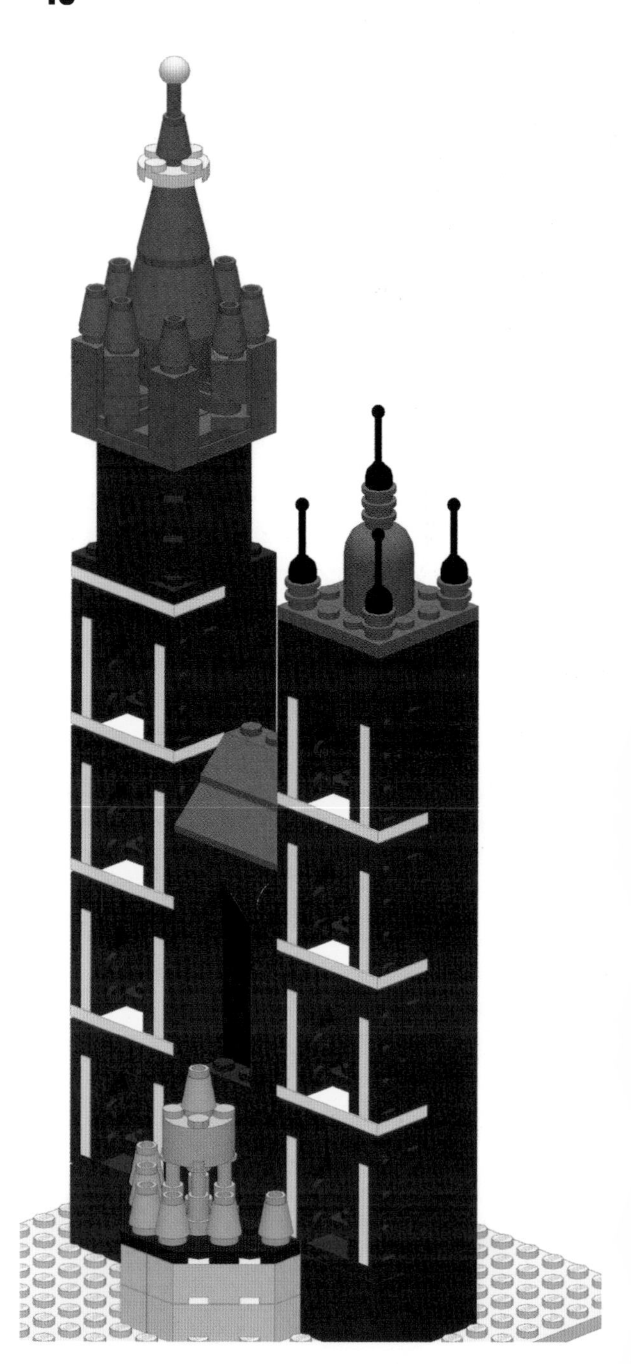

MOSCOW

BOLSHOI BALLET

This is the home of the Bolshoi Ballet and Bolshoi Opera, two of the greatest and oldest theatre companies in the world. The columns used on the outside are pieces called 1x2 plate with bar, used sideways to emulate columns. This technique was used on the 'New York-New York' hotel's skyline as well.

The scene in the inset picture (right) is my artist's impression of what a show at the Bolshoi might look like. (Can you tell I've never been?)

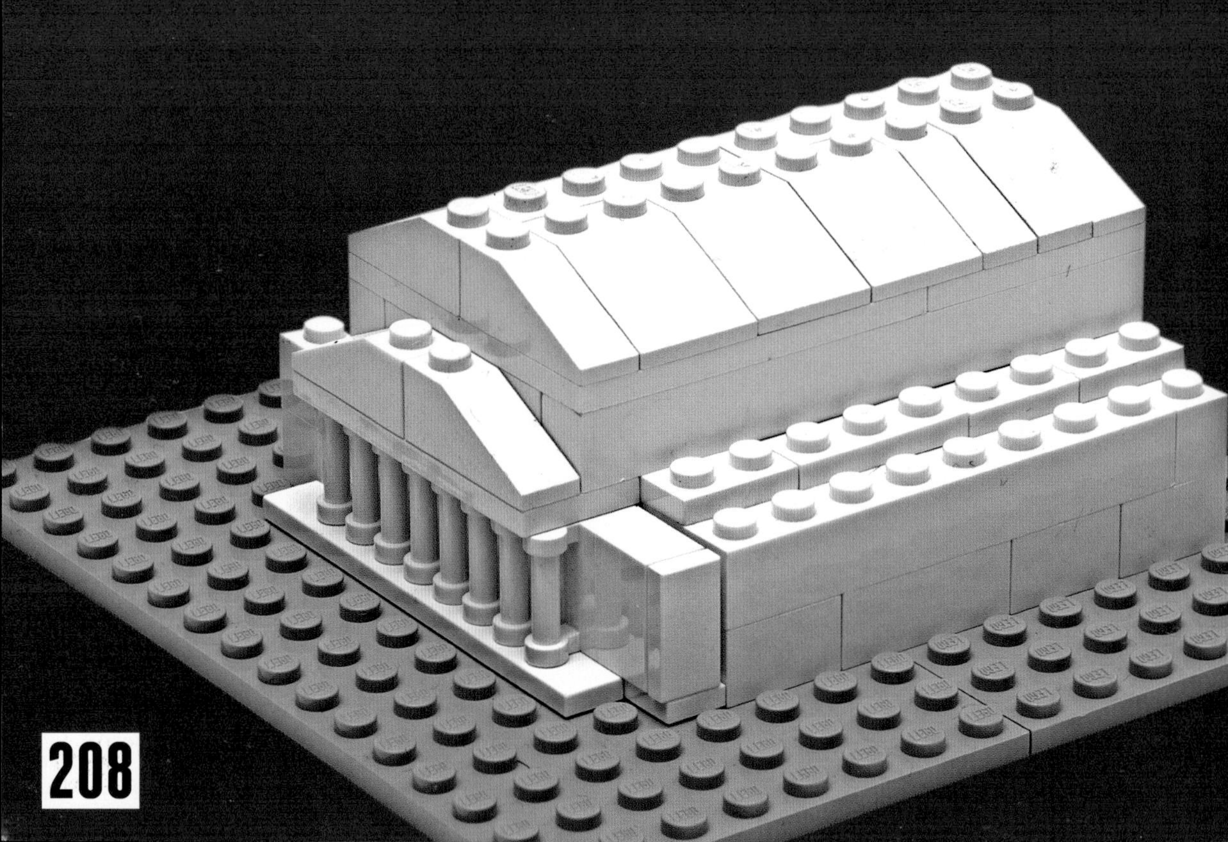

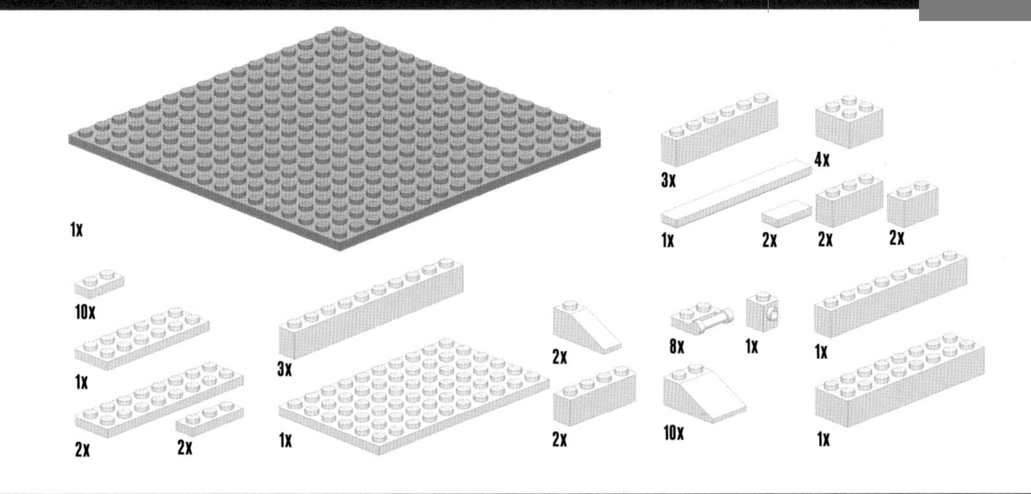
1x
3x
4x
1x
2x
2x
2x
10x
1x
2x
2x
3x
1x
2x
2x
8x
1x
1x
10x
1x

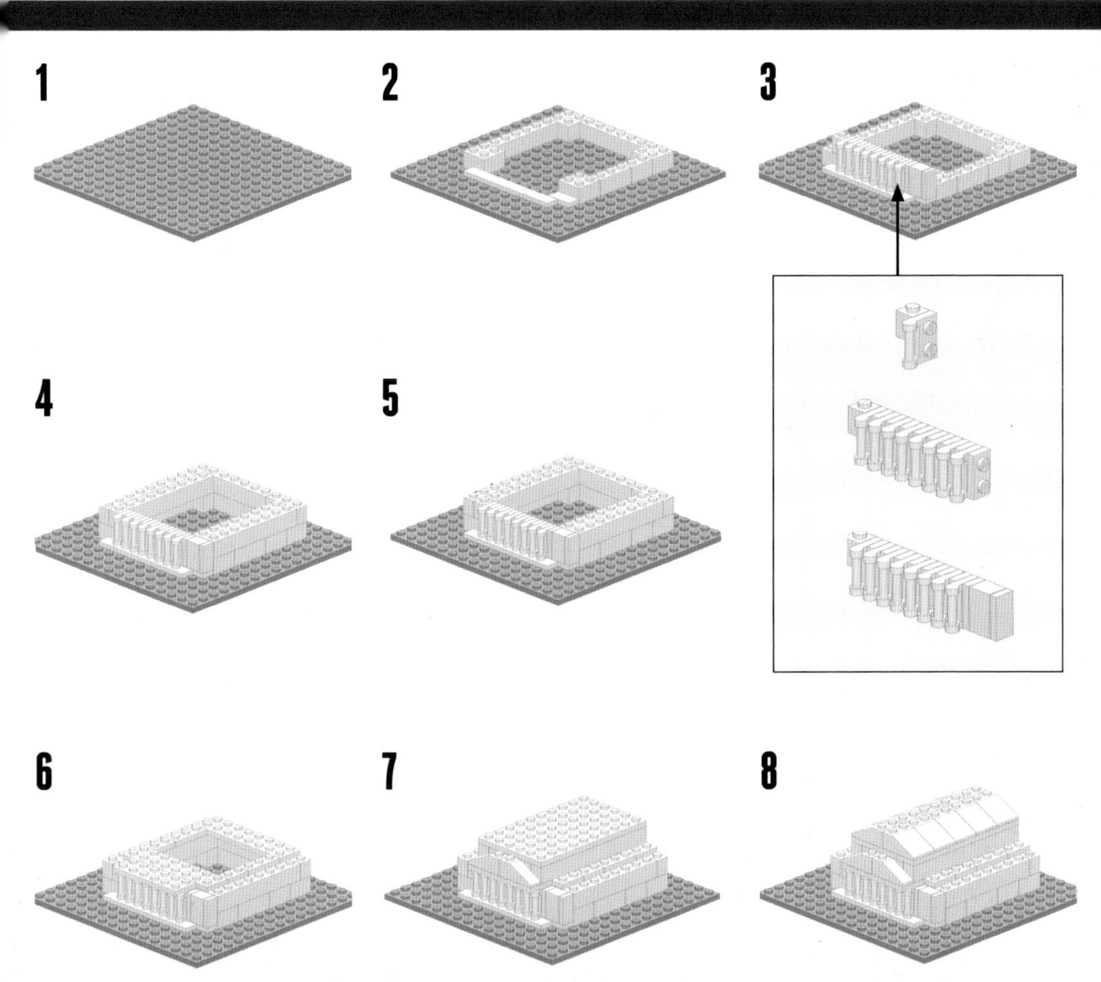
1
2
3
4
5
6
7
8

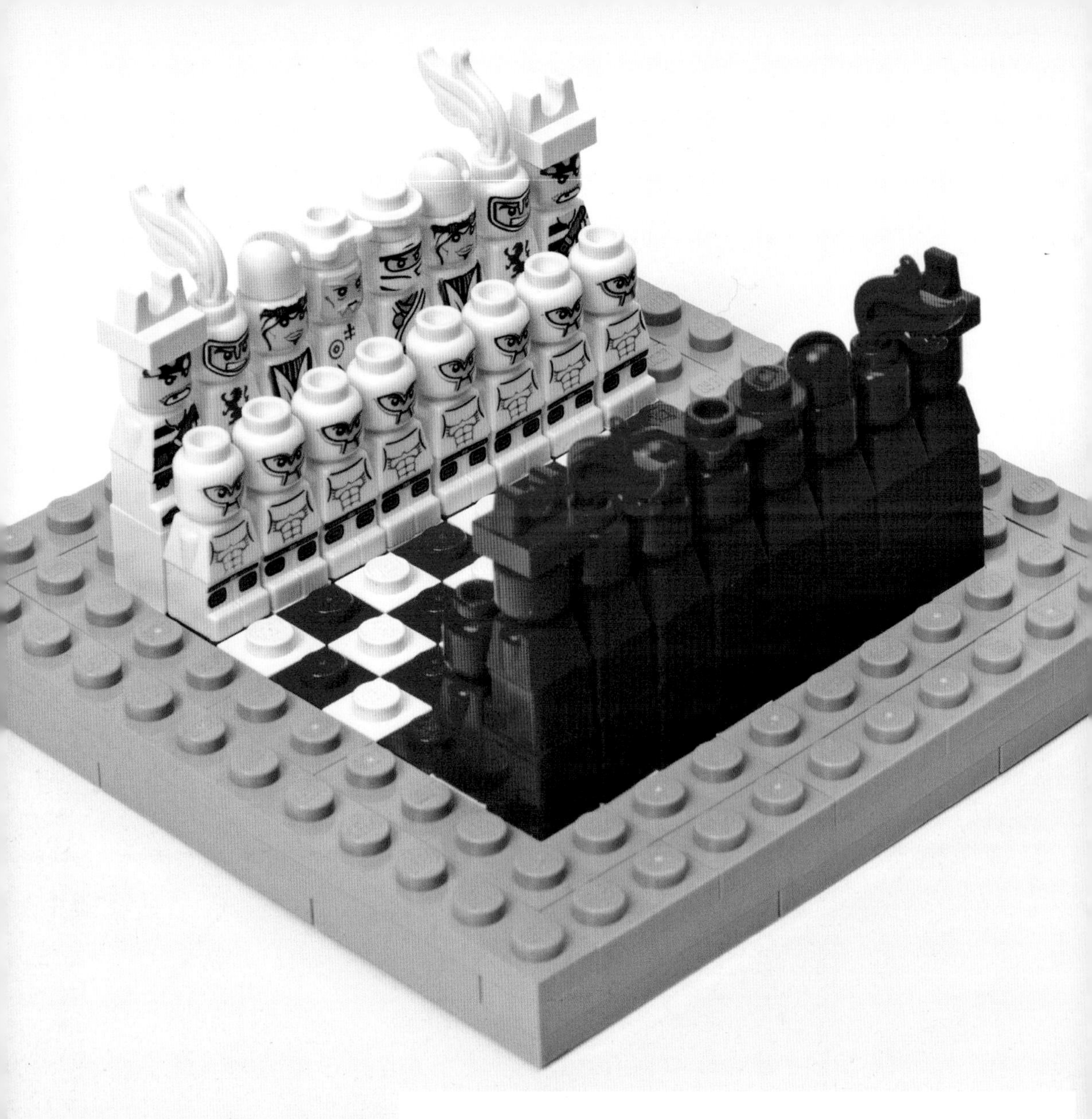

CHESS BOARD

LEGO® Construction by Teresa 'Kitty' Elsmore

Size: 5 cm (2 in) high, 10 cm (4 in) long and wide

Bricks: 170

Scale: Minifig scale

The inspiration for this model was a LEGO walled garden, which Kitty is creating, and she wanted a chess set for her minifigs to move around on as life-sized pieces.

The challenge in constructing this model was finding the microfigs used to build it, which not only had to match and come in pairs, but also had to be in both red and white. For the non-pawn pieces, Kitty had to find tiny elements she could use for their headwear to differentiate them, also in red and white.

FOUNTAIN OF THE PEOPLE'S FRIENDSHIP

Architects: K.G. Topuradze & G.D. Konstantinovskiy

Sculptors: Joseph Chaikov, E.V. Bazhenova, P.I. Dobrynin et al (1954)

LEGO® Edition by Warren Elsmore

Size: 10 cm (4 in) high, 25 cm (10 in) long and wide

Bricks: 200

Scale: Minifig scale

This is a well-known fountain built during the Soviet Era – and is the largest in Moscow. Covered in gold plate and featuring statues that represent the different nationalities and republics of the then Soviet Union, the real fountain is extraordinarily lavish. We hope the LEGO version also looks appropriately opulent.

ST. BASIL'S CATHEDRAL

Architects: Barma & Postnik Yakovlev (1555)

LEGO® Edition by Arthur Gugick

Size: Over 51 cm (20 in) wide and tall

Bricks: Over 20,000

Scale: approximately 1:110

St. Basil's was built by Ivan the Terrible to commemorate a series of military victories in present-day Bulgaria, and stands in the geometric centre of Moscow – the city has grown around it for more than 500 years. After the Taj Mahal, it was the second most complex model Arthur had ever built. It measures 51 cm (20 in) square and incorporates over 20,000 pieces. The onion domes with the embedded spirals were so complicated that Arthur actually wrote his own computer software to help him construct them.

CAPE TOWN

LIGHTHOUSE

The diagonal stripe across this lighthouse, which was the first solid lighthouse built on the South African coast (its first light was lit in 1824), is very distinctive and had to be painstakingly re-created. The effect is very pleasing, though, making it all worthwhile.

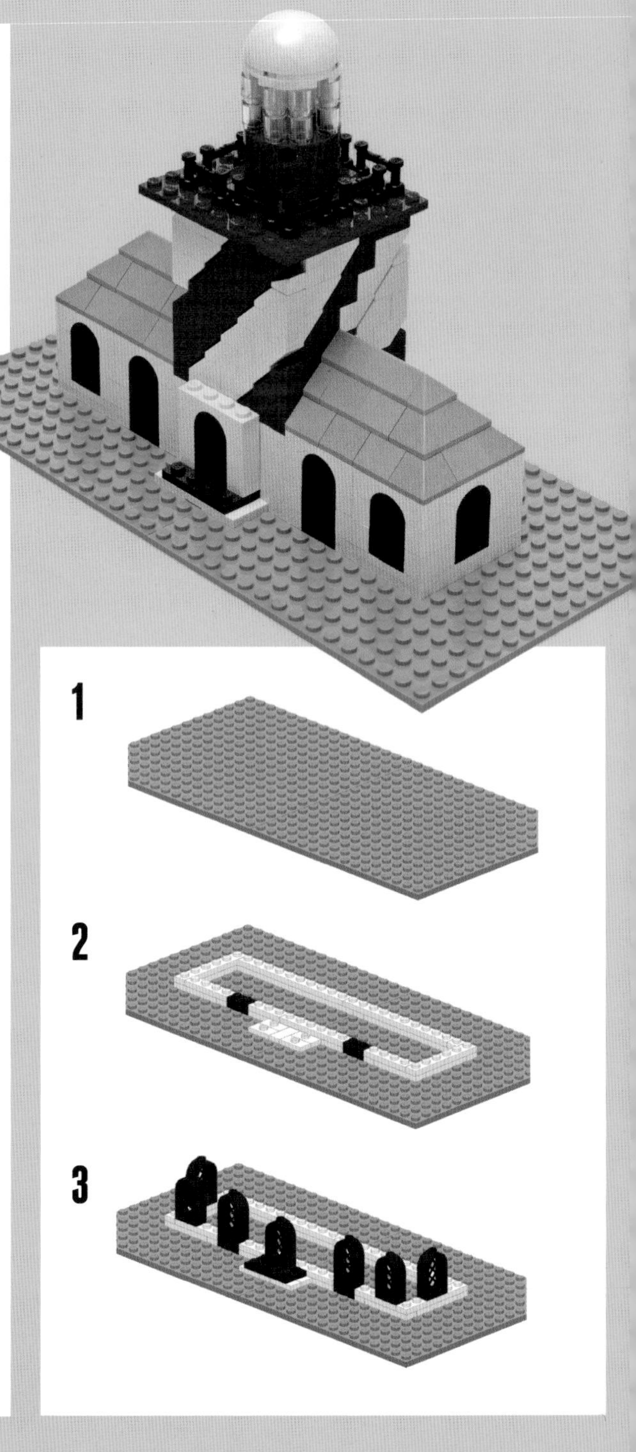

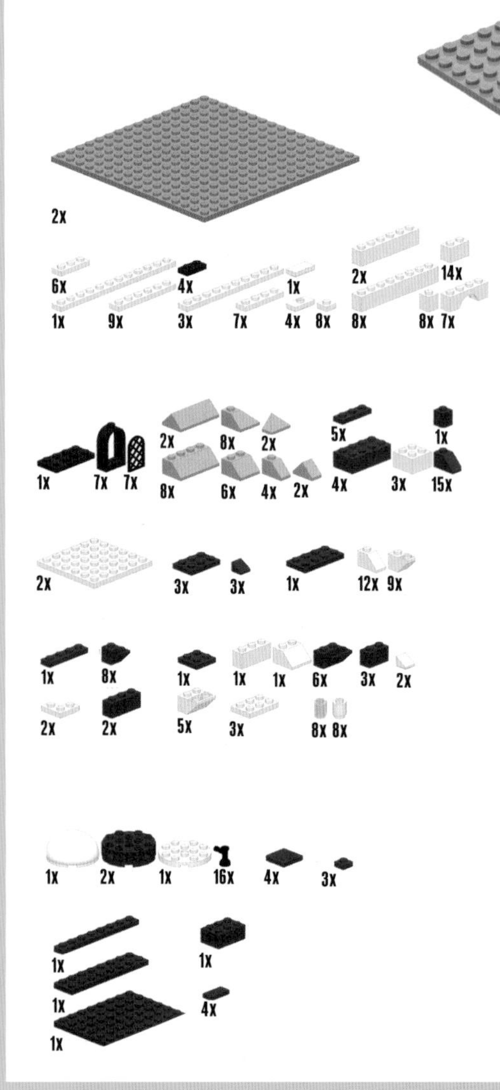

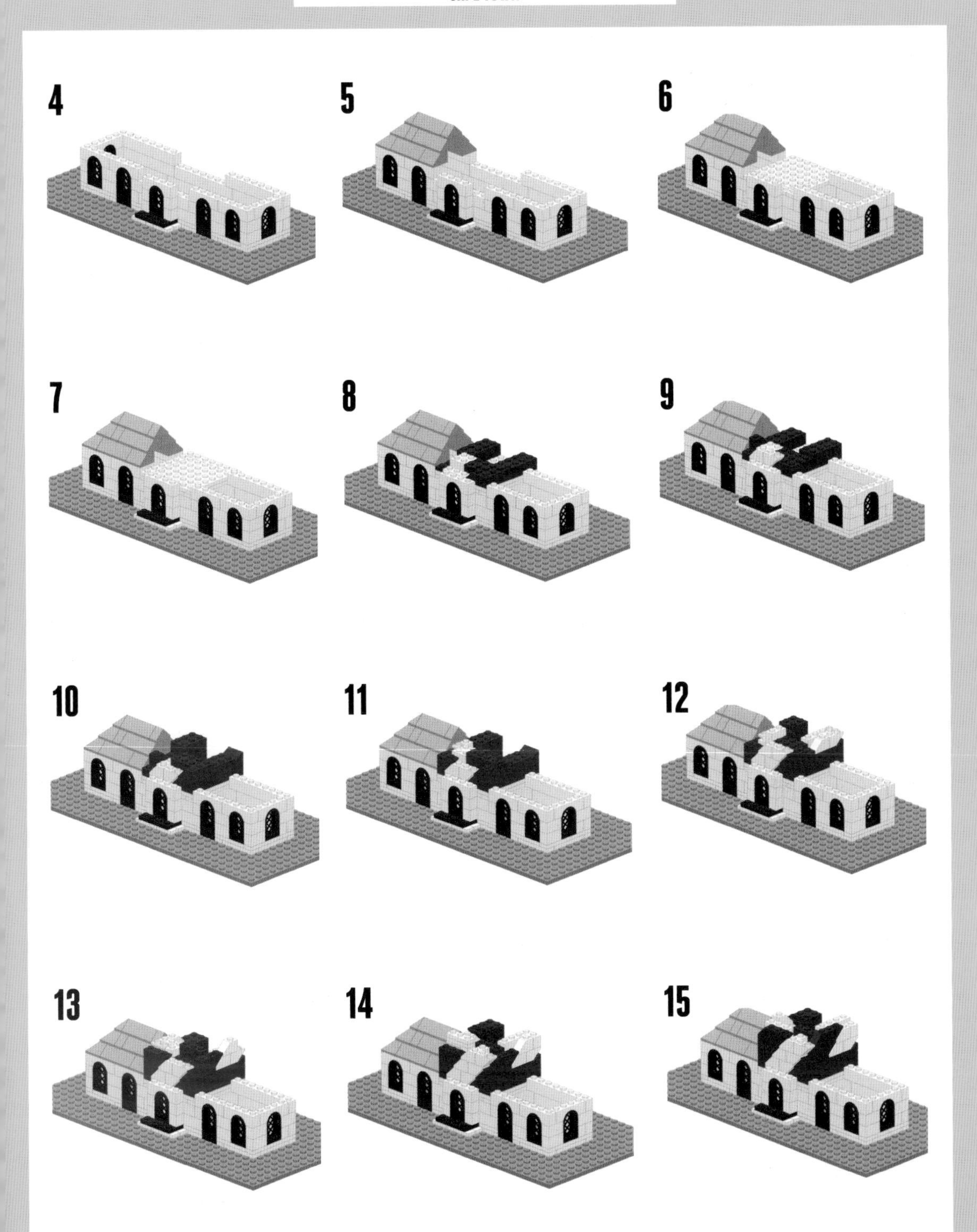
4
5
6
7
8
9
10
11
12
13
14
15

16

17

18

19

20

21

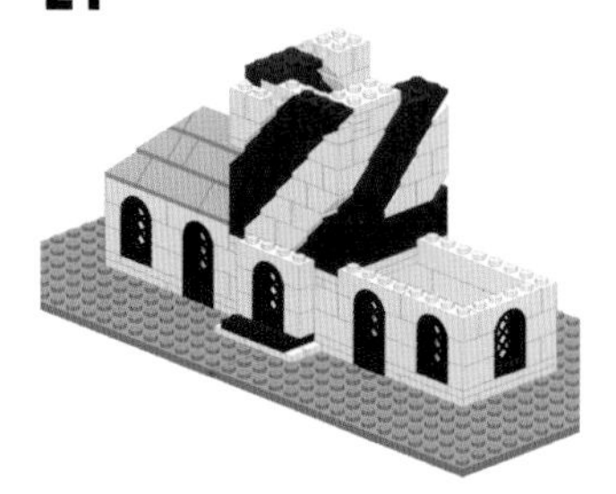

22

23

24

25

26

PENGUIN COLONY

These very cute African penguins are made out of LEGO® bricks. Their beaks are special pieces usually used to hold a minifig accessory or a horizontal bar in a larger structure.

Penguins have established large colonies on two beaches near Cape Town – Boulders Beach and Stony Point – where you can get almost as close to them as the man below, who is making himself very popular by feeding them fish!

TABLE MOUNTAIN AERIAL CABLEWAY

The cable car has microfigs inside because it's on such a small scale. The pieces, which make up the actual cable car, are probably ten years old and are no longer available. We were lucky to come across them, as they are crucial to this model. In the photo, the car is hanging from a genuine wire, which can be reproduced – the cable car can be pushed backwards and forwards along it.

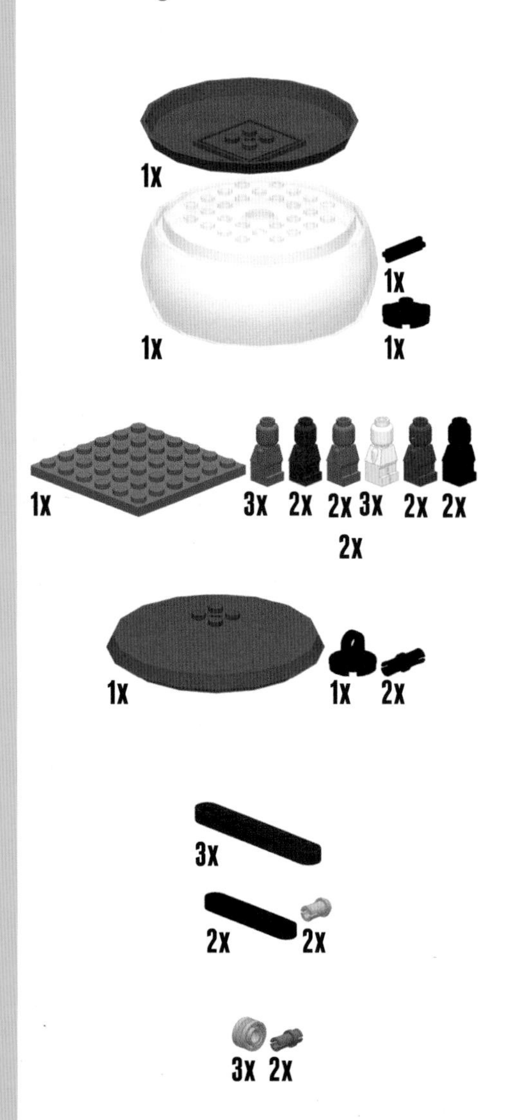

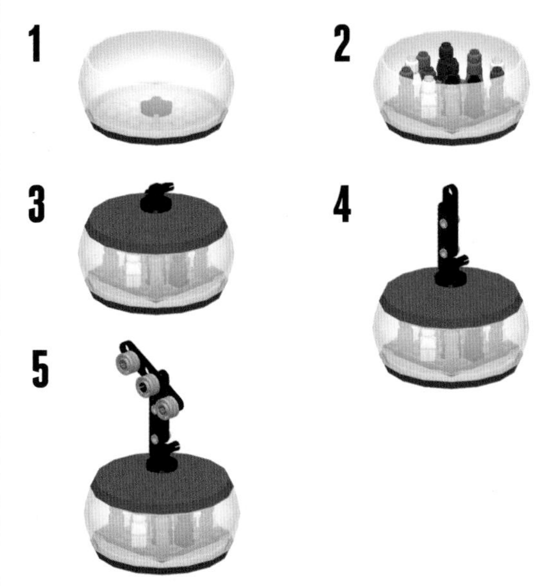

DUBAI

PALM JUMEIRAH

Architects: HHCP Architects
LEGO® Edition by Teresa 'Kitty' Elsmore
Size: 51 cm (20 in) tall and wide
Bricks: 4,100

This is a flat 2-D mosaic that attempts to represent one of the three massive and extraordinary Dubai Palm Islands, artificial archipelegos created using land reclamation. Dark blue was used for the sea, and a mixture of grey and beige represent the land and beach elements, that provide the palm shape.

THE BURJ AL ARAB

Architect: Tom Wright (1999)

LEGO® Edition by Spencer Rezkalla

Size: 49 cm (19½ in) high, 38 cm (15 in) long and wide

Bricks: 5,621

Scale: approximately 1:650

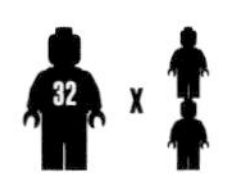

This massive model took nearly seven months to design and build. Reproducing the hotel's billowing sail-shaped form became possible by employing LEGO Flexi-tubes to outline the curving edges of outer trusses and the central sweeping white curtain wall. The model sits on a base plate composed of three layers of plate elements working together to reproduce the appearance of the Persian Gulf's sparking blue waters. The topmost layer consists of rare trans-light blue plates. Beneath lies a layer of transparent plates, diffusing the appearance of the studs below. The lowest level is composed of solid coloured plates of varying shades of blue. They are arranged in a gradual gradient of ever-darkening colour, giving the appearance of deeper water further from the shoreline.

AGRA

TAJ MAHAL

Architect: Ustad Ahmad Lahauri (1632)
LEGO® Edition by Arthur Gugick
Size: 65 cm (25½ in) high, 76 cm (30 in) long, 127 cm (50 in) wide.
Bricks: 28,000
Scale: approximately 1:265

Built by Mughal emperor Shah Jahan to commemorate his third wife, the Taj Mahal is one of the most beautiful tombs in the world and a masterpiece of Muslim architecture. Re-creating it proved to be the largest and most complex LEGO project that Arthur had ever undertaken. It took him more than four months, and the final model measures 76 by 127 cm (30 by 50 in) and contains over 28,000 pieces. It was built for an independent Australian movie called *Taj*. Winston Furlong, the movie's director, asked for some of the dimensions to be distorted to make sure that it looked more accurate on film.

KUALA LUMPUR

PETRONAS TOWERS

This model was very interesting to build. To re-create the style of the building, with its many floors and many differently angled edges, the model was built almost entirely out of layers of 1x1 round plates, using a combination of grey and clear ones. These were arranged into circles that, due to the nature of LEGO®, would only work at certain scales. That's why one level is actually square, when it should be round. At this scale, certain compromises will always have to be made. If you have more than 1,000 1x1 plates lying around (and why wouldn't you?), this is the ideal model to build.

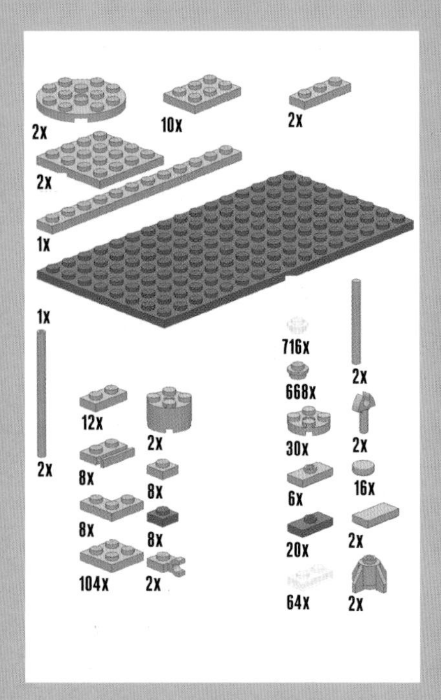

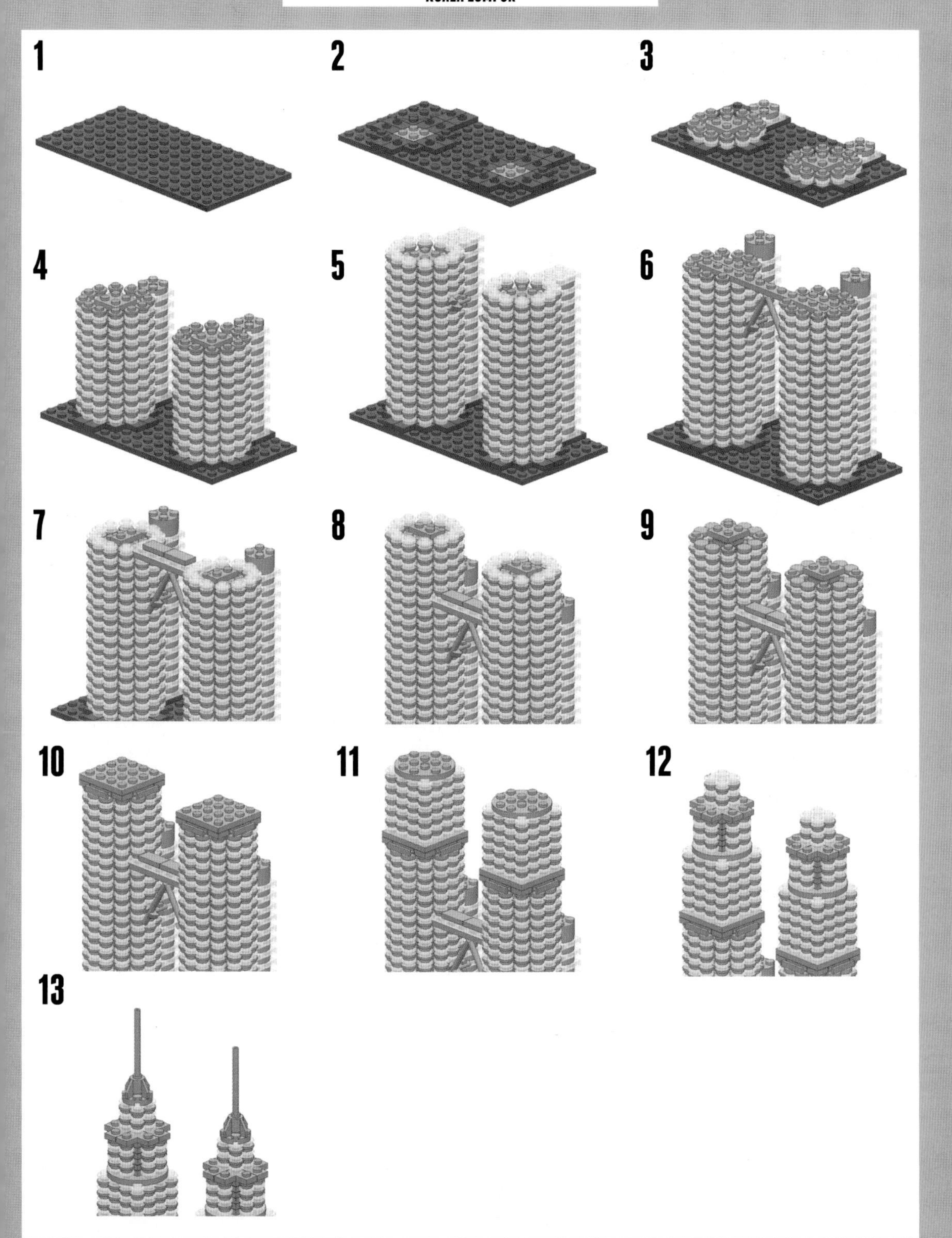
1
2
3
4
5
6
7
8
9
10
11
12
13

SINGAPORE

MARINA BAY SANDS

A spectacular hotel which also touts itself as the most expensive casino in the world, costing more than $8 billion to construct (including the price of the land). Luckily the LEGO® model wasn't quite that expensive...

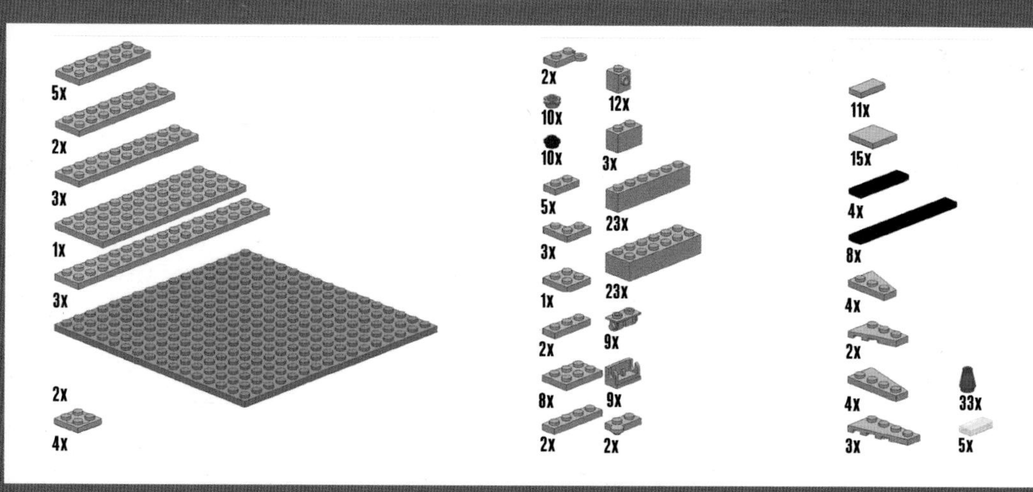
5x
2x
3x
1x
3x
2x
4x
2x
12x
10x
10x
3x
5x
23x
3x
23x
1x
2x
9x
8x
9x
2x
2x
11x
15x
4x
8x
4x
2x
4x
33x
3x
5x

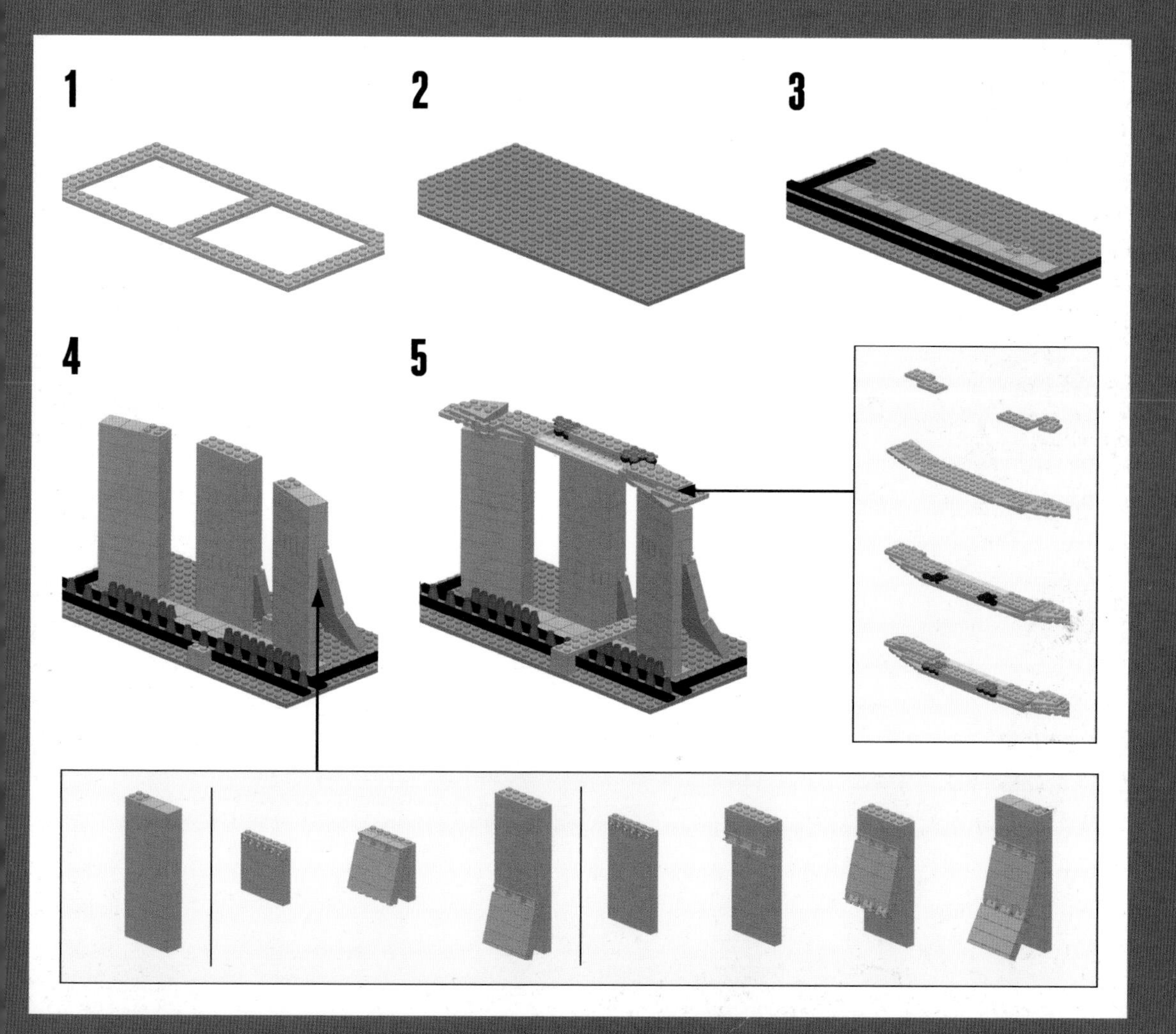
1
2
3
4
5

MERLION

LEGO® Construction by Warren Elsmore
Size: 56 cm (22 in) tall, 25.5 cm (10 in) wide
Bricks: 2,050

The merlion is a mythical creature with the head of a lion and the body of a fish. It's the national symbol of Singapore, which reflects two important influences – the city's beginnings as a fishing village, and the definition of the name Singapore itself, which means 'lion city'. This model was created using a straightforward mosaic technique.

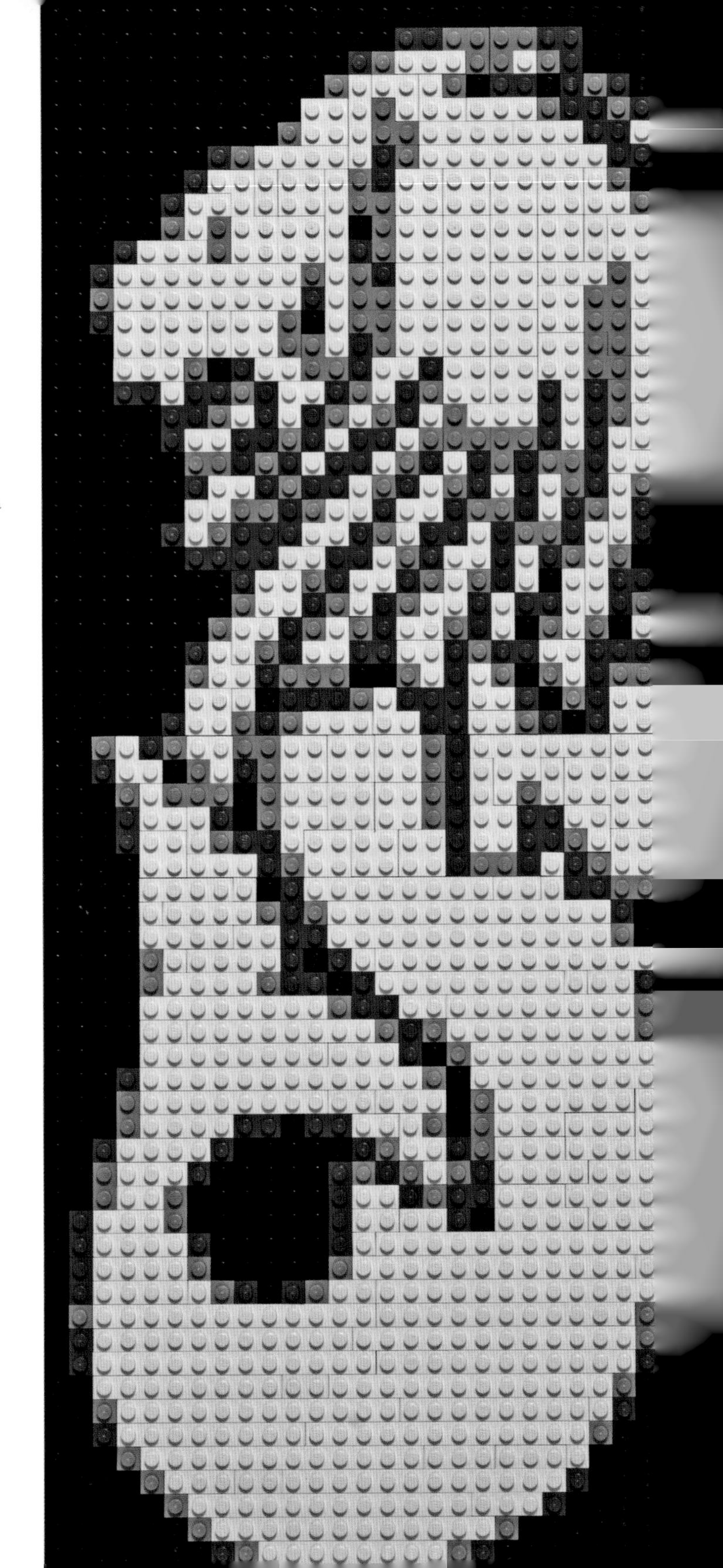

HONG KONG

JUNK

This is a strikingly convincing representation of the famous boats that sail in the Hong Kong harbour. Junks have been in use since ancient times, and are thought to have developed from simple bamboo rafts with high sterns. This is a rewarding model for the novice LEGO® builder: it is easy to construct and looks very distinctive when finished.

2x

1x 2x

2x 2x

2x

1x 1x 1x 1x

3x 2x 2x

1x 4x

1x 1x 2x

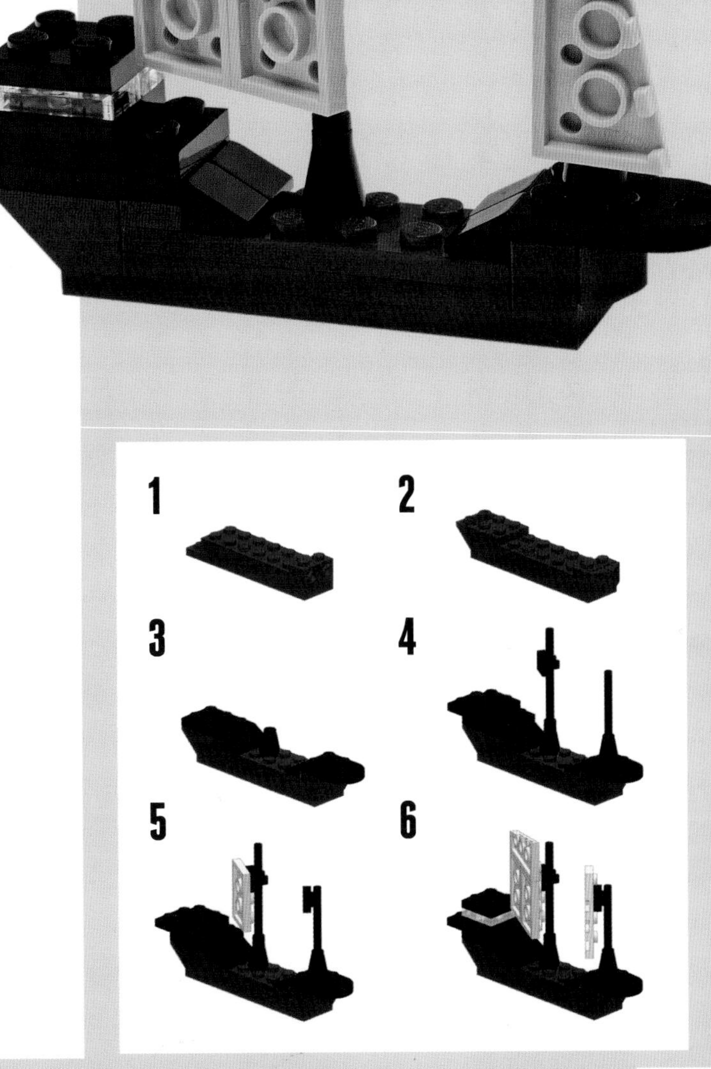

STAR FERRY

This is quite different from the junk vessel. It's a representation of the ferries that run constantly between Hong Kong island and Kowloon. The model uses relatively few parts, but those that are used are pointing in different directions and have to be assembled with care.

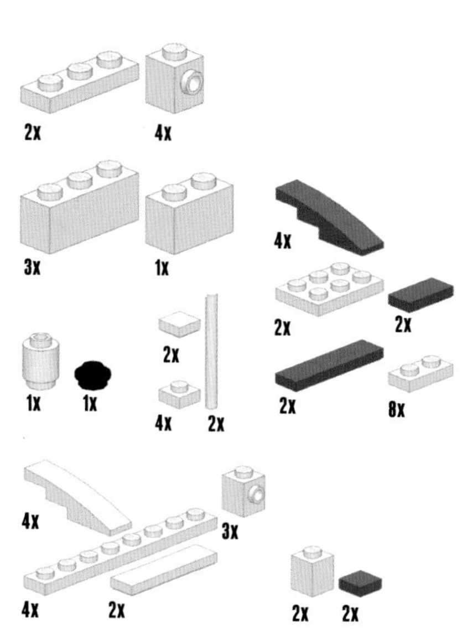

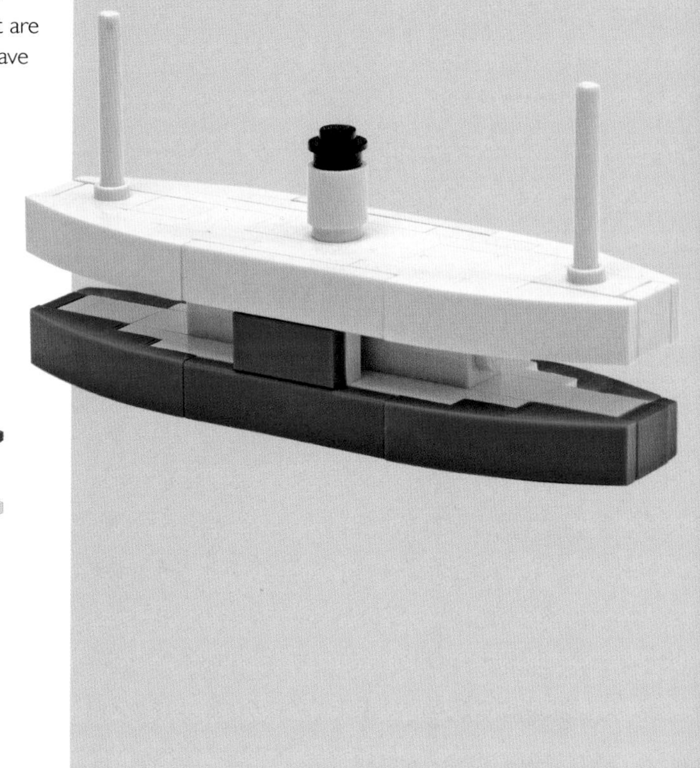

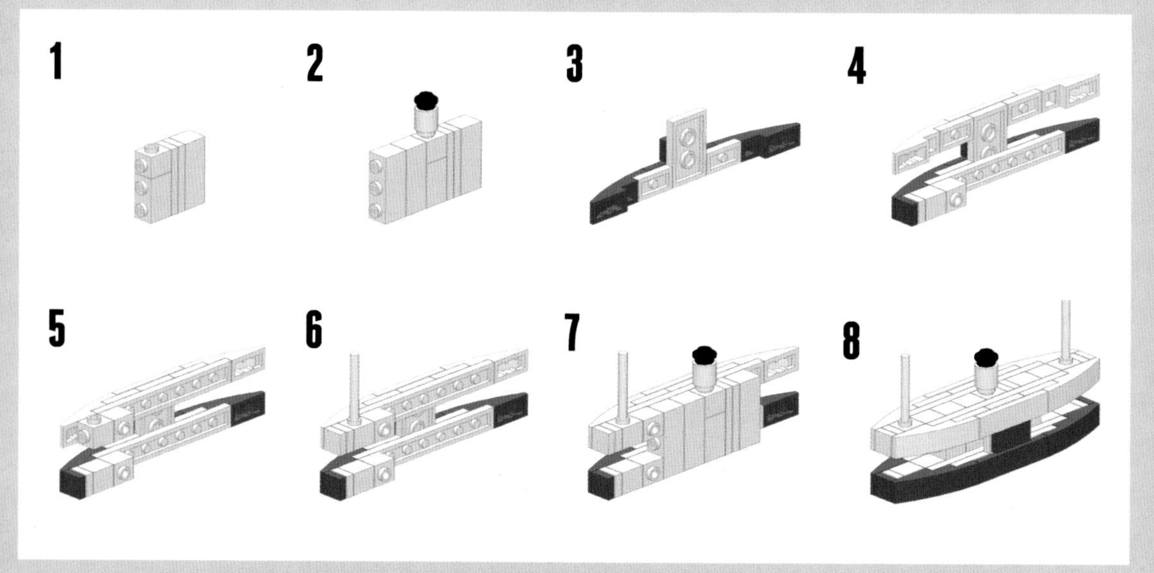

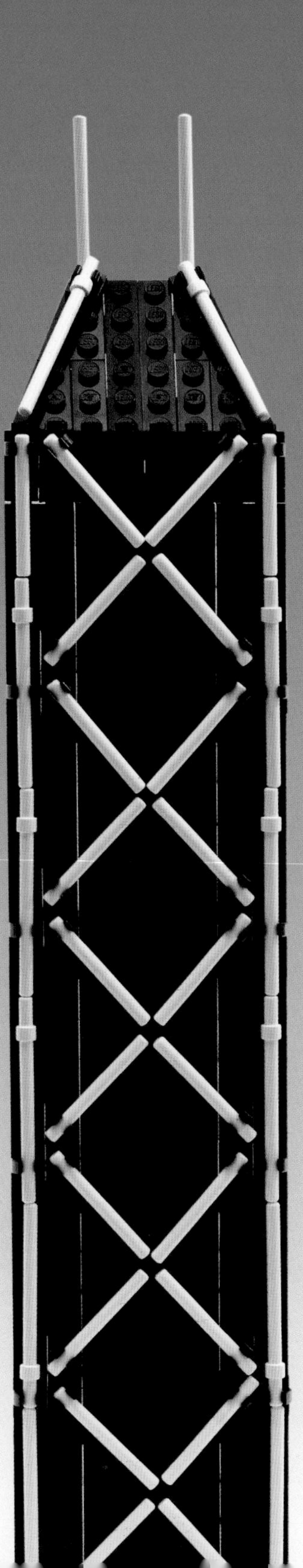

BANK OF CHINA TOWER

Architect: I.M. Pei (1985)

LEGO® Edition by Warren Elsmore

Size: 32 cm (12½ in) high, 7 cm (2¾ in) wide
Bricks: 240
Scale: 1:700

The white crisscross structure in this model is actually made from pieces stuck onto the front. On the original building, however, they are the steel girders that perform the essential load-bearing task of holding the whole thing up. The real tower is also clad with reflective glass, rather than being jet black as it is here, which gives the distinct impression of an evil wizard's tower.

CONTAINER SHIP

LEGO® Edition by Tom Groombridge

Size: 87 cm (2 ft 2 in) high, 3.15 m (10 ft 4 in) long, 56 cm (1 ft 10 in) wide

Bricks: Over 25,000

Scale: 1:65

This was quite an arduous build, to say the least! First, Tom Groombridge tried to design it on the computer and got as far as the hull – by which time the computer model already had 10,000 parts – before he got impatient and started on the real thing.

He started on the bow of the ship, and when it was really starting to take shape, he moved it and the whole thing imploded – eight hours of work and hundreds of bricks ended up in a big mess on the floor. The next version had a lot of internal added support, with the first 20 cm (7¾ inches) being almost solid brick. It was then safe to move, but was extremely heavy. Tom's favourite part was building the superstructure, adding all the details and dealing with challenges, such as attaching the handrails to the stairs and connecting the doors – although they might look simple, getting them to recess by half a stud meant a lot of parts were needed behind the wall to make it work.

Photography by Gareth Butterworth

LIPPO CENTRE ('THE KOALA TREE')

Architect: Paul Rudolph (1986)

LEGO® Edition by Warren Elsmore

Size: 36 cm (14 in) high, 10 cm (4 in) deep, 10 cm (4 in) wide

Bricks: 321

Scale: 1:450

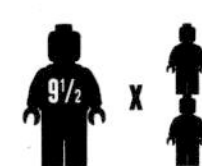

This famous skyscraper in Hong Kong is nicknamed the Koala Tree because its design looks as if koalas are climbing up on either side of the building towards the roof. It is a square tower with chamfered corners, and there is only one LEGO piece that works well for that effect. Unfortunately, this piece is only available in four colours: it should be grey, but by necessity it's black here.

SHANGHAI

PEARL TOWER

This tourist attraction was, for a long time, the tallest structure in China. There are a lot of pieces of LEGO® Technic in this model, including gears, rods and axles. The vertical parts in the tower are all Technic pieces, which are needed to connect to each other to represent the columns.

The parts listed in the bill of materials at the top of p.236 include all elements required for the boxed-out sections.

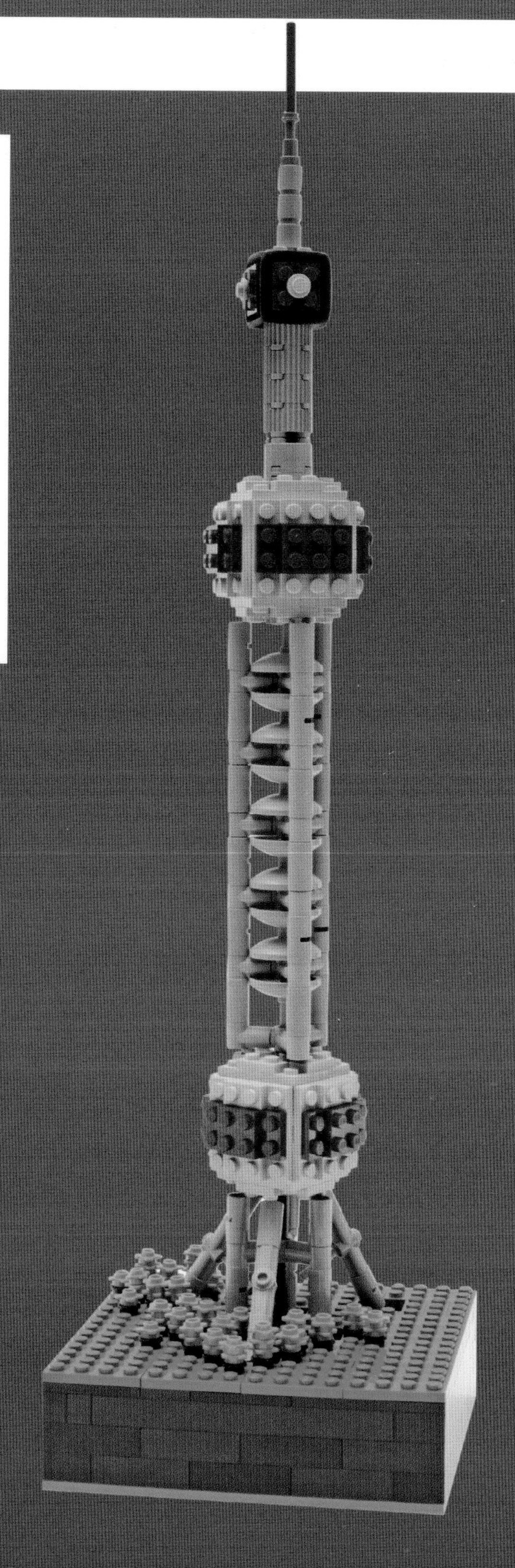

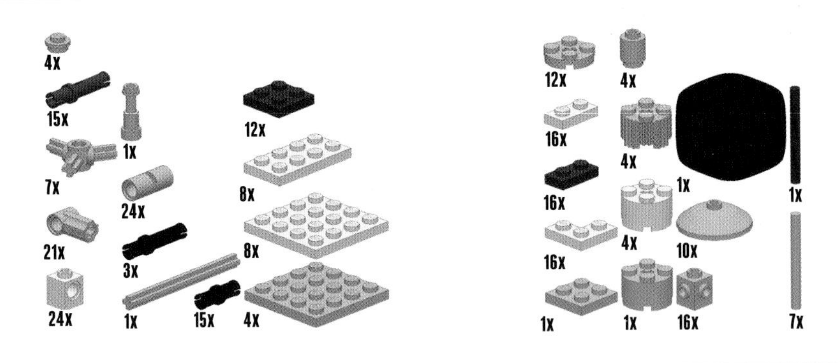
4x
15x
1x
7x
24x
21x
3x
24x
1x
15x
12x
8x
8x
4x
12x
4x
16x
4x
16x
1x
4x
16x
10x
1x
1x
1x
16x
1x
7x

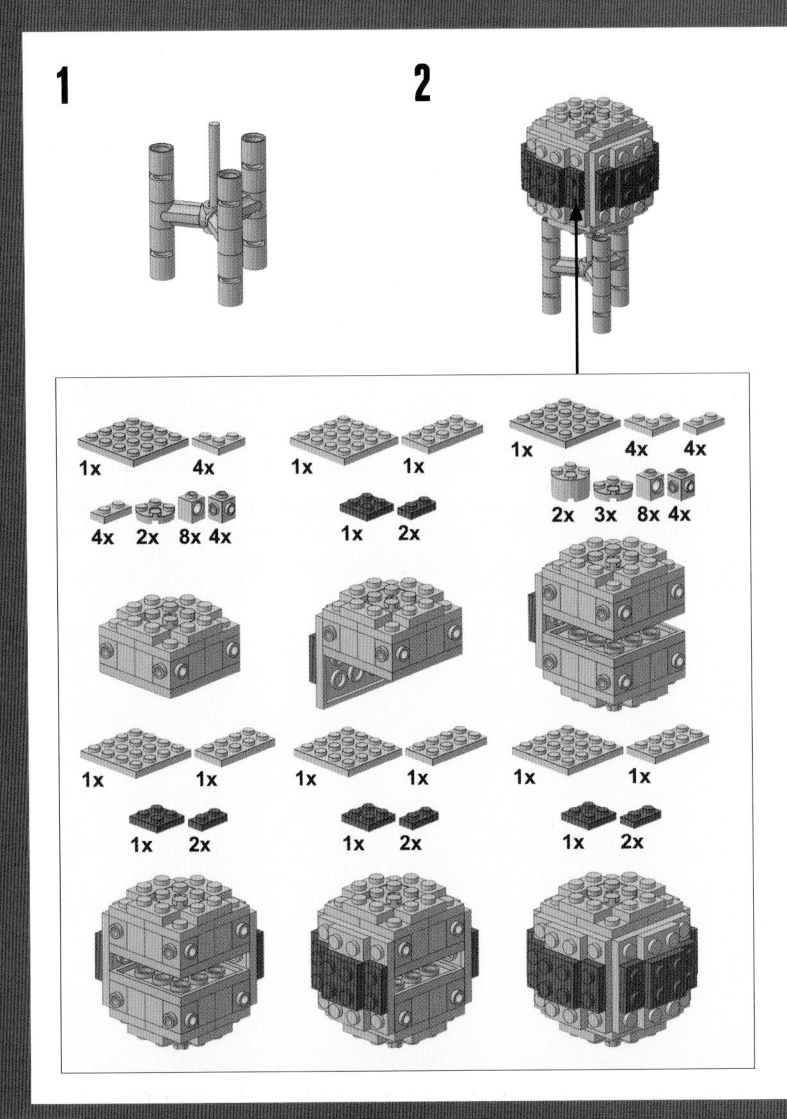
1
2
1x
4x
4x
2x
8x
4x
1x
1x
1x
2x
1x
4x
4x
2x
3x
8x
4x
1x
1x
1x
2x
1x
1x
1x
2x
1x
1x
1x
2x

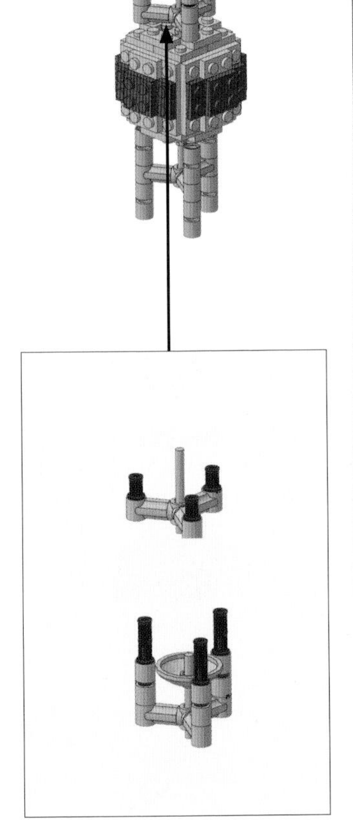
3

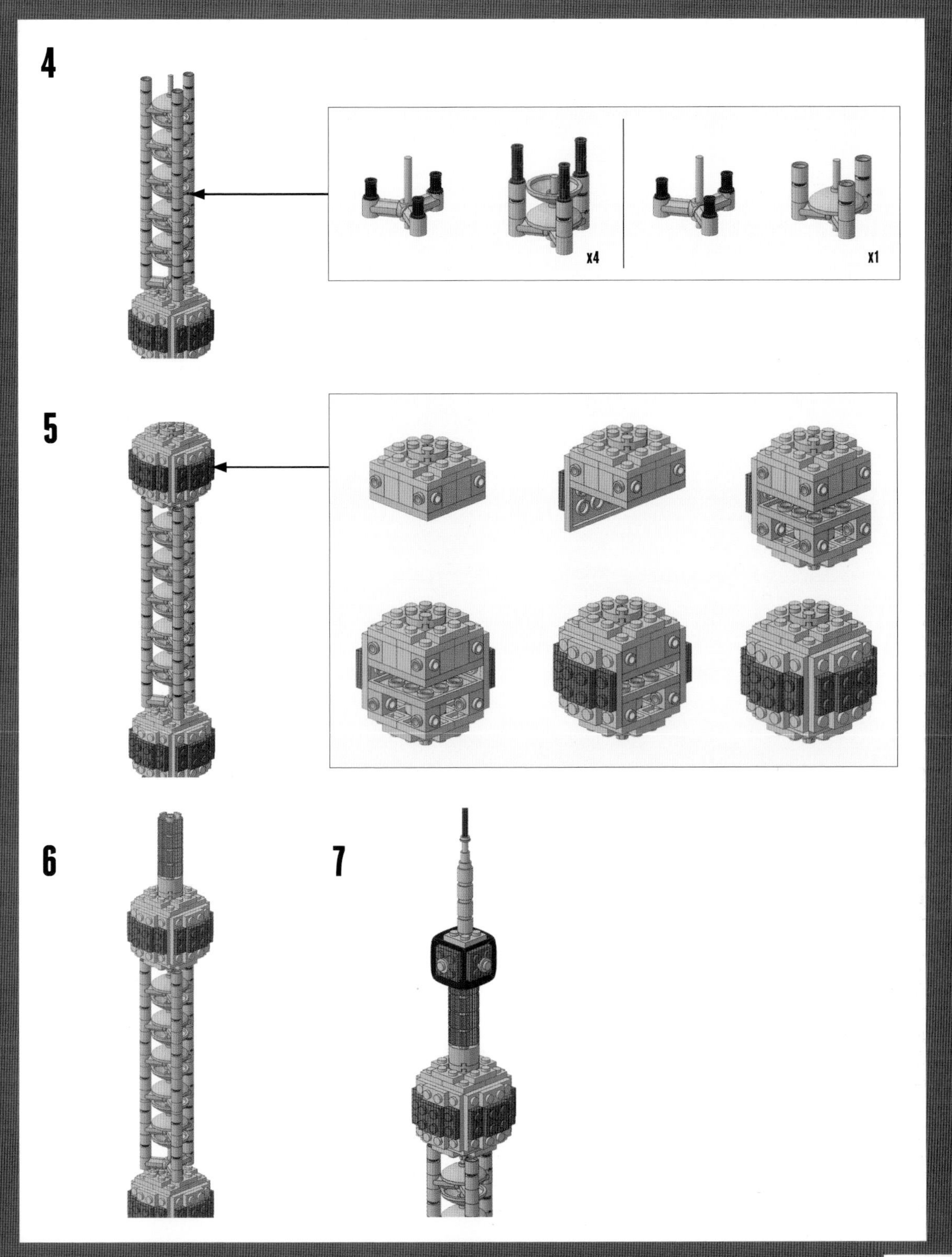
4
x4
x1
5
6
7

CHINESE GATE

LEGO® Construction by Warren Elsmore

Size: 19 cm (7½ in) high, 35 cm (13¾ in) wide, 10 cm (4 in) deep

Bricks: 2,500

Scale: 1:60

This is a representation of the traditional style of Chinese gates known as 'paifangs', of which there are many highly decorated and very beautiful examples. They originally separated cities into separate administrative blocks (or 'fangs'), but they now serve chiefly as stylistic ornaments.

SEOUL

CITY HALL

The blue part of this large government building in South Korea's capital is the new city hall, designed to look like a big wave. The old city hall underneath the wave, built in 1926, has been converted into a library.

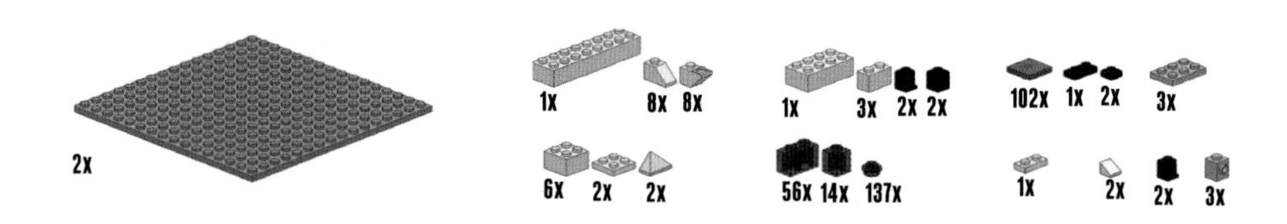
2x
1x
8x
8x
6x
2x
2x
1x
3x
2x
2x
56x
14x
137x
102x
1x
2x
3x
1x
2x
2x
3x

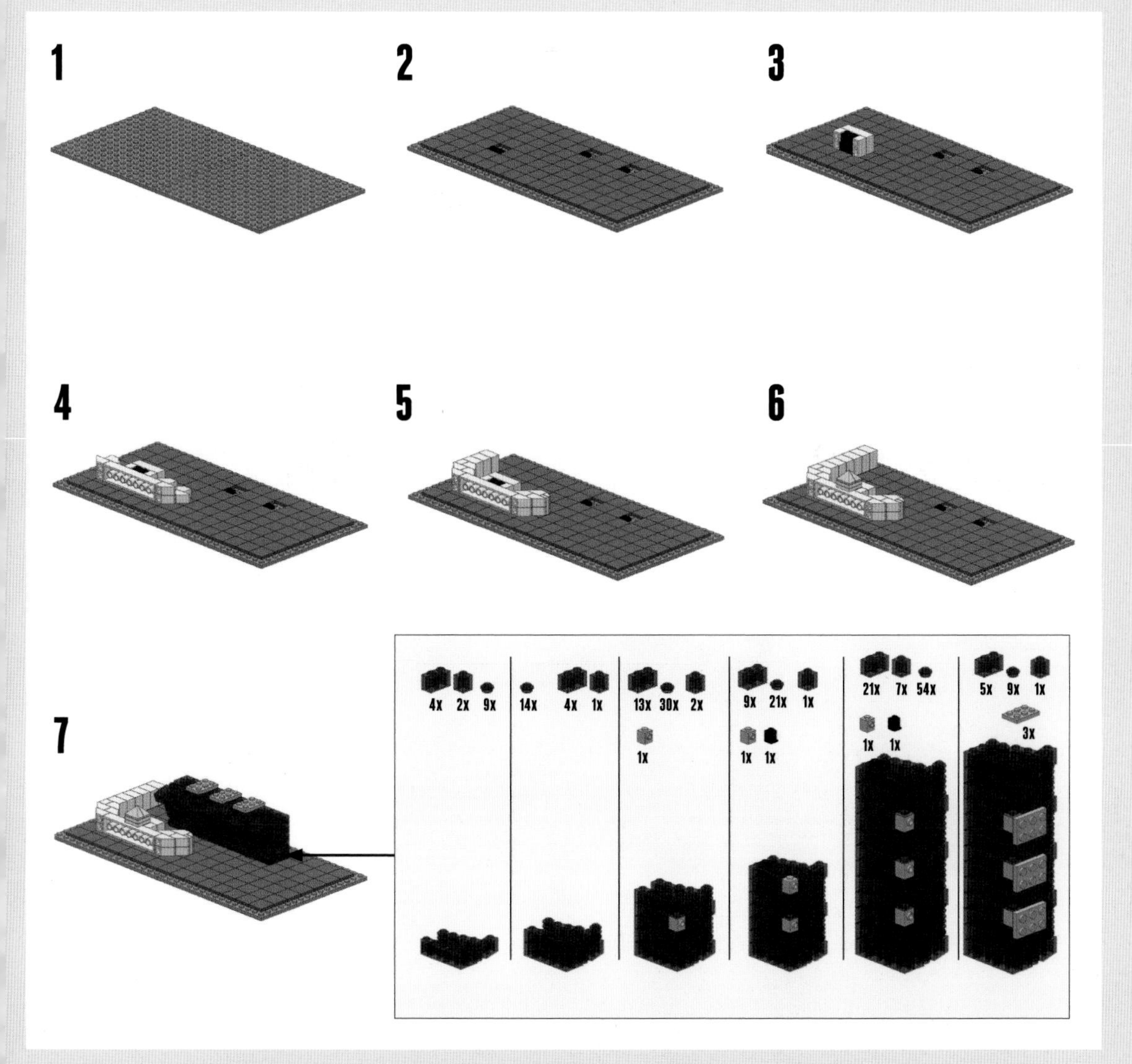
1
2
3
4
5
6
7
4x
2x
9x
14x
4x
1x
13x
30x
2x
1x
9x
21x
1x
1x
1x
21x
7x
54x
1x
1x
5x
9x
1x
3x

TOKYO

PICNIC SCENE

The famous Japanese cherry trees are represented here in their beautiful blossom. What was exciting about this model was coming up with a repeatable technique for making the trees look both convincing and attractive. There is no specific design to making a realistic-looking tree – a degree of randomness actually makes it look more natural. Simply build a trunk to the desired height as shown in the numbered steps opposite, then combine both large and small foliage pieces into shapes of various sizes like those shown below opposite, following no set pattern; the number of pieces specified opposite is a guide only. Thread these combined shapes onto the Flexi-tube as shown in step three, first using progressively wider shapes then progressively smaller ones again, until you have a rounded tree foliage shape as shown in the picture below; with this done, top the central column with a green 1x1 cone. To add the cherry blossom, add round, one-stud pieces in pink and/or white to the studs on the foliage pieces.

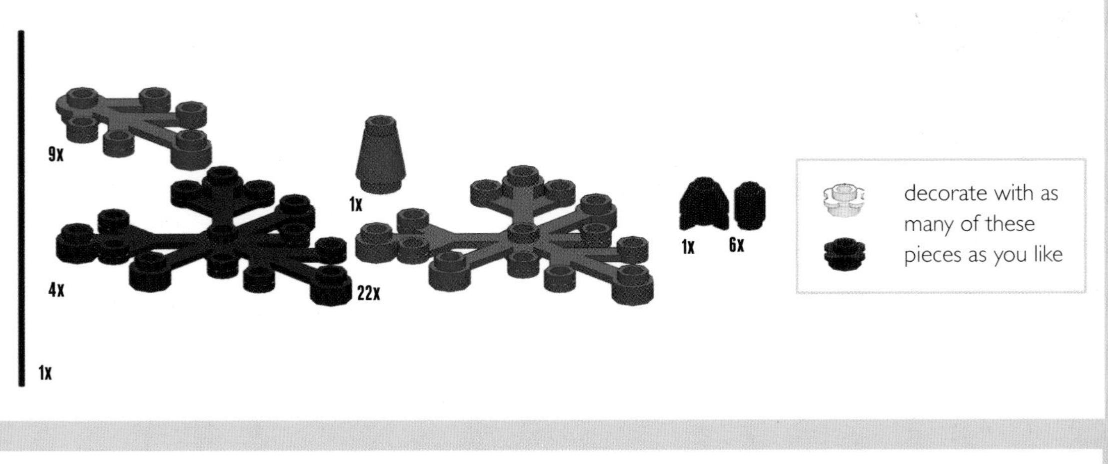
9x
1x
4x
22x
1x
6x
1x
decorate with as
many of these
pieces as you like

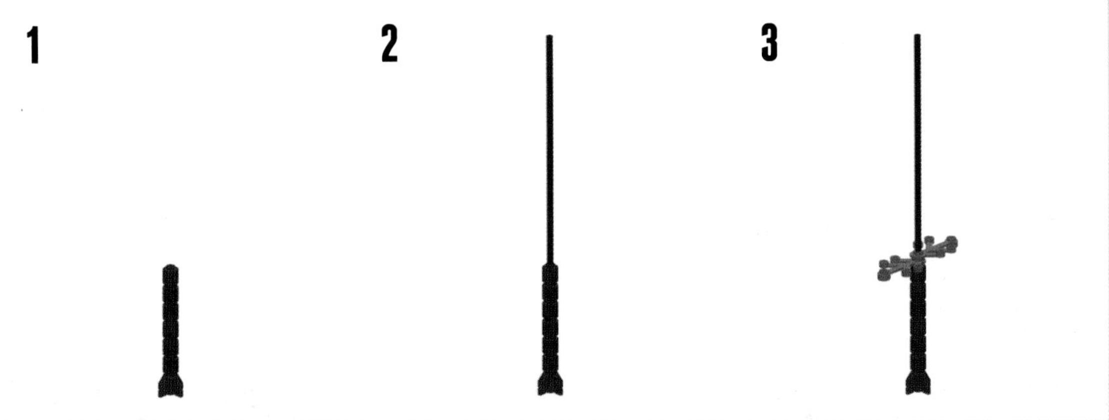
1
2
3

x2
x2
x2
x2
x2
x2

HIMEJI

HIMEJI CASTLE

LEGO® Edition by Warren Elsmore

Size: 19 cm (7½ in) high, 14 cm (5½ in) wide, 16 cm (6¼ in) deep

Bricks: 788

Scale: approximately 1:245

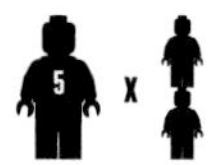

Like most Japanese castles, Himeji Castle is built from wood and plaster rather than stone. It is known as the 'White Heron' castle because of its white plaster walls, which are both fireproof and very strong – the castle has stood in its current form since 1601. This hilltop castle is also a fiendishly complicated model to build, involving a maze of layers, supporting struts and angled roof

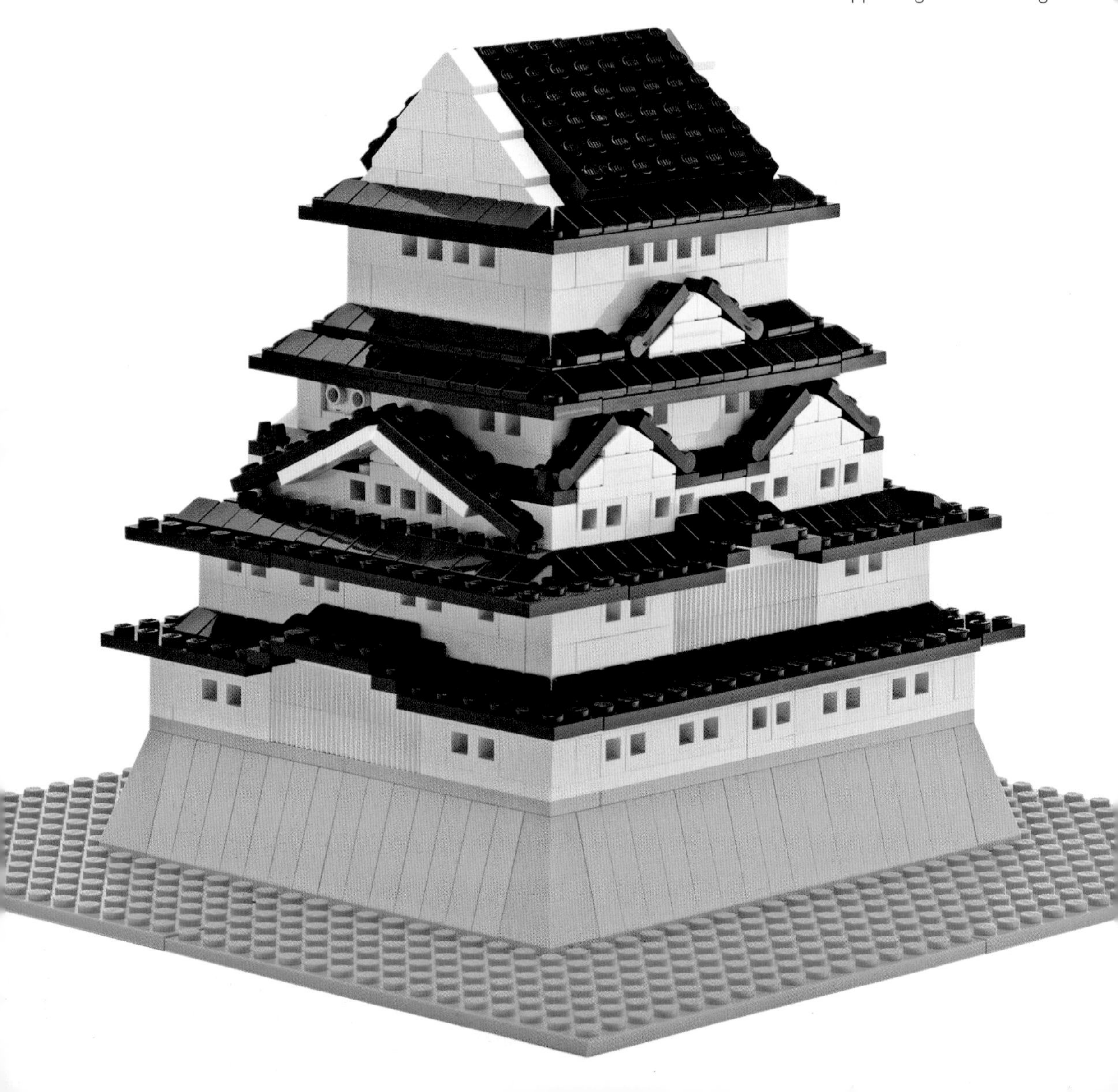

MELBOURNE

EUREKA TOWER

Architect: Fender Katsalidis (2006)

LEGO® Edition by Aaron Amatnieks
Size: 100 cm (3 ft 4 in) high, 40 cm (1 ft 4 in) wide, 30 cm (1 ft) deep

Bricks: 10,000

Scale: 1:300

In contrast to the Flinders Street scene that follows, the Eureka Tower model was planned weeks in advance using drawings, floor plans and photographs to work out the scale and a design based on the surveyor's scale of the building. Weeks of trial and error were needed to perfect the diamond shape of the main building, as well as to design and conceal the motor and gears in the golden section – these power the viewing deck, which extends, waits and then retracts at periodic intervals.

This model was designed to break down into four easy-to-transport pieces, with the centre section built upside down to allow the lip of the 2x2 tiles to act as balcony railings. The Eureka Tower was chosen due to its distinctive shape, design, and use of colour: the blue and white represent the Eureka flag, the gold represents the gold mines, the markings are for the surveyors' poles used on the mines, and the sliver of red is the blood spilled at the Eureka Stockade, a key historical event in the state of Victoria, when gold miners rebelled against British colonial soldiers in 1854.

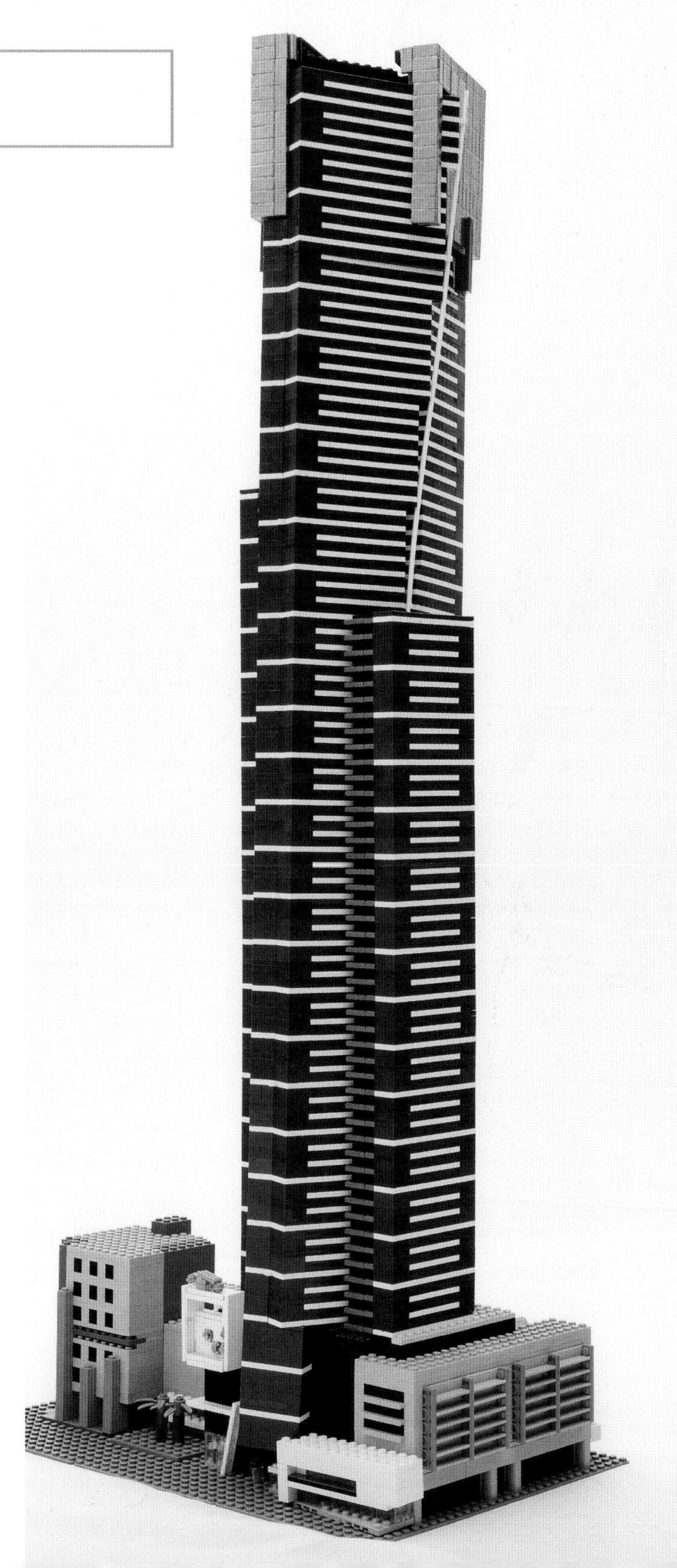

Photography by James Lauritz

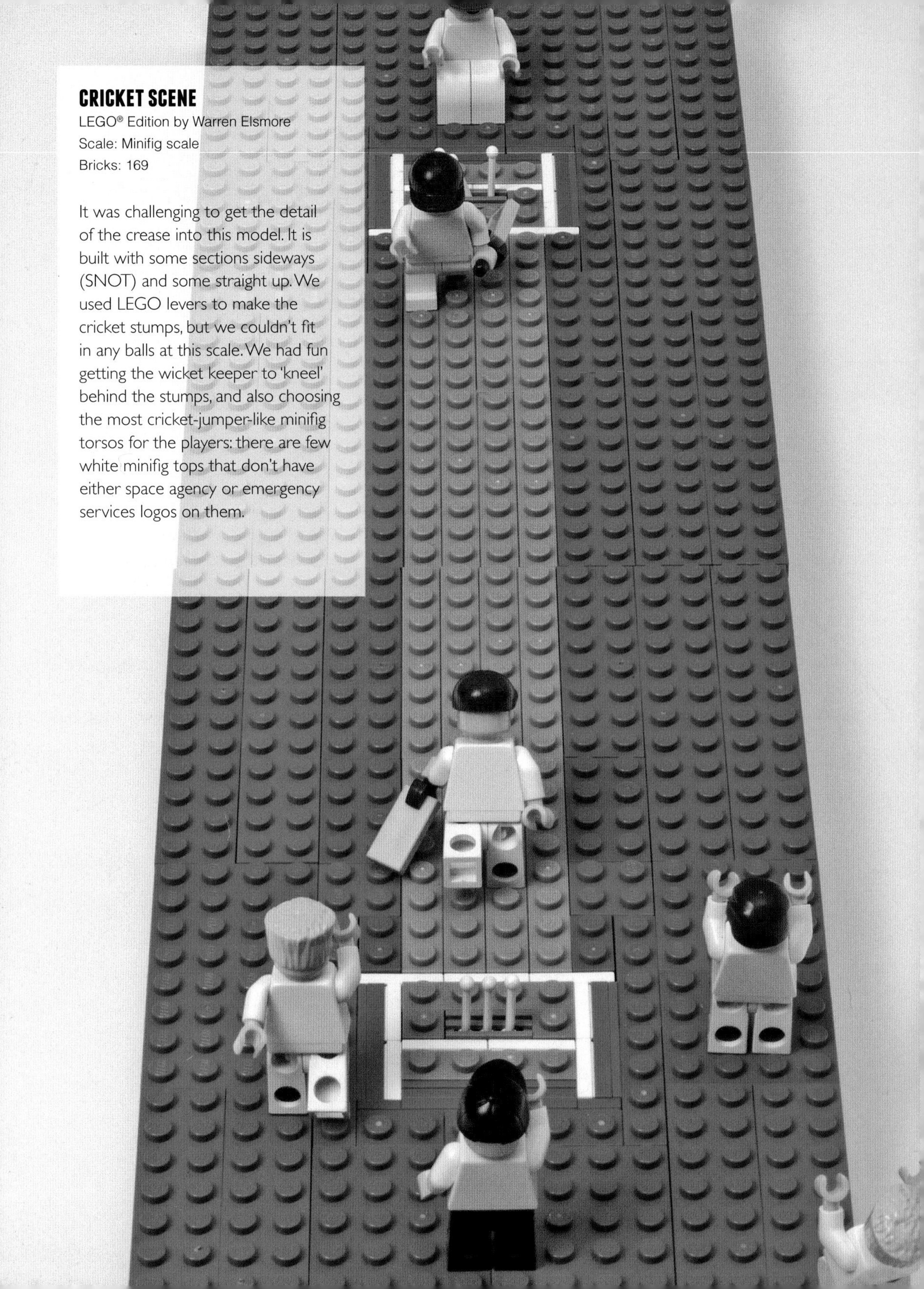

CRICKET SCENE

LEGO® Edition by Warren Elsmore
Scale: Minifig scale
Bricks: 169

It was challenging to get the detail of the crease into this model. It is built with some sections sideways (SNOT) and some straight up. We used LEGO levers to make the cricket stumps, but we couldn't fit in any balls at this scale. We had fun getting the wicket keeper to 'kneel' behind the stumps, and also choosing the most cricket-jumper-like minifig torsos for the players: there are few white minifig tops that don't have either space agency or emergency services logos on them.

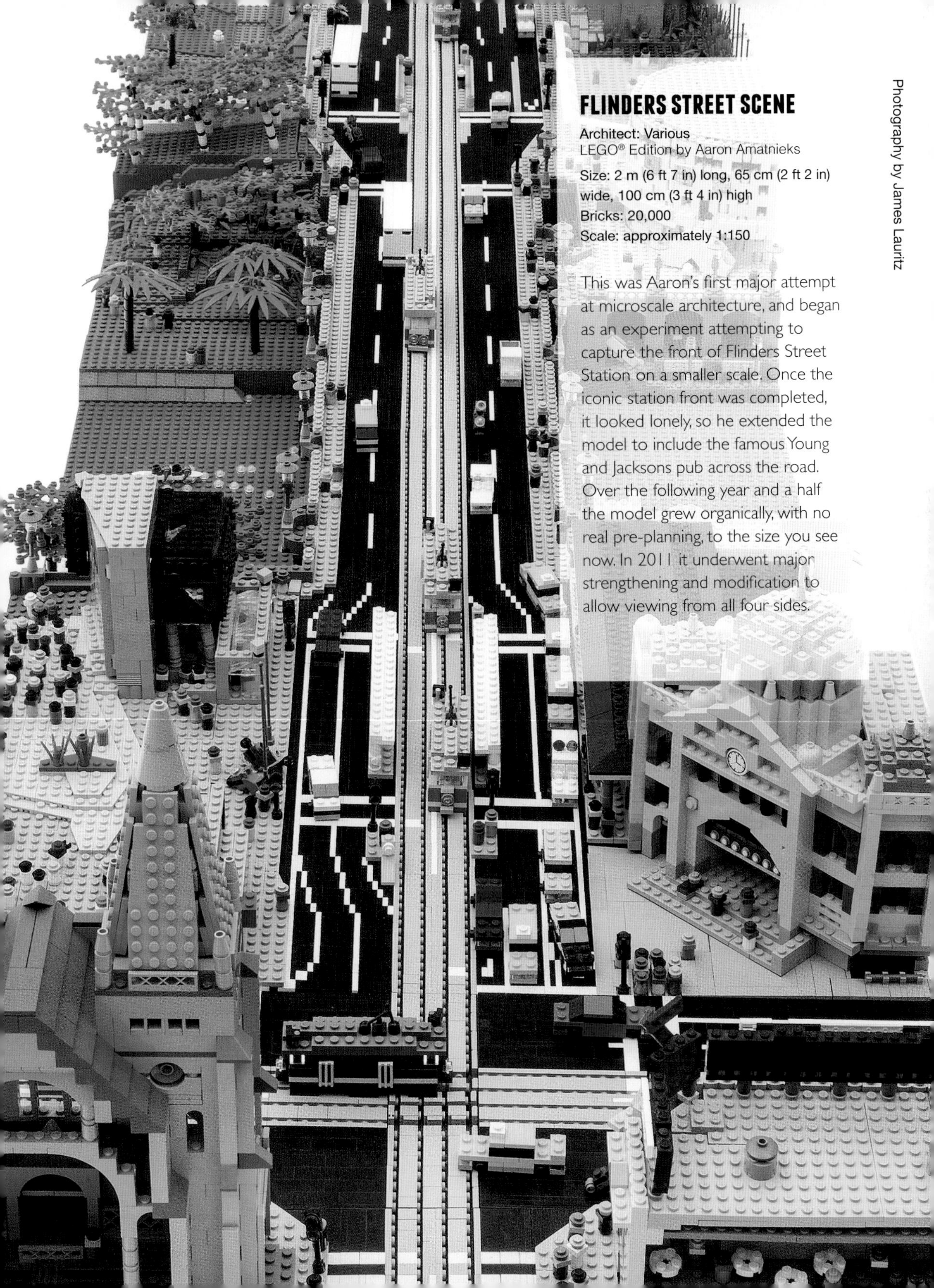

FLINDERS STREET SCENE

Architect: Various
LEGO® Edition by Aaron Amatnieks

Size: 2 m (6 ft 7 in) long, 65 cm (2 ft 2 in) wide, 100 cm (3 ft 4 in) high
Bricks: 20,000
Scale: approximately 1:150

This was Aaron's first major attempt at microscale architecture, and began as an experiment attempting to capture the front of Flinders Street Station on a smaller scale. Once the iconic station front was completed, it looked lonely, so he extended the model to include the famous Young and Jacksons pub across the road. Over the following year and a half the model grew organically, with no real pre-planning, to the size you see now. In 2011 it underwent major strengthening and modification to allow viewing from all four sides.

Photography by James Lauritz

Although not an exact replica, this scene includes the many sights that can been seen around this Melbourne landmark: the morning rowers, the buses dropping off tourists, the people sitting under the clocks, crowds watching the Australian Football League (AFL) on the big screen and the famous Melbourne trams passing by.

SYDNEY

SYDNEY HARBOUR BRIDGE

Engineer: John Bradfield

LEGO® Edition by Ross Crawford

Size: 1 m (3 ft 3 in) high, 2.5 m (8 ft 2 in) long, 90 cm (2 ft 11 in) wide

Bricks: 11,000

Scale: approximately 1:200 lengthwise

This model has actually been built twice. The first time was in 2001 from Ross Crawford's personal collection, and was dismantled when he needed the parts for other projects. The bridge photographed here was built in 2007 for an exhibition at the Museum of Sydney, *Bridging Sydney*, to commemorate the seventy-fifth anniversary of the landmark's opening. LEGO Australia provided the parts, and it was built in situ, with museum visitors asking Ross questions as he worked.

The most technically difficult parts are the support hinges, which are almost totally hidden inside the end pylons and carry the entire weight of the arch. The blue 'harbour' base is a structural element: without it, the ends would spread quite considerably.

The only non-LEGO parts are the Australian and New South Wales flags at the top, and there is no glue used at all. It is also very strong – Ross loaded it up with books as an experiment and piled on over 20 kg (44 lbs) before he decided it was strong enough!

Photography by James Lauritz

AUCKLAND

Architects: Craig Craig Moller Ltd.

LEGO® Edition by Warren Elsmore

Size: 120 cm (47¼ in) high, 17 cm (7½ in) wide and deep

Bricks: 111

Scale: 1:230

This is a circular tower with numerous layers above the elevator shaft. To decide upon a scale for this model I had to look at all the circular plates, cones and cylinder LEGO elements that were available. The main component that shaped this build is the LEGO hinge plate. This is an ingenious element that allows you to choose the angle that the bricks sit at, so you can, in this instance, create a circular tower base. Above the lift shaft, we had to look at what elements would allow us to re-create the different layers and diameters of the top part of the structure.

SKY TOWER BASE JUMP

The Sky Tower is the tallest free-standing structure in the southern hemisphere, at 328 m (1,076 feet). From the observation deck people can see as far as 82 km (50 miles) away! The tower pierces the Auckland skyline, and one if its most famous features is the Skyjump, a base jump to the ground from a platform 192 m (119 yards) high. A base jump is like a bungee jump, but without bouncing back up – but don't worry, jumpers are guided by a cord so that even in high winds they will stay well clear of the building. This is where we have to jump off as well, so we hope the models we've showcased in this book have brought you as much fun and excitement as they did us. Happy building!

INDEX

(Bold entries = buildable projects)
(Italic entries = featured cities)

BUYING BRICKS ONLINE

If you don't have all of the parts required for some of the models featured in this book, or can't quite decide which bricks I've used, then help is at hand. Complete lists of the parts you will need for each of the buildable projects featured in this book are available on my website, *warrenelsmore.com.*

If you need some but not all of the parts, I recommend working from the full list and simply deleting the bricks (or the quantities of them) that you already have, which will give you exactly the parts that you need. Not that having a few spares ever hurt anyone...

BIOGRAPHIES OF FEATURED ARTISTS

Warren Elsmore is an Adult Fan of LEGO® ("AFOL") based in Edinburgh. He has been in love with the plastic brick since the age of four and is now heavily involved in the LEGO fan community, as well as working as a commercial artist helping companies to realise their own dreams in plastic. Since rediscovering his love of LEGO at age 24, Warren has never looked back. Warren is best known for his model of St. Pancras station in London (p. 102–3). A 150,000-brick, 13-foot (4-metre) behemoth, this model has been featured in numerous news articles, and was the subject of a BBC article alongside Warren's 20-foot (6-metre) long model of the Forth Bridge.
Warren also organises "AFOLCON", a dedicated LEGO fan convention, and The LEGO® Show – the largest public LEGO event in the UK, which attracts many thousands of fans. You can see more about Warren and his brick masterpieces at *warrenelsmore.com*.

Teresa "Kitty" Elsmore was a LEGO fan as a child and continues to enjoy creating models with LEGO bricks today. Her passion is for organic forms such as the trees and gardens you see in this book (e.g. on p.219, p.242–3). Since their marriage in 2005, Teresa and Warren have collaborated on many projects, and she is responsible for many of the minifig characters that bring models such as St. Pancras (p102–3), the Oscars (p.34–5) and the Rio Carnival (p.82–5) to life. She has also been involved in many of the large projects in *Brick City* – whether inspiring ideas or helping place the tens of thousands of bricks!

Aaron Amatnieks is a Melbournian IT worker and Melbourne LEGO Club member. His model of Eureka Tower (p.245) so impressed the construction firm behind the real tower that they put it on display on the building's Skydeck observation area.

Ross Crawford is a Melbourne-based computer analyst, LEGO engineer, and member of the Melbourne LEGO Club. Besides his monumental Sydney Harbour Bridge (p.250–1), he has also created a fully-functional LEGO ukulele.

Ed Diment, **Annie Diment**, **Naomi Farr**, and **Stuart Crawshaw** are all members of the Brickish Association, and are based in Portsmouth. They collaborated on the gargantuan Westminster Abbey model (p.104–7) with Warren Elsmore.

Alastair Disley is a lecturer and researcher based in Kent. He is married, and has a one-year-old who is already fascinated by LEGO. The Reichstag model (p.192–3) was his first microscale model. His other hobbies are music and architectural history.

Tom Groombridge lives in Kent, and is married with four children. A LEGO builder since the age of five, the Container Ship (p.232–3) was only his second large-scale original model. He is also a keen archer and cyclist.

Arthur Gugick is a high school maths teacher based in Cleveland, Ohio. Born and raised in New York City, he has been a LEGO fan for over 40 years. You can see more of his creations at *gugick.com*.

Sean Kenney was, in 2005, named the first of now only eleven 'LEGO® Certified Professionals' in the world. Based in Manhattan, he has created pieces on commission for television, celebrities, tourist attractions, galleries, museums, and corporations; his work has been featured widely in the media. He also founded *MOCpages.com*, the world's largest LEGO fan community. His own website is *seankenney.com*.

James Pegrum is based in Colchester, and specialises in historical LEGO models, particularly those themed on the Roman Empire (see p.170–1 and p.180–3) and the Medieval era. Among his creations are a series of builds illustrating the history of Britain.

J. Spencer Rezkalla was born just outside New York City, and his lifelong fascination with tall buildings began with family trips into Manhattan. He has assembled a collection of more than 25 world-famous skyscraper models, built to roughly 1:650 scale and informed by comprehensive research into the landmarks' architectural theory, engineering, and developmental history. An automotive engineer by profession, his LEGO work has been displayed at the Henry Ford Museum, the Alden B. Dow Museum of Science and Art, and numerous LEGO fan events.

Ralph Savelsberg is a physicist in his daily life, which gives his LEGO modelling a particular edge; you can see more of his creations on *flickr.com* under the name "Mad Physicist." Ralph lives in Holland.